Mastering Tools, Taming Daemons

Mastering Tools, Taming Daemons

UNIX FOR THE WIZARD APPRENTICE

Dean Brock

**with Bob Benites, Jack V. Briner Jr.,
Lynne Cohen Duncan, Stefan Gottschalk,
Anselmo Lastra, Jon Mauney,
Kenneth Pugh, and Sue Stigleman**

MANNING

Greenwich
(74° w. long.)

The publisher offers discounts on this book when ordered in quantity.
For more information, please contact:

Special Sales Department
Manning Publications Co.
3 Lewis Street
Greenwich, CT 06830

Fax: (203) 661-9018
email: 73150.1431@compuserve.com

Recognizing the importance of preserving what has been written, it is the policy of
Manning to have the books they publish printed on acid-free paper, and we exert our
best efforts to that end.

Library of Congress Cataloging-in-Publication Data
Mastering Tools, Taming Daemons: UNIX for the Wizard Apprentice/Dean Brock, editor
      p.   cm.
   Includes bibliographical references and index.
   ISBN 1-884777-07-4

   (To come...)

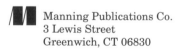 Manning Publications Co.
3 Lewis Street
Greenwich, CT 06830

Managing editor: Lee E. Fitzpatrick
Copyeditor: Margaret Marynowski
Typesetter: Aaron Lyon

Printed in the United States of America
1 2 3 4 5 6 7 8 9 10 - BB - 98 97 96 95

Authors

Bob Benites is currently a graduate student in the MLA program at the University of North Carolina at Asheville. He also supports all of the university's UNIX computers. Bob received a BS in computer science from UNCA in 1992. Before that, he worked for several years in Geographic Information Systems software and application development for San Diego Gas and Electric Company, Integrated Information Systems, and IBM Corporation.

Jack V. Briner Jr. taught computer science and obtained a number of grants at The University of North Carolina at Greensboro before moving to Plano, Texas, where he runs a consulting company. His areas of expertise are parallel and distributed simulations. His interests include operating systems, computer-aided design, computer architecture, parallel and distributed processing, human–computer interaction, object-oriented programming, and performance analysis. He received his BS, MS, and PhD in computer science from Duke University. When not lost in the computer network (or about town), he enjoys spending time with his two children, Clarissa and Christopher, and his wife, Sue.

Dean Brock is chair and associate professor of computer science at the University of North Carolina at Asheville. During the summer, he runs the UNCA Workstation Workshop, a NSF-funded program which teaches college science faculty how to use UNIX workstations in their classes. He is interested in computer networks and operating systems. Dean has been using UNIX computers for over fifteen years now and can't imagine typing left-leaning slashes in file names. Many years ago, he received a BS in mathematics from Duke University, and a MS and PhD in computer science from MIT.

Lynne Cohen Duncan is a systems programmer supervisor with the department of computer science at the University of North Carolina at Chapel Hill. She received her BA in earth science from Wesleyan University in Middletown, Connecticut and her MA in prehistory and archaeology from the University of Sheffield in Sheffield, England. In 1985, she received her MS in computer science from the department in which she now works. Lynne's interests include large scale UNIX system administration tools, historical linguistics, geology, and lighthouse preservation.

Stefan Gottschalk received his BS in applied science from the University of North Carolina at Chapel Hill in 1991. Subsequently, he worked for the computer science department at UNC-CH for two years before joining its graduate program, where he is currently enrolled. At present, he works on wide area tracking systems for use in virtual environments.

Anselmo Lastra is a research assistant professor in the graphics group of the computer science department at the University of North Carolina at Chapel Hill. His current work is in interactive computer graphics and virtual environments. He received his BS in electrical engineering from the Georgia Institute of Technology, and his MS and PhD from Duke University.

Jon Mauney is an independent consultant in Raleigh, North Carolina. He first encountered UNIX (6th Edition) in 1977, while pursuing his PhD in computer science at the University of Wisconsin, Madison. After nine years as a full-time faculty member and part-time UNIX systems administrator in the computer science department at North Carolina State University, he reversed roles: now he plays at being a professor part-time, while devoting his full-time efforts to providing consulting and training in UNIX-related software, including compiler construction, distributed computing, and of course, the X Window System.

Kenneth Pugh is a principal in Pugh-Killeen Associates in Durham, North Carolina. He consults for companies around the world in the areas of SystemArchitectonics^{SM}, object-oriented design, and operating systems. He has taught and lectured in locales ranging from London, England to Sydney, Australia. He holds a BS in electrical engineering from Duke University and a MS from the University of Maryland.

Sue Stigleman is the education services librarian at the Mountain Area Health Education Center of Asheville, North Carolina. At MAHEC she is responsible for training health professionals about information retrieval and using the Internet. For the last two summers, she has been on the staff for the UNCA Workstation Workshop, teaching UNIX basics and navigating the Internet. She has a BS in zoology from Northern Arizona University, an MA in dance, and an Master of Library Science from UCLA.

Contents

Introduction

There are many excellent books that can tell you what to do those first few times you login to a UNIX workstation. This isn't one of them. This book is written for two groups of people.

The first group consists of people who have been using UNIX for a while, and no longer get lost making their way through the system. If you are one of this crowd, you can create directories and edit files with ease. You `grep` at least twice a week, and may have written a couple of simple shell scripts. The more experienced members of the group may even write C programs and manage their own systems and networks. This book is a good readable overview of the UNIX operating system that will give you a broad understanding of the system. Here you'll learn what it means to write a graphical application with the X Window System and to export a directory under the Network File System, along with many other useful facts, such as how the UNIX kernel manages open files.

The second group consists of the UNIX neophytes. This book isn't a reference manual. If it were a travel guide, it would point out all the noteworthy views, but not the bus routes and motel rates. This is an exposition of UNIX that will show you the features that make UNIX worth using. It may be a while before you encounter all of them, but be prepared!

The alert reader may have noticed that when you put these two groups of people together you come up with practically everyone interested in UNIX. However, there is no reason to stop there. If you are a serious user of MS/DOS or Macintosh systems, or even mainframes, you should read this book to find out what you are missing. Maybe you will defect.

This book is a collection of eight chapters written by nine authors. Each chapter may be read, and reread, independently of the others. Here you'll learn how to

- Create a regular expression
- Write a shell script
- Find programs on the Internet
- Compile C programs

- Manage UNIX software development

- Write graphical applications for X and Motif

- Explain the workings of the UNIX kernel

- Create new user accounts

- Add much needed disk storage

- Attach a computer to the Internet

- Use the Distributed Computing Environment

Chapter 1, written by Jack Briner of the department of mathematics at the University of North Carolina at Greensboro, is entitled "UNIX for the Nonprogrammer." Jack introduces important UNIX concepts, such as filter processes and regular expressions, along with the standard UNIX tools that manage, process, digest, and present data. The shells, or command interpreters, of UNIX provide users of the system with a "friendly" means of writing simple scripts (*batch files,* to you MS/DOS users) for frequently preformed tasks. The Internet is a useful source of public domain information and programs for UNIX users. The chapter describes shell programming and Internet usage at a level suitable for almost all users of the UNIX system.

The next two chapters of the book describe the state of the art in programming applications for UNIX workstations. Chapter 2, "UNIX Programming Environment," was written by Anselmo Lastra of the department of computer science at the University of North Carolina at Chapel Hill. UNIX is often considered the ultimate programmer playpen. This chapter examines the toys of the playpen. It talks about C, the C compiler, the loader, as well as tools for managing object code libraries. This is followed by a discussion of make, a tool for automating compilation, dbx, an interactive debugger, and SCCS, a set of tools for managing source code.

Jon Mauney, of Mauney Computer Consulting in Raleigh, North Carolina, wrote Chapter 3, "The X Window System." For years, the X Window system has been the *de facto* standard for windowed applications on UNIX workstations, and now that all the major UNIX vendors have pledged support for the Common Desktop Environment (CDE), the Motif *toolkit* will certainly become the dominant UNIX graphical user interface (GUI). Unfortunately, GUI programming is a complicated and sticky chore, even with Motif and X. This chapter presents the X Window System and pays particular attention to the programming of Motif applications. Jon does not go into the details of those popular multivolume reference manuals anchoring the desks of many programmers, but he does present a good overview of X and Motif that should be read first by anyone contemplating writing their first application.

The core of UNIX is the operating system kernel. Chapter 4, "UNIX Internals," describes the operation of the UNIX operating system kernel. The ways in which the kernel manages processes, virtual memory, file systems, devices, and networks are explained. The major in-core data structures, such as the process and file tables, are presented, and the means by which files and directories are stored on disks are explained. This chapter was written by Dean Brock, the book's editor and chair of the department of computer science at the University of North Carolina at Asheville.

The next three chapters of the book deal with the administration and customization of a UNIX computer. "UNIX System Administration," Chapter 5, examines what is required to install and manage a UNIX system. Lynne Duncan, a UNIX system administrator in the department of computer science at the University of North Carolina at Chapel Hill, has considerable experience in this domain. She describes the creation of user accounts, the management of file systems, and system monitoring in a way that will benefit users and administrators of UNIX computers.

Everyone wants to personalize their accounts. Chapter 6, "Customizing the UNIX User Environment," was written by Stefan Gottschalk, a graduate student of computer science at the University of North Carolina at Chapel Hill, and by Sue Stigleman, a librarian specializing in computer and Internet education at the Mountain Area Health Education Center of Asheville, North Carolina. They show you how to create a UNIX environment that is all your own using the basic tools: shells, variables, aliases, programs, commands, shell scripts, and initialization files. The chapter also looks briefly at customizing mail and the X Window environment.

In Chapter 7, Sue Stigleman teams up with Robert Benites, system administrator for all UNIX systems at the University of North Carolina at Asheville and a former IBM mainframe system administrator who has seen the light (though he may not admit it), to discuss "Network Administration." They take a down-home how-to approach to their task, and describe the steps required to configure network interfaces and software. The chapter concludes with a discussion of network security and debugging tools.

The book concludes with Ken Pugh's chapter, "Distributed Computing Environment." Ken, one half of Pugh-Killeen Associates of Durham, North Carolina has been teaching courses on the Distributed Computing Environment (DCE) for several years. DCE integrates a network into a single computing system, and provides a naming structure and security system for networked objects. Ken provides an overview of the facilities and management of DCE in his chapter.

The writing of this book started when Marjan Bace of Manning Publications asked some UNIX experts in the microelectronics laboratory of the department of computer science at UNC-Chapel Hill what they thought about a suggestion he had heard at a party. The suggestion was to develop a book for readers who were neither UNIX power users nor novices. The party opinion was that there were many intermediate level users of UNIX who were not directly served by existing books. To Marjan's surprise the experts agreed, and one thing led to another— resulting in this book.

Several people helped out with this book. Lee Fitzpatrick, the managing editor for the book, tied up many of the project's loose ends and has been patient in dealing with people who don't always know how to keep to a schedule. Margaret Marynowski, the copyeditor, has wielded her green pencil with great skill—we've learned quite a bit about writing style by paying attention to her suggestions. Aaron Lyon, the typesetter, has also been diligent and understanding in dealing with *all* **these** strange ᶠᵒⁿᵗ **changes**. Brad Bennett of UNC-Chapel Hill played an active role in the development of the book and was particularly helpful in identifying the subjects the book should cover. Both Mike McMullen and Bill Howell of the Glaxo RTP research center made their own valuable contributions. Mike McMullen provided useful technical advice to several of the chapter authors, and Bill Howell, in his previous position as director of computer facilities for the department of computer science at UNC-Chapel Hill, was the ultimate overseer of the UNIX workstations on which several of the authors have earned their UNIX guruship. I thank all of the above. I'd also like to thank John Fauerbach and Scott McMahan, two students in my recent Special Topics class, who wrote thoughtful reviews of some of the book chapters.

Of course, the real work on this book was done by my friends, the many chapter authors. I thank them all for a job well done.

DEAN BROCK
brock@cs.unca.edu

1

UNIX for the Nonprogrammer

Jack V. Briner, Jr.

1.1 Introduction

The ability to program in C is useful in a UNIX environment, but is not essential. UNIX systems support a number of programs that can solve many tasks without formal programming. In some cases, a single UNIX program cannot solve the problem. However, several programs tied together with the simple programming capabilities of the shell and the programming language awk can solve many problems.

If your problem does not seem to be solvable with the tools discussed in this chapter, it is likely that someone else has come across a similar problem. There are many individuals associated with UNIX who seek to keep people from reinventing the wheel. In fact, these individuals want to give you the wheel for free. The later part of this chapter discusses ways to obtain free software and free advice by using news and software archives.

1.2 The On-Line Manual

One of the best resources available to the user is the command man. While it does not perform any of the data manipulation or transformation functions described below, it does provide access to a brief description of each command. The collection of standard commands and local commands of your system should be stored in a directory called man (usually /usr/man) and should contain a directory of all the

commands available to the user from the shell, in a subdirectory man1.
These commands are known as section 1 or user commands. Other
directories contain information on system calls, file formats, and system administration programs. All of the programs that we will be concerned with are in section 1 of the manual (some nonstandard
commands may be installed and stored in section l of the manual). All
the manual pages are stored in troff(1) format and are displayed
using a combination of nroff(1) and more(1). If you don't have a
copy of a man page, you can always get one by formatting the page by
hand. For example, to get a copy of the man page for sort, type

```
% nroff -man -Tlpr /usr/man/man1/sort.1 | lpr
```

The option -man indicates to the nroff typesetting package that a set
of macros for printing manual pages should be used. The option -Tlpr
tells the package to print in a style suitable for a line printer. (Type
man nroff for more detailed formatting options.)

Of course, there is the old problem of the chicken and the egg: What
if we do not know which command to use? One solution would be to
look in a book. Such a recourse is good for authors, but runs against
the nature of UNIX. man has an option -k which looks for a word on
the headers of all man pages. For example, suppose we wanted to
know the last time the system administrator was logged in, but we did
not know which command would yield this information. We could type

```
% man -k last
```

The system responds with

```
end, ext, edata (3)   - last locations in a program
last (1)              - indicate last logins of users
                        and teletypes
lastcomm (1)          - indicate last commands executed
                        in reverse order
```

This shows the three commands which have *last* in either their names
or in their one-line definitions. From this, we could then print the
manual page for last:

```
% man last
```

1.3   The Philosophy of UNIX Tools

Most of this chapter will focus on software which comes with UNIX systems. This software is designed mainly for the manipulation of existing data: sorting, table handling, character substitution, text searching, and graphing. We will focus on these tools for the majority of the chapter, and will talk about the shells as a mechanism for tying everything together.

Most of the standard programs on UNIX systems are intended to work with standard ASCII text files. This has been considered inefficient because programs must first convert the ASCII representation to an internal format for processing. However, the common interchange format of text allows different computers and programs to share the same data, and can be read by people, as well. The concept of using ASCII as the interchange format allows programs to function independently, and is one of the major reasons for the success of UNIX.

Consider the following problem: removing repeated elements in a list. Suppose we had a file, items, that contained the following numbers:

```
27
19
83
22
19
27
99
42
```

One way to remove the second instance of 27 and 19 from the list would be to sort the list and to remove lines that were multiple instances of the same number. If we were to do this on the computer, we could imagine the flow of data shown in Figure 1.1.

In UNIX, we could simulate the process by

```
% sort < items > sorted_items
% uniq < sorted_items > unique_items
```

We could avoid the intermediate file sorted_items by using a pipe:

```
% sort < items | uniq > unique_items
```

This example shows the power of UNIX tools for manipulating files using text as the communication medium. Other tools exist for further manipulation and extraction of data stored as text. These tools are discussed in the next section.

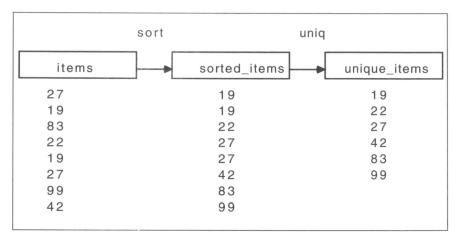

Figure 1.1   Removing repeated elements in a file

1.4   Standard UNIX Text Manipulation Tools

In this section, programs are ordered by topic rather than alphabetically. A complete description of each command is available on-line using man.

1.4.1   sort

sort provides a facility for sorting files written in ASCII. The options available for sorting will vary from flavor to flavor of UNIX. Some of the more useful flags are:

- -b   Ignore leading blanks.

- -d   Sort according to usual dictionary practices, letters and digits, and then blanks.

- -f   Fold uppercase letters to lowercase letters.

- -i   Ignore characters which are earlier than ! (33) in the ASCII alphabet and after the space character (126).

- -n   Sort numeric fields numerically.

- -r   Sort in reverse order.

- -tx   Use the character x instead of a space for separating fields.

- -u   Sort only unique items.

`sort` is also controlled by selecting the fields upon which to perform the sort. By default, the sorting starts with the first field, 0. Fields are separated by spaces unless the option `-t` is used. Suppose we wanted to sort a list of names and telephone numbers stored in the file `phone`:

```
Jack Briner     919-555-1212
John Doe         201-555-7893
Jan Keppler     212-555-8999
Jim Jones        713-555-8772
Janet Adams 814-555-8888
```

Doing a sort (`% sort phone`) without options would give us the list

```
Jack Briner     919-555-1212
Jan Keppler     212-555-8999
Janet Adams 814-555-8888
Jim Jones        713-555-8772
John Doe         201-555-7893
```

It would make sense that we would want to sort the list by last names rather than first names. Thus, we can sort on the second field (the last name) with the command

```
% sort +1 phone
```

yielding the file

```
Janet Adams 814-555-8888
Jack Briner     919-555-1212
John Doe         201-555-7893
Jim Jones        713-555-8772
Jan Keppler     212-555-8999
```

If we wanted to sort the list by phone numbers we might suspect that we could use the third field:

```
% sort +2 phone
```

This yields

```
John Doe         201-555-7893
Jim Jones        713-555-8772
Jan Keppler     212-555-8999
Jack Briner     919-555-1212
Janet Adams 814-555-8888
```

The sort seems to have worked. However, notice that Adams' phone number occurred after Briner's. The problem is that only the first space is considered a separator. Thus, we need to use the option -b to ignore the extraneous spaces:

```
% sort -b +2 phone
```

This yields

```
John Doe          201-555-7893
Jan Keppler       212-555-8999
Jim Jones         713-555-8772
Janet Adams 814-555-8888
Jack Briner       919-555-1212
```

Suppose that our phone list also contained people who have the same last name. Then we would want to sort on the last name first, and then on the first name. If we add John Adams 215-555-6945 and perform a sort, we should use the following command:

```
% sort +1 +0 phone
```

which yields

```
John Adams 215-555-8888
Janet Adams 814-555-8888
Jack Briner       919-555-1212
John Doe          201-555-7893
Jim Jones         713-555-8772
Jan Keppler       212-555-8999
```

However, Janet Adams does not appear at the top as expected. This is because the command sort +num really means *sort from the position starting at* num *to the end of the line.* Instead, we want to sort only on the second field. So we should specify the range of fields to search by +num and -num. Thus, what we really want is

```
sort +1 -2 +0 phone
```

which yields

```
Janet Adams 814-555-8888
John Adams 215-555-8888
Jack Briner       919-555-1212
John Doe          201-555-7893
Jim Jones         713-555-8772
Jan Keppler       212-555-8999
```

Each field can optionally specify the r, n, b, d, and f options. The r option sorts the field in reverse order. The n option sorts the field in numerical order (i.e., 5 is considered to be less than 15, in contrast to lexigraphical order in which 15 is considered to be less than 5 because of the leading 1).

One of the problems with many UNIX utilities is the assumption of line length. Only the first 1024 or so characters of each line are used in sorting, and the remaining characters may be lost. On some systems you may be out of luck. The Sun and System V versions of the system provide some assistance with the problem. The flag -z allows the length of the longest line to be specified. If your files have excessively long lines, use the command

```
sort -z10000
```

This will allow lines up to 10,000 character lines to be sorted. Be aware that such lines may cause memory allocation problems. This, too, is addressed by the Sun and System V variants with option -y, which allows you to specify the amount of main memory to be used before using the disk to perform the sort.

sort -u performs a sort on the data and then removes duplicate lines. Thus, this command performs the same operation discussed in the introduction.

1.4.2 uniq

uniq, which stands for *unique,* is a tool for handling repetitious lines in files. In all cases, it assumes that the input is sorted. By using uniq following a sort, one can do more than with sort -u. Below is a summary of the commands:

- -u Display the lines which are not repeated in the input.
- -d Display the lines which are repeated.
- -c Precede each line displayed by the number of times it occurs.
- -m Ignore the first m fields and any blanks before them.
- +n Ignore the first n characters (including spaces).

Consider the file data, which contains the following data:

```
5    57.3
8    87.9
9    88.7
53   88
53   88
5    57.3
9    88
```

One question we might ask is, "What is not repeated in this file?" The
answer is found by using the switch -u:

```
% sort data | uniq -u
```

This yields

```
8   87.9
9   88
9   88.7
```

So what was repeated? That can be found with

```
% sort data | uniq -d
```

which yields

```
5   57.3
53 88
```

Applying uniq without any option,

```
% sort data | uniq
```

yields

```
5   57.3
53 88
8   87.9
9   88
9   88.7
```

This gives us one copy of each line without any repetition.
   Input does not need to be sorted if only consecutive lines in the file
are to be found or deleted. For example, running uniq on the file data
will get rid of one of the repeated 53 88 lines, but will not delete the
repeated 5   57.3 lines, because they are not next to each other:

```
% uniq data

5   57.3
8   87.9
9   88.7
53 88
5   57.3
9   88
```

1.4.3   cut

Frequently, programs output tables for processing. Tables are made of records and fields. In UNIX, the usual record consists of a line in a text file. Each record is then broken into a fixed number of fields separated by tabs or spaces. In viewing or processing a table, some fields may be unwanted. cut removes the unwanted fields from records. The usage is as follows for Berkeley flavors of UNIX:

```
cut -clist [file1 file2 ... ]
cut -flist [-dchar][-s] [file1 file2 ... ]
```

The options for each of the uses is

- −c*list*   Treat each character position as a column, extracting those characters in a comma separated list. A range of characters may be specified with a dash (−).

- −f*list*   Using the separation character (which by default is a tab) to demark columns, extract those columns in a comma separated list. A range of columns may be specified with a dash (−).

- −d*char* Use the character *char* instead of tab as the separation character.

- −s   Do not print lines which have no separation character on them.

Consider some weather data in the file weather:

```
Houston 56   75   0.02
Dallas 60 77 0.00
Philadelphia 65 66 1.20
Washington 50 55 0.00
Seattle 66 77 1.20
```

Each record contains a city name, its lowest temperature, its highest temperature, and the amount of rainfall it received. If we were interested only in the highs, we could use cut to get the first and third fields, as shown in Figure 1.2.

The format of cut in Figure 1.2 requires the delimiter between fields to be a tab. However, the weather file uses spaces. So we must use the option −d to change the delimiter:

```
% cut -f1,3 -d" " weather
```

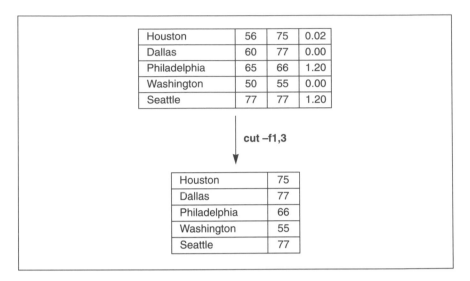

Figure 1.2   Removing fields using `cut`

yielding

```
Houston 75
Dallas 77
Philadelphia 66
Washington 55
Seattle 77
```

The quotes after the `-d` are significant. The option `-d` needs a character for separating the fields. To tell the `cut` program that the character is a space, we need to assure that the space is passed to the program. Unfortunately, the shell strips spaces and tabs sent to programs unless they are enclosed in quotes.

A similar command is `colrm`, column remove. For more information on that command, see your man pages.

1.4.4   paste

`cut` takes files apart; `paste` joins files. That is, `paste` puts lines in two or more files together. Possible usages are

```
paste file1 file2 ...
paste -dlist file1 file2 ...
paste -s [-d] file1 file2 ...
```

The options for each of the uses is:

- -d*list* Use the characters in *list* to separate the columns of the joined files in a circular fashion. That is, if more than one character is specified, use the first character to separate the first and second files, the second character to separate the second and third files, etc. If the number of files exceeds the number of characters in the list, restart separation with the first character in the list.

- -s Merge consecutive lines together. The number of lines to merge into one line is given by the number of characters specified by the option -d.

A second file, weather2, is displayed below:

```
Houston 66 88 0.00
Dallas 56 79 0.15
Philadelphia 62 65 0.01
Washington 51 55 0.01
Seattle 55 62 0.00
```

If we wanted to see the files together, we would use

```
% paste weather weather2
```

which yields

```
Houston 56   75   0.02      Houston 66 88 0.00
Dallas 60 77 0.00           Dallas 56 79 0.15
Philadelphia 65 66 1.20     Philadelphia 62 65 0.01
Washington 50 55 0.00       Washington 51 55 0.01
Seattle 66 77 1.20          Seattle 55 62 0.00
```

Suppose, however, we want to see only the name and the two highs. We can do this by using paste and cut together:

```
% paste -d" " weather weather2 | cut -f1,3,7 -d" "
```

This yields

```
Houston 75 88
Dallas 77 66
Philadelphia 66 75
Washington 55 55
Seattle 77 62
```

The -d option was necessary for both cut and paste. When using paste, we needed it to use a space as the delimiter instead of the usual tab. cut would not see the tab as a separator.

One thing to note about paste is that you need to be careful that there is a one-to-one correspondence between lines of the files. In our example, if the second set of data had been missing a city, the results would have been incorrect. Of course, the ordering of the data also must be the same in both files.

The -s option allows consecutive lines in a file to be merged together. The number of lines to be merged depends on the character set defined by the -d option. For example, to print three files per line of an ls command, the following command could be issued:

```
% ls | paste -d"\t\t\n"
```

1.4.5 Regular Expressions

Many UNIX tools use regular expressions to describe a sought item. However, it is frequently difficult to find an explanation of these expressions. The most general description is found in the manual page for the line editor ed. However, line editors are not regularly used anymore, and most users are unfamiliar with the ed manual page.

A regular expression defines a set. Frequently, when we wish to find something in some text, we are looking for one of a set of items. For example, if we were to look for numbers in an ASCII file, we could look for 1, 2, 3, 4, 5, ..., 4019, etc. However, it is impossible to enumerate the entire set of numbers. Thus, we need some mechanism for expressing this and other sets. A regular expression is made up of a series of operators (see also Table 1.1):

- Concatenation (the juxtaposition of items)
- Alternation (one of two items)
- Repetition (0 or more repetitions, 1 or more items)
- Optional (0 or 1 items)
- Grouping
- Set definition

operating on a regular expression, which can be:

- A literal string
- A character from a set
- Any character
- Begin of string mark
- End of string mark
- The result of applying a regular expression operator

and limited by meta characters (characters used as operators, as well as those in Table 1.2).

Operator	Name	Usage	Meaning
	Concatenation	abc	abc
|	Alternation	a|b|c	a,b,c
*	Repetition, 0 or more times		a,ab,abb,...
+	Repetition, 1 or more times	ab+	ab,abb,...
?	Optional, 0 or 1 times	ab?	a,ab
( )	Grouping	(ab)+	ab,abab,...
[ ]	Set definition	[a-z]	a,b,c,...,z

Table 1.1   Regular expression operators

Operator	Name	Usage	Meaning
\	Escape sequence	\\	\
		*	*
		\t	Tab
		\f	Formfeed
		\b	Backspace
		\n	Newline
$	End of line	a$	An a at the end of a line
^	Beginning of line	^a	An a at the beginning of a line

Table 1.2   Additional meta characters

Unfortunately, each UNIX program has slightly different ideas about what constitutes a regular expression. We will try to comment on the forms used by different programs as they are encountered. A summary of the supported regular expression operators and some of the tools that use them is given in Table 1.3.

In the examples below, we show a regular expression in the first column and the set which it represents in the last column. For example, the simplest regular expression is a literal string. Here, the first regular expression is a, and the set of possibilities is the letter *a*:

Operator	grep	egrep	ed	vi	sed	awk
Concatenation	√	√	√	√	√	√
Alternation (|)	X	√	X	X	X	√
Set of literals ([ ])	√	√	√	√	√	√
Zero or more (*)	√	√	√	√	√	√
One or more (+)	X	√	X	X	X	√
Zero or one (?)	X	√	X	X	X	√
Ordering (( ))	\ (\ )	( )	\ (\ )	\ (\ )	\ (\ )	( )
Registers (\1)	X	X	√	X/√	√	X
Begin of string (^)	√	√	√	√	√	√
End of string ($)	√	√	√	√	√	√

Table 1.3   Regular expression capabilities of UNIX programs
(√ = supported, X = not supported)

```
a                 {'a'}            The letter a
d                 {'d'}            The letter d
```

A character from a set is defined by listing the possible characters within square brackets [ ]. Thus [abc] means one of the characters a, b, or c. Ranges of characters can be separated by a dash (-). Below, the set of uppercase and lowercase letters is given by a-zA-Z. The complement of the set can be defined if the first character in the square brackets is a caret ^.

```
[abc]            {'a','b','c'}      One of the letters a, b, or c
[def]            {'d','e','f'}      One of the letters d, e, or f
[a-zA-Z]         {'a','b',...,'z','A','B',...,'Z'}
                                    The letters of the alphabet
[^a-zA-Z]        {'1','2','+','/',...}
                                    Any character but a letter
```

Concatenation is implicit when two regular expressions are juxtaposed. If A is a regular expression and B is a regular expression, then AB is a regular expression:

```
abc              {'abc'}
abc[abc]         {'abca','abcb','abcc'}
[def]abc         {'dabc','eabc','fabc'}
[abc][def]       {'ad','ae','af','bd','be','bf','cd',
                  'ce','cf'}
```

The operator for alternation is a bar `|`. It is used between two regular expressions. If A is a regular expression and B is a regular expression, then A|B is a regular expression, and it contains a union of the elements described by A and by B:

```
abc|[abc]              {'abc','a','b','c'}
[def]|[abc]            {'d','e','f','a','b','c'}
```

Alternation is not available in `vi`, `ed`, `sed` or `grep`, but is available in `egrep` and `awk`.

The grouping operator `()` guarantees the order of evaluation of regular expressions in a complicated expression. If A is a regular expression, then (A) is a regular expression, and it contains the same elements as in A:

```
(abc)                  {'abc'}
(abc|[abc])            {'abc','a','b','c'}
((abc)|[abc])          {'abc','a','b','c'}
```

Many programs, like `vi`, `sed`, and `awk`, backslash \ the parentheses when used as an operator. Unbackslashed parentheses are treated as literals. So, for example, one may have to use the forms below:

```
(abc)                  {'(abc)'}
\(abc\)                {'abc'}
((abc)|[abc])          {'((abc)','a)','b)','c)'}
\(\(abc\)|[abc]\)      {'abc','a','b','c'}
```

The optional operator `?` says that its operand is optional. If A is a regular expression, then A? is a regular expression. It contains the same elements as A plus the empty string, which we will denote as ' ':

```
(abc)?                 {'abc',''}
(abc|[abc])?           {'abc','a','b','c',''}
```

The zero or more repetitions operator `*` says that its operand may be repeated zero or more times. If A is a regular expression, then A* is a regular expression which contains the same elements as A, plus the empty element, and as many repetitions of A as can be concatenated together.

```
(abc)*                 {'abc','','abcabc','abcabcabc', ...}
(abc|[abc])*           {'abc','a','b','c','','aa',
                        'abcabc','bbb', ...}
```

The one or more repetitions operator + says that its operand may be repeated one or more times. If A is a regular expression, then A+ is a regular expression which contains the same elements as A and as many repetitions of A as can be concatenated together:

```
(abc)+                 {'abc','abcabc','abcabcabc', ...}
(abc|[abc])+           {'abc','a','b','c','aa',
                        'abcabc','bbb', ...}
```

Notice the primary difference between + and * is that the empty string ' ' is a member of A* but not of A+.

In equations, some operators are performed first not because of the order of symbols but because of the precedence of the arithmetic. For example, a * b + c = c + a * b is TRUE because multiplication is always performed before addition. Regular expressions also have an order in which the operators are applied:

1. ()

2. ?,+,*

3. Concatenation

4. Alternation

Some examples with explicit ordering with parentheses are given below:

```
abc+                   ab(c+)
abc|def                (abc)|(def)
abc[def]*              abc(d|e|f)*
```

Some programs, e.g., sed and ed, allow a test to see if a pattern is repeated within a string. For example, perhaps we are interested in finding all words that begin and end with the same letter. We can do this by remembering part of a match and storing it in a register. The part of the matched expression to be remembered is placed in matched parentheses (). We use \n to refer to the register containing the matched string. There are 9 registers, numbered from 1 to 9, left to right.

The regular expression ([a-zA-Z]*)\1 describes the set of strings which begin with the same string of letters. The (and) are applied first, and the letters which are matched are stored in register 1. Finally, the string stored in register 1 must make up the rest of the string. This set would contain ' ', 'aa', 'AzAz', etc.

The regular expression \(.\).\(.\).*\2\1 matches only if the first and third characters match the last two characters. The expression can be understood as follows: the first character (which does not need to be a letter) is stored in register 1; a second character must be present but is not stored in a register; and the third character is stored in register 2. Next, any number of characters are matched, and finally, the last two characters must be the same as the third character of the string (stored in register 2) and the first character (in register 1).

Other characters such as, ., ^, and $, have special meanings. The symbol . can be used to recognize any character. ^ is the beginning-of-string mark, while $ is the end-of-string mark. Both are used in pattern matching, where a match exists if the string match must begin or end appropriately for a match to occur.

Clearly, the characters ., $, ^, +, *, [,],), and (have special meanings. These characters, along with \, are known as meta characters (see Table 1.2). To differentiate the literal characters from their special meanings, we precede them with a backslash \. To represent a * or a $, we would use * or \$, respectively:

.[abc]	{'aa',',b','!c', ...}
	One of the letters *a*, *b*, or *c* preceded by any character
[def].	{'d3','e?','fx'}
	One of the letters *d*, *e*, or *f* followed by any character
[a-zA-Z]$	{'a','b',...,'z','A','B',...,'Z'}
	A letter of the alphabet at the end of a string
^[a-z]$	{'a','b',...,'z','A','B',...,'Z'}
	A string which consists only of a letter of the alphabet

In several sections in this chapter we will see how regular expressions are used.

1.4.6 grep/fgrep/egrep

The cut command removes fields of all the records in a file. What if not all the records are to be considered? How can the important records be found? One of the grep family of commands can be used to cut along records. There are three members in the family: grep, egrep, and fgrep. fgrep is usually the fastest, but is also the most limited version. egrep is the most flexible, allowing full regular expressions but is usually the slowest. grep is the middle of the road, allowing limited regular expressions. The most useful options available are:

- -c   Output the number of matched lines.

- -e*expression*   The expression that follows begins with a -. This allows the program to distinguish *expression* from a command.

- -f*file*   *file* contains strings to be matched for `fgrep`, or regular expressions to be matched for `egrep`.

- -i   Ignore case only (`fgrep` and `grep`).

- -l   List files with matching lines only once.

- -n   As each match is printed, include the line number of the match.

- -s   Silent operation. The error code returned by the program will be 0 if a match is found, 1 otherwise. This option is useful in shell scripts.

- -v   Displays all lines that do not match specified expression.

- -x   Print only those lines that exactly match the given string.

For example, suppose we are interested only in cities which had no rain. Thus, we want to find lines in a file which have 0.00 in the "rain" record. The commands

```
% grep 0.00 weather
```

or

```
% fgrep 0.00 weather
```

or

```
% egrep 0.00 weather
```

all yield

```
Dallas 60 77 0.00
Washington 50 55 0.00
```

Likewise, if we want a list only of cities which did receive rain, we would use the -v option. This option prints only those lines which do not have the desired pattern. Using the fastest option, fgrep,

```
% fgrep -v 0.0 weather
```

yields

```
Houston 56   75   0.02
Philadelphia 65 66 1.20
Seattle 66 77 1.20
```

Of course, if we want to list cities which had a temperature greater than 100, we would have to use a more flexible search. The use of regular expressions gives us some flexibility.

In the previous section, we saw that a regular expression is a notation for describing possible patterns which match a word or words. The simplest regular expression is just a literal. This is what is done with fgrep:

```
% fgrep Houston weather

Houston 56   75   0.02
```

The word *Houston* is a literal. Another regular expression operator is the alternation operator |. The alternation matches either the regular expression on the left or the right. Such expressions with alternation are supported only by egrep (see Table 1.3). For example, to match either *Houston* or *Dallas* using egrep,

```
% egrep "Houston|Dallas" weather
```

yields

```
Houston 56   75   0.02
Dallas 60 77 0.00
```

If the pattern string begins with a ^ the match must be at the beginning of a line. To match lines which start with the string *all*:

```
% grep "^all" weather
```

yields

```
< nothing >
```

and

```
% grep "^Dall" weather
```

yields

```
Dallas 60 77 0.00
```

The character $ is used to denote the end of a line. For example, to be sure that only towns with zero rainfall are printed:

```
% grep '0[.]00$' weather
```

This ensures that *0.00* was the last entry on the line. Note, that the . was put into the bracket notation so as not to match any character, as . normally does. Otherwise, a line like

```
Honolulu 72 75 10000
```

would have been recognized because the . would have matched the second 0 in 10000. This could have also been expressed using the escape sequence \ ., as in

```
% grep '0\.00$' weather
```

Note that single quotes were used because the shell would otherwise attempt to interpret the meaning of $ as a shell variable reference.

If a regular expression begins with a ^ and ends with a $, the entire line must match the expression given with grep or egrep. If you are using fgrep, the same task is accomplished with the -x option.

Regular expressions can have limited memory abilities. As we saw earlier, if a regular expression is surrounded by \(and \) the regular expression matched is remembered and can be used later in the matching process. Since each \(is numbered, we can match repeated substrings in an expression by using the construct \n to denote the *n*th matched substring. An example would be if we wanted to see if any city had the same high twice in a row:

```
% paste -d" " weather weather2 | cut -f1,3,7 -d" " > temp
% egrep "\( [0-9]*\)\1" temp
```

yields

```
Washington 55 55
```

This works by combining two days, as done earlier with the `paste`
command, using the `-d` option so that only spaces are used between
files. Finally, the file is cut apart to look at the highs, and `egrep` is run
over the file to search for repeats on the same line.

In searching for words in a file, you must know the case of all the
words. For example, given the following file,

```
The quick brown
fox jumped over
the lazy dog.
```

a search using `fgrep` for the word *the*

```
% fgrep 'the' typing
```

would return the single line

```
the lazy dog.
```

This search missed the first line because the *T* was capitalized. The `-i`
flag makes the search insensitive to case.

```
% fgrep -i 'the' typing

The quick brown
the lazy dog.
```

If more than one file name is part of the command, the matched
lines are prepended with the file that caused the match:

```
% fgrep -i dallas weather weather2

weather: Dallas 60 77 0.00
weather2: Dallas 56 79 0.15
```

The file names can be suppressed with the `-h` flag. It is also useful to
know where a match occurs. The `-n` option prepends the line number
to the output of the matching line.

The `-f` option allows the expressions of the `grep` family to be stored
in a file. If there are several search patterns, this makes entering the
patterns easier. For example, consider the problem of finding unique
lines, but suppose that we also want the output to be in the order of
the original file. Because `uniq` requires that the input be sorted, the

original order of lines is lost. Consider the file data again, with the
following data:

```
5   57.3
8   87.9
9   88.7
53  88
5   57.3
9   88
```

Recall that removing repeats changed the original order:

```
% sort data | uniq -u
```

This yielded

```
53  88
8   87.9
9   88
9   88.7
```

However, we can save the data into a file, matches:

```
% sort data | uniq -u > matches
```

With the data stored in matches, fgrep can search data for matches
in matches:

```
% fgrep -xf matches data
```

yielding

```
8   87.9
9   88.7
53  88
9   88
```

The -f option has a limit on the number of patterns which may be
used. If you exceed the limit, grep will fail.

1.4.7   head/tail

Having found the line number in which a particular pattern occurs, it
would be useful to have a tool which allows a view of material

surrounding the line in question. head allows the first n lines of a file to be viewed, while tail allows the last n lines of a file to be viewed. The usage for each is:

```
head [-count] [file ...]
tail [+|-number][lbc][fr] [file ...]
```

The options for head are:

- *-count*   The number *count* of lines to print from the top of the concatenated set of files.

The options for tail are:

- *+number*   Print after the first *number* of lines, characters, or blocks.
- *-number*   Print the last *number* of lines, characters or blocks.
- l   Print by lines.
- c   Print by characters.
- b   Print by blocks.
- f   Keep reading the file as information is appended.
- r   Print the output in reverse order.

As an example, consider the file, colors:

```
red
yellow
blue
green
black
white
purple
```

The command

```
% head -2 colors
```

yields

```
red
yellow
```

while the command

```
% tail -2 colors
```

yields

```
white
purple
```

The command

```
% tail +4 colors
```

yields

```
black
white
purple
```

The `-f` option is useful for watching a file being generated by another program (perhaps in the background or by another user). For example, suppose that we send the command:

```
% dosomething > output &
```

Now suppose that we are interested in how far along the program has come and we use `tail`:

```
% tail output
```

```
12
18
17
...
```

However, `tail` stops before the program generating `output`. To keep it watching `output` we must use the command

```
% tail -f output
```

1.4.8 sed

`sed` stands for *stream editor*. It allows editing of long files and standard input. It is useful for converting formats, deleting lines, adding lines, and printing portions of files. sed is a powerful but complicated command. We will present only the vital parts of sed. Its usage is

```
sed [-n] [-e expression] [-f sfile] [file ...]
```

and its options are

- -n   Do not output to standard out. However, do set the error flags after completion.

- -e*expression*   Apply *expression* to a file. More than one expression may be applied by using additional -e commands.

- -f*sfile*   The file *sfile* contains multiple expressions to be applied to the file.

A sed expression consists of three parts. The first part is the address (the lines) for which commands are to be applied. The second part is the function to be applied, and the final part contains the options to apply. The format is expressed as

```
[address] [command] [options]
```

The address can be a single line or a set of lines. It can be a specific line number or numbers or can be addressed by a regular expression. For example, /Dallas/,/Houston/ would address all the lines which contain a line matching *Dallas* and *Houston* inclusive. The address space, in either number or regular expression format, bridges files. It is as if the files had first been put together using cat. There are a number of commands available:

- a*text*   Append *text* after the selected address.

- c*text*   Delete the lines in the selected address and replace them with *text*.

- d   Delete the lines in the selected address.

- D   Delete the first line in the selected address.

- g   Replace the address with the information in the hold space.

- G   Append the hold space to the addressed lines.

- h   Replace the hold space with the lines in the address space.

- H   Append the hold space with the lines in the address space.

- i \ *text*   Insert *text* before the address space

- n   Copy the pattern space to the standard output. Replace the pattern space with the next line of input.

- N   Append the next line of input to the pattern space with an embedded newline.

- p   Print the pattern space to the standard output.

- P   Print the first line of the pattern space to the standard output.

- q   Quit.

- r *rfile*   Read the contents of *rfile*. Place them on the standard output before reading the next line.

- s / *regular expression* / *replacement string* / *flags*
           Substitute *replacement string* for instances of *regular expression*. A symbol other than / may be used instead. The flags available are: b to print the pattern space, g to replace more than one regular expression per line (by default only one is replaced), and w*wfile* to append the pattern space to *wfile* if a replacement was made.

- x   Exchange the pattern and hold spaces.

- y / *string1* / *string2* /
           Substitute the individual characters in *string1* with the corresponding characters in *string2* (like tr, described in Section 1.4.9).

- ! *function*
           Apply the function to lines which are not in the address space only.

- {   Execute the commands given through a matching } .

- =   Place the current line number on the standard output.

Perhaps the most common use of sed is to change a word in a file. Suppose that we are making a form letter and we want to use a standard template in a file called form:

```
Dear XXX:
We understand that you are just becoming familiar with
UNIX and that you are confused. Well, XXX, we can make
the problem of learning UNIX much easier. With this
book, you will be able to perform lots of tasks that
you thought required special programmers.
                    Sincerely,
                    ACME Publishing
```

To prepare this letter for John, we would use the command

```
sed 's/XXX/John/g' < form
```

In this example there is no address; thus the entire file is to have the substitution of *XXX* for *John*. The g says that multiple occurrences of *XXX* are to be changed on a line. By default, only one change per line is normally made.

Care must be taken with pattern matching, especially when performing substitutions. For example, if we want to substitute all occurrences of the word *the* for *that*, using the command

```
sed 's/the/that/'
```

with the input

```
The dog barked at the cat and together they ran away.
```

would yeild

```
The dog barked at that cat and togethatr thaty ran
away.
```

The concept of a word needs to be better defined. A word starts a line, is preceded by a space and ends the line, or is followed by a space. To handle capital letters we use the set notation and the capability of remembering a match to keep the first letter capitalized if appropriate:

```
% sed -e 's/\( [tT]\)he / \1hat /' -e 's/\(^[tT]\)he
/\1hat /'
```

This yeilds

```
That dog barked at that cat and together they ran away.
```

While substitutions are the most common use of sed, record editing
(see grep also) is also possible. sed allows contextual inclusion of
information. For example, the first part of a mail message is garbage,
and we may want to delete up to some line. If we had a file called mail
containing the following:

```
to:   brinerj@hamlet.acc.uncg.edu
from:   jvb@cs.duke.edu
date:   01-JAN-91 00:02:03
subj:   sed
message:

Dear Jack,
I am having problems with sed. I think I can do many
things with it, but I don't have a clue. Could you
send me some examples?
```

we could delete the header information with the command

```
% sed '1,/message:/d' mail
```

yeilding

```
Dear Jack,
I am having problems with sed. I think I can do many
things with it, but I don't have a clue. Could you
send me some examples?
```

Suppose that we want to add a line, after the subject line, to tell us
that the file had been read. This requires the use of a sed script file,
which allows very complicated actions. To do the simple task of adding
a line, we need to create a file, add.sed, which contains

```
/subj:/a\
read: yes
```

This finds the "address" of the subject line and appends the line *read:
yes*. To execute the script, we type

```
% sed -f add.sed mail
```

which yields

```
to:   brinerj@hamlet.acc.uncg.edu
from:  jvb@cs.duke.edu
date:  01-JAN-91 00:02:03
subj:  sed
read:  yes
message:

Dear Jack,
I am having problems with sed. I think I can do many
things with it, but I don't have a clue. Could you
send me some examples?
```

   sed can be used like grep if the -n option of sed is used. Normally, all lines are output. However, we can specify, for instance, that only lines in the address space are to be printed. For example, to print only the lines that have *XXX* in the file form, we would use

```
% sed -n '/XXX/p' form
```

which yields

```
Dear XXX:
and that you are confused. Well, XXX, we can make the
```

   sed is a difficult command to use and understand. For a more thorough review, *Sed & Awk* by Dale Dougherty (O'Reilly and Associates, Inc., 1990) is a good reference.

1.4.9 tr

It is frequently necessary to translate characters to other characters. For example, a file may need to be converted to all capital letters. tr is the fastest UNIX mechanism available for this kind of conversion. Its usage is

```
tr [-[ds]] [string1 [string2]]
```

and its options are

- -d   Delete all the characters in *string1*.
- -s   Squeeze all the matching characters in *string2* into one occurrence.

   tr takes input only from standard input and outputs to standard out. Thus, we need either to use indirection or pipe input from another program such as cat.

To convert lowercase to uppercase using indirection, we could type

```
% tr 'a-z' 'A-Z' < weather
```

or use an input pipe:

```
% cat weather | tr 'a-z' 'A-Z'
```

to yield

```
HOUSTON 56   75   0.02
DALLAS 60 77 0.00
PHILADELPHIA 65 66 1.20
WASHINGTON 50 55 0.00
SEATTLE 66 77 1.20
```

Any characters can be converted, including newlines. Special characters, such as newlines, are represented by a backslash \ followed by their octal equivalent. A newline is character 10 (decimal), which is 12 (octal). All octal numbers should be preceded by a zero. Thus, to convert all the spaces in a file to newlines, we type

```
% head -2 weather | tr ' ' '\012'
```

which yields

```
Houston
56
75
0.02
Dallas
60
77
0.00
```

To get rid of multiple spaces in a file, the squeeze option is very useful. Consider the file wasted:

```
This      file    has unnecessary    spaces. It    would
be nice   to have  something to get  rid of the spaces.
```

The tr command can convert spaces to a different number of spaces, but with the -s option, the translation process deletes repeats:

```
% tr -s ' ' ' ' < wasted
```

The result is

```
This file has unnecessary spaces. It would
be nice to have something to get rid of the spaces.
```

To delete all the spaces, the command

```
% tr -s ' ' < wasted
```

yields

```
Thisfilehasunnecessaryspaces.Itwould
benicetohavesomethingtogetridofthespaces.
```

1.4.10 tee

As you become more comfortable with the programs discussed here, you will be likely to create long pipes. One problem with long pipes is that it is difficult to determine where errors occur. tee is a program to help with these problems. tee allows standard input to flow in two directions: to a file and to standard output.

Suppose we wanted to look at the results of the sort of the sort-uniq pipeline. We could make the middle file using the following:

```
% sort < input > sorted
% uniq < sorted > uniqitems
```

or with tee,

```
% sort < input | tee sorted | uniq > uniqitems
```

1.4.11 Advanced Text Processing Tools

There are a number of other programs that can assist in transforming data. These include the C preprocessor and the M4 preprocessor. These programs generally require much more knowledge and have more specific usage needs.

The C preprocessor is accessible from the C compiler (cc) with the -E option or directly with cpp, which is usually located in /lib. The compiler expects input from a file with a .c extension, while the preprocessor expects input from standard in. Both send the output to standard out. cpp outputs line information for the C compiler.

M4 provides more flexibility than cpp. It does not have to have the line information output by cpp, and has built-in string handling for macros that are defined.

1.5   Information About Files

It can be difficult to judge the contents a file by its name. Sometimes we are interested in figuring out what kinds of data the file contains. Other times we actually need to see the file. We may be interested in the size of the file or in how it has changed. At other times we just need to be able to find a particular file. This section discusses each of these problems in turn.

1.5.1   File

The command `file` determines the type of a file. In particular, it looks at magic numbers. If it cannot find a valid magic number, then it tries to read the first few lines to determine the file's type. For example, suppose that we want to determine the type of file `/usr/ucb/vi`. The command

```
% file /usr/ucb/vi
```

yeilds

```
/usr/ucb/vi:   mipsel demand paged sticky executable
```

This tells us that the file is for a mips machine, is demand paged, has the sticky bit set, and is executable.

1.5.2   page/more/pg/less

There are a number of programs that allow you to view a file. Of course, there are the editors: ed, ex, vi, and emacs. However, data are frequently viewed as the standard output result of a command. Rather than taking disk space, using these commands at the end of a pipe gives one a quick view of the output. They can also be used to view a file. Each program is slightly different. We mention them here only to get your attention. Table 1.4 summarizes the differences between them. In general, less is the most flexible and powerful program. It is available from software archives (Section 1.9). The other commands come with the operating system.

	more/page	**pg**	**less**
Availability	UCB	System V	Public Domain
Movement	Forward or backward are now supported	Forward or backward	Forward or backward
Pattern search	Supported	Supported, plus capability to match nth pattern	Forward and backward movement supported
Scrolling	By page or line	By page or line	Flexible, easy to move a specified number of lines or go to a certain percentage of the file
Brace matching	Unsupported	Unsupported	Supported
Options	Command line	Command line	Command line and environment variables
Tags	Unsupported	Unsupported	Fully supported
Key bindings	Fixed	Fixed	Adjustable

Table 1.4   File viewing options

1.5.3 wc

The size of a file tells us quite a bit about it. The ls command can provide information about the number of bytes in a file, as well as whether the file is executable and what permissions exist on it. Other information that might be useful is the number of lines or words in a file. wc provides the number of bytes, words, and characters in a file or files. Its usage is

```
wc [-l][-w][-c]  [file ...]
```

and its options are

- -l   List the number of lines.
- -w   List the number of words (space separated items).
- -c   List the number of characters.

If more than one file is named in the command, each file is listed and a total reported. If no file is provided, standard input is used. Below is a command to determine the number of users on the system:

```
% who | wc -l
```

Of course, the command uptime would be just as effective.

1.5.4   diff/cmp

A common problem is determining whether two files are identical, and if not, how they differ. diff allows comparison of text files. It does a comparison which attempts to determine the least number of inserts, deletes, and changes that are necessary to translate one of the files to the other. It outputs the changes by displaying commands similar to ed which could be used to translate from one to the other. diff has many options which we won't discuss here. The ones that are most frequently useful are: directory comparison (-r), the merge option (-D), and the ignore trailing white space (-b).

cmp (compare) is used to detect if two files are exactly the same. If they are different, the byte number of the difference is reported. cmp is used mostly to compare binary files.

1.5.5   find/whereis/which

Sometimes it is difficult to find a file in a complicated tree structure. Worse yet, sometimes you need a program but do not know its exact name or where it is located.

If you have a program in your path but want to know exactly where it is, the which command will search your path for the program after checking any aliases in your .cshrc.

If you know the name of the program but it is not in your path, whereis will search a system database to find the name. For example,

```
% whereis vi
```

yields

```
vi: /usr/ucb/vi /usr/man/man1/vi.1
```

This tells you that vi is located in /usr/ucb, and that the manual pages are in /usr/man/man1/man1. Thus, you can add /usr/ucb to your path so that vi will be immediately available.

However, if you don't know the name of the program (and `apropos` does not help), or if the program is not a system program, you may need to perform a broader search.

`find` is one of the most powerful and flexible commands. It searches a directory and subdirectories and performs tests to determine where to search and what to do if a particular pattern is found. Its usage is

`find` *pathname-list expression*

pathname-list is a list of directories to search (use `.` for current directory). *expression* is an expression consisting of

- `-fstype` *type*   TRUE if the file system is of type *type* (nfs, 4.2, ufs).

- `-name` *name*   TRUE if the current filename matches the regular expression contained in *name*.

- `-perm` *onum*   TRUE if the permission is exactly the octal number, *onum* (see `chmod`).

- `-prune`   Always returns TRUE. A way to stop a search after a certain level.

- `-type` *c*   TRUE if the file is of type *c* given below:
  - · b   for block special file
  - · c   for character special file
  - · d   for directory
  - · f   for plain file
  - · l   for symbolic link

- `-l` *n*   TRUE if the file has *n* links.

- `-user` *uname*   TRUE if the file belongs to user (by name or `uid`).

- `-group` *gname*   TRUE if the file belongs to group (by name or `gid`).

- `-size` *n*   TRUE if file is *n* blocks long.

- `-inum` *n*   TRUE if the file is `inode` number *n*.

- `-atime` *n*   TRUE if the file was accessed *n* days ago. (You can use +n to mean *n* or more days or -n to mean *n* or fewer days.)

- -mtime *n*   TRUE if the file was modified *n* days ago. (You can use the +n and -n notation above.)

- -exec *command*   TRUE if the executed command returns with a zero status. The end of the command must be an escaped semicolon. An argument of the form { } represents the current program.

- -ok *command*   Like exec except that the user is requested to enter y to execute the command.

- -print   Print the path of the file.

- -newer *file*   TRUE if the current file has been modified more recently than file.

- ( )   Parenthesis may be used to group operators. The parenthesis should be escaped by a \ to avoid conflict with the shell.

- !   Negation of the expression (should be escaped).

- -o   TRUE if the command to the left or the command to the right is TRUE.

To use the program to find a particular file called letter in your home directory structure, type

```
% find ~ -name letter -print
```

This will start a search in your home directory (denoted by the ~) and then search files in that directory to see if they have the name letter. If there is one, the program prints the path to that file relative to the starting point. The search continues down any subdirectories (even if letter was found) looking for more matches.

Another common use of find is to compress files (see Section 1.8.3) which have not been used lately. By compressing files, space is saved. The problem is deciding which files should be compressed. The find command has the capability to test certain attributes of a file such as its type, its permissions, its owner, and when it was last accessed. The -exec option allows a program to be executed when a match is found. The executed command can have arguments, one of which may be the most recently matched file which is designated by { }. The command is terminated by \ ; and takes the following form:

```
% find ~ -atime +120 -type f \! -name "*.Z" -exec
compress {} \;
```

This command starts a search in your home directory and compresses each file in that directory or any subdirectories which was last accessed more than 120 days ago—provided that the name of the file does not end in a .z which means it has already been compressed. If you do not want to automatically have everything compressed, use -ok instead of -exec, which gives you the choice of whether to execute compress.

The + sign is significant in a find operation. Without it, find looks for files that were changed exactly 120 days ago.

1.6   awk: Programming Without Hassles

awk is a simple programming language for manipulating ASCII data files. awk gets its unusual name from its authors, Alfred W. Aho, Peter J. Weingerger and Brian W. Kernighan. Brian Kernighan was one of the authors of C, and thus C's influence is seen in awk. However, awk is much simpler to learn and use.

There are currently two versions of awk on most systems. The original version is called awk, and the newer version is called nawk. The new version provides better file-handling, pipes, functions and a few other improvements. Our discussion will draw from nawk; however, all of the examples, except for functions, should work with awk.

1.6.1   General Organization

In its simplest form, an awk program consists of pattern and action sets. A pattern is a Boolean expression. The most common Boolean expression used in awk is a string pattern match based on regular expressions. awk actions have a C-like syntax, but there are no variable declarations and no variable types. All variables hold strings of characters.

Pattern and action sets are acted upon during awk's main input cycle, which repeatedly performs the following steps until there is no more input:

1. A line of input is read.

2. The line is broken into fields delineated by white spaces.

3. Patterns described in the pattern action set are matched.

4. The actions of matched patterns are performed.

Below is a simple program to print out all lines which have the words *awk* or *UNIX* in them.

```
$0 ~ /awk/ { print }
$0 ~ /UNIX/ { print }
```

The part of each line before the the brackets is the pattern and the part in the brackets is the action. In this simple program, the input is to be scanned and each line is to be tested if it has the word *awk*. If a match is found, the action print will be performed, printing the input line. Likewise, the input will be checked to see if *UNIX* is in the line, and will print the line if it is.

The program can be stored in a file such as AU.awk. Then the program can be executed by typing:

```
% nawk -f AU.awk
```

Now, awk reads the file AU.awk for the set of pattern and actions which make up the program. The input is now assumed to be coming from the terminal. If instead we wanted it to come from a file we could use indirection from a file, input:

```
UNIX is an operating system that was developed at Bell
Labs. The first real users of the operating system were
at universities. UNIX provided a number of tools
besides the usual tools for looking at directories,
printing files and accessing other computers. One of
the best tools is awk. The authors of awk were guided
by the need for quick data manipulation.
```

This is accomplished using the command

```
% nawk -f AU.awk < input
```

which yields

```
UNIX is an operating system that was developed at Bell
at universities. UNIX provided a number of tools
the best tools is awk. The authors of awk were guided
```

A shortcut is to use a shell feature. If the first line of our awk program begins with #!/bin/nawk -f, nawk is automatically called. Thus, to run automatically we have:

```
#!/bin/nawk -f
$0 ~ /awk/ { print }
$0 ~ /UNIX/ { print }
```

If the file is made executable using chmod:

```
% chmod a+x AU.awk
```

then the program can be executed:

```
% AU.awk < input
```

nawk is started for us automatically, and yields the same output as before:

```
UNIX is an operating system that was developed at Bell
at universities. UNIX provided a number of tools
the best tools is awk. The authors of awk were guided
```

1.6.2 Pattern Matching

Pattern matching is the problem of finding if, for a given string of characters, there is a subsequence of characters in the string which is also in the regular expression set.

String pattern matching in awk uses the ~ operator. A regular expression is defined within //. A string can be the value stored in a variable, the contents of a string within " ", or even an arithmetic expression. For example,

```
"abc" ~ /abc/        Matches
"abc" ~ /[abc]/      Matches
"abc" ~ /[abc]+/     Matches
"a" ~ /abc/          Does not match
"ab" ~ /abc/         Does not match
```

We can also pattern match if no match occurs. This is done with the !~ operator. For example,

```
"abc" !~ /abc/        Does not match
"abc" !~ /[abc]/      Does not match
"abc" !~ /[abc]+/     Does not match
"a" !~ /abc/          Matches
"ab" !~ /abc/         Matches
```

A pattern match doesn't care exactly where in the string the regular expression is found. Sometimes, it is necessary to root the match so that it occurs at the beginning. For example, suppose we want to find all the strings that start with an a.

```
"abc" ~ /a/          Matches
"cba" ~ /a/          Also matches
```

To root the match, we use a caret ^ to say that the following regular expression matches only if the string starts with the regular expression.

```
"abc" ~ /^a/          Matches
"cba" ~ /^a/          Does not match
"cba" !~ /^a/         Matches because the !~ operator was used
```

Sometimes, it is necessary to root the match so that it occurs at the end. For example, suppose we want all the strings that end with a *c*.

```
"abc" ~ /c/           Matches
"cba" ~ /c/           Also matches
```

To root the match on the end, we use a $ to say that the following regular expression matches only if the string ends with the regular expression:

```
"abc" ~ /c$/          Matches
"cba" ~ /c$/          Does not match
```

Remember that pattern matching is not just string pattern matching, it is really a Boolean expression. The ~ operator is just a fancy equivalence test. Thus, a larger Boolean expression can be performed. Something like, line ~ /c$/ && a == 3, is also acceptable and may have the interpretation, "If the string line ends in a *c* and the variable a has the value 3, the pattern match is TRUE." Variables like a are good as state variables, which may be used to tackle a more complicated programming problem in which a string pattern match is not always supposed to be performed.

Two special patterns exist, BEGIN and END. BEGIN is a pattern which is matched before any input is read, while END is a pattern which is matched upon the end-of-file being reached.

BEGIN might be useful for initializing a variable. For example, if we were to count the number of lines that have the word *Zoo* in them, we would initialize a counter before we started matching. When all the lines had been read, we would want to print the number of lines with matches. This would be matched with the END pattern. The total program would look like:

```
BEGIN { count = 0}
$0 ~ /Zoo/ {count = count + 1}
END {print "Zoo was in " count " lines"}
```

1.6.3 Actions

The actions available in awk are nearly the same as those provided by C. Most obvious are the arithmetic, and Boolean operators as well as assignment. If you are familiar with C, you can also take advantage of the prefix and postfix operators, ++ and --. The operation assignment operator, +=, format is also available.

There are four basic statements for control within an action:

- if
- while
- do-while
- for

The if statement allows the flow of control between one of two possibilities. Any integer expression can be used to decided which action to follow. If the expression results in a nonzero result, the first action is performed. With a zero result, the second action is performed.

However, be careful with your test statements. The use of = is for assignment whether in a Boolean expression or in an assignment statement. == is used for comparison. For example, consider

```
if (a = 1)
      print "this is always executed"
else
      print "this is never executed"
```

The first part of the if statement is always executed and the value of a is changed to 1.

With ==, as shown below, the value of a is not changed and which print statement will be performed depends on the value of a.

```
if (a==1)
      print "only executed if a has the value 1"
else
      print "executed whenever a is not 1"
```

If we need to perform more than one action with an if statement or any of the other control programs, we must make a compound statement using {}. The brackets allow multiple statements, including other if statements, while statements, etc. For example, if we wanted to print all the lines containing *Duke* or *UNC* and count them, we need to conditionally perform two actions instead of just one. Thus, a compound statement is necessary:

```
if ($0 ~/Duke|UNC/) {
    print $0;
    count = count + 1;
    }
```

Another useful control statement is the `while` statement. The `while` statement allows code between braces `{ }` to be repeated while the Boolean expression is nonzero. For example, if we wanted to count the number of times the word *letter* occurs on a line, we could use the following actions:

```
i = 1;
count = 0;
while (i <= NF) {
    if ($i == "leter")
            count = count +1;
    i = i + 1;
    }
print "letter occurred " count " times on line: " NR
```

The first assignment, `i = 1`, says that the first word to be searched is the first word. The second assignment statement, `count = 0`, initializes a count that will keep track of how many lines had *letter* in them. The next statement declares that the next three lines are to be executed while `i` is less than the number of fields on the current line (`NF` is a variable which is automatically set on each line read). The next statement says that if the `i`th word on the line is *letter* (but not *letterman*, for example), the variable count will be incremented by 1. The next statement, `i = i + 1`, says that `i` is to be incremented by 1 on each pass through the loop. The loop will terminate when `i` exceeds the number of fields (words) on the line. After the `while` completes, the number of times *letter* was found and the record number for the line being processed are printed.

The effects of both the `do-while` and `for` statement can be mimicked with the `if` and and `while` statements. For those familiar with C, the statements are equivalent. However, the `for` statement has one special case not handled in C. With an array, the elements of the array can be sequentially accessed with the `in` variation.

Arrays in awk have strings as subscripts, so anything goes. For example, to store phone numbers we might have a file that looks like:

```
Jack   555-1212
John   555-8128
Jane   555-8273
```

We could read the file with:

```
{ phone[$1] = $2}
```

After reading all the numbers, we could print them out in nonalpha-numeric order:

```
END { for (i in phone)
        print i "'s phone number is " phone[i]
    }
```

Here the `in` operator allows each subscript of the array to be operated on. The order in which the subscripts are returned is not specified, and the list is not necessarily in alphabetic order:

```
John's phone number is 555-8128
Jane's phone number is 555-8273
Jack's phone number is 555-1212
```

1.6.4 Functions

awk programs can become complicated very quickly. To reduce the complexity, the new version of awk (nawk) allows repeated actions to be made into user functions. Thus, if we frequently need to perform a complicated procedure, we can make the procedure into a function.

A function is declared before all actions, including `BEGIN`. A function is defined `func`, followed by the function name and a parenthesized formal argument list. For example, if we frequently needed to put two lists together, we could use the following:

```
func join(a,b,c) {
    for (i in a)
          c[i] = a[i]
    for (i in b)
          c[i] = c[i] " " b[i]
}
```

Now to join two lists into a third, we just say

```
join(phone,address,joint);
```

This will create a new list called joint which contains both phone numbers and addresses. The function works by initializing c with each element of a. If the lists of a and b have different indices, those which are not in both will be put in c. If we only want ones that are in both, we could use the in operator to test to see if an element in b is also in a. For example, we could use

```
func join(a,b,c) {
     for (i in a)
           if (i in b)
                c[i] = a[i] " " b[i]
}
```

This function ensures that only elements which are both in a and b are included in c. Note that you should not attempt to perform a test like b[i] != "" because this will create an element in b if one did not already exist.

Functions may also return a string. Thus if we wanted to count the number of times that a string occurred in a list, we could use

```
func count(a,b) {
total = 0;
for (i in b)
     if (b[i] ~ a)
           total += 1;
     return total;
     }
```

One problem with functions in awk is that variables that are not in the parameter list are global. Thus, the variable i may destroy another i already in use. For example, problems are sure to ensue if we call the function count in a program like:

```
BEGIN {
     . . .
     for (i in list)
           print i "occurs " count(i,somelist) " times
           in somelist"
     }
```

The i used in the BEGIN is the same as the one used in the function call; thus the for loops are working on the same variables. To remedy this we can add extra parameters:

```
func count(a,b,total,i) {
        total = 0;
        for (i in b)
              if (b[i] ~ a)
                    total += 1;
        return total;
        }
```

Here both i and total are local to the function count. Note that the call to count need only have the first two arguments as before:

```
count(i,somelist);
```

1.6.5 Advanced Features

Because not all files are broken into fields by spaces and tabs, the variable FS can be used to break fields on any particular regular expression. Likewise, the variable RS can be used to separate records based on a regular expression. Suppose that we had a file, phone, that looked like

```
Jack Briner, 555-1234;John Smith, 555-9876;
Abby Jones, 555-6543; Melissa Fee, 555-8793
```

To write a program, tele, that could print the names and phone numbers for a directory, we would want a comma to separate fields and a semicolon to separate records:

```
#!/bin/nawk -f
BEGIN {
        FS = ","
        RS = ";"
        }
{list[$1] = $2}
END{
        for (i in list)
              print i " " list[i]
        }
```

Executing the program on phone:

```
% tele phone
Jack Briner 555-1234
John Smith 555-9876
Melissa Fee 555-8793
Abby Jones 555-6543
```

Suppose that we had different phone formats and that we wanted to specify a command line argument to distinguish between formats. In general, command line arguments are interpreted as files against which to run the awk program. However, before this is done, the BEGIN action is executed, allowing time to look and even modify the arguments. The variable ARGC has the number of command line arguments (not including commands directed to awk, such as -f) plus the command itself. Let us assume that the input is always from standard input. If the number of inputs to the command is greater than 1, then there are arguments. We will assign the first argument to be the field separator and the second, if present, to be the record separator. Adding the following BEGIN allows us to select the separator by accessing the ARGV array, which contains the arguments:

```
BEGIN {
      if (ARGC > 1) {
            FS = ARGV[1]
            ARGV[1]= "";
            }
      if (ARGC > 2) {
            RS = ARGV[2]
            ARGV[2]= "";
            }
      }
```

If fields in our file were separated by semicolons and records were separated by newlines, we would need to specify only the ; argument because the default record separator is a newline. A sample command would thus be:

```
% tele ";" < phone2
```

The sub, gsub, and split commands allow string processing after a match has been found. The < and > operations used in getline and print statements allow the redirection of input and output, respectively. | allows output to be sent directly to a UNIX command. For more detailed information on these advanced commands, consult the book by the awk authors.

When you are writing a program, you know how the problem is solved, who wrote the code, and when. Later, when something needs to be changed, you or someone who uses your code will need to know these things. Comments allow this information to be stored in the program but are ignored by the awk system. Comments consist of all the characters on a line after a sharp #. For example, for the program we might have:

```
#!/bin/nawk -f
# Created by Jack Briner 9/1/91
#
# This program allows viewing of a phone
# directory which can have arbitrary field
# and record separators.
#
# The format of the file should be:
# <name> <FS> <number> <RS>
#
# Where <name> is the name. <FS> is a field
# separator. <number> is the phone number. <RS> is
# the separator between fields.
#
# By default the field separator is a space and the
# record separator is a newline.
#
# Usage:
#   tele [FS [RS]]
#
BEGIN {
     if (ARGC > 1) {
          FS = ARGV[1]
          ARGV[1]= "";
          }
     if (ARGC > 2) {
          RS = ARGV[2]
          ARGV[2]= "";
          }
     }
{list[$1] = $2}
END{
     for (i in list)
          print i " " list[i]
     }
```

1.7   The Shell as Glue

In testing the programs in this chapter you have been using a command line interpreter known as a shell. However, as you have probably learned, it is difficult to remember the many steps necessary to solve a task. It would be nice to bundle them into a simple package or script which allows the commands to be performed automatically. Depending on which shell you are using, you have different options available. We will disuss the C-shell in some depth. If you are using another shell, you should examine the man pages or a book on the topic. Small sections on the Bourne shell and ksh follow and there is a table describing the differences between them and the csh.

1.7.1   The C-Shell (csh)

The C-Shell is the most commonly used shell in the academic community, because of its heritage. It was invented at UC-Berkeley by Bill Joy to add more flexible job control. The two most important added capabilities over the earlier Bourne shell are its history mechanism and aliases. The history mechanism allows the editing and reexecution of commands previously executed.

The alias mechanism allows complicated commands to be abbreviated. For example, suppose we wanted to see if John was logged onto the computer, but did not want to search through the output of the who command. That could be done with the command:

```
who | fgrep john
```

However, this is rather cumbersome, so we might make an alias:

```
alias john 'who | fgrep john'
```

The single quotes ' are significant. Without the single quotes the bar | would cause the alias command to end, and would cause the result of performing the alias (nothing) to be searched for the string *john*. The quotes allow the pipeline to be executed when john is entered from the keyboard.

Now, suppose that we would rather find out if a particular person, not necessarily John, is here. We could write the alias,

```
alias here 'who | fgrep'
```

This allows us to say

```
% here sandy
```

This may give us

```
sandy ttypa Nov 8 14:00
sandy ttypb Nov 8 14:00
sandy ttypc Nov 8 14:01
```

This is more information than we want, if we just want to know if `sandy` is here. Instead, we want to perform some post processing after we do the `grep`. This poses a problem. If we tried to create an alias:

```
alias here 'who | fgrep | head -1'
```

the pattern matching string *sandy* is an argument to `head` and not `fgrep`. To allow arguments to an aliased command to be substituted other than at the end of the alias, the escape sequence \ ! * is added at the appropriate place:

```
alias here 'who | fgrep \!* | head -1'
```

To make an alias part of your permanent work environment, you should save your alias in your `.cshrc` file.

Sometimes what needs to be done is more than can be done in a pipe. Frequently, tasks must be repeated or alternatives taken based upon the result of another operation. In order to automate the actions necessary for decisions, you need to create a shell script.

For example, suppose that we wanted the capability to send a form letter like the one described in Section 1.4.8. Recall that we have a file `form` which contains *XXX* where a name was to be substituted. The command:

```
sed 's/XXX/John/g' form
```

substitutes the name *John* for *XXX* in the file `form` and outputs the results to standard output. Suppose we had a list of people to whom we wanted to send the form letter and that their names were their electronic mail addresses. We could create a file `sendform` which looks like:

```
foreach i ($*)
    echo Sending form letter \"form\" to $i "."
    sed "s/XXX/$i/g" form | mail $i
    end
```

In order for the system to know that it can execute the file, we must mark it executable:

```
chmod a+x sendform
```

Now we can use the script:

```
% sendform Jack John Mary
```

This sends a letter to each person and works as follows. The `foreach` construct allows the variable `i` to take on each of the values specified in the parentheses. The arguments, `Jack`, `John`, and `Mary` are passed to the script as shell variables. As a group, they are accessed as `$*`. In the parentheses, the expanded list determines that `$i` will become `Jack`, `John`, and `Mary` in turn. As `$i` changes, the commands between the `foreach` and `end` will be executed, with `$i` substituted appropriately. Thus, the `sed` and `echo` lines become

```
echo Sending form letter \"form\" to Jack "."
sed "s/XXX/Jack/g" form | mail Jack
```

The echo line forces the line

```
Sending form letter "form" to Jack.
```

to appear. In order for the metacharacters . and " to appear, they need to be escaped with a backslash \.

The `sed` line translates *XXX* to *Jack* and sends Jack mail. Note that double quotes " were used rather than single quotes. If single quotes ' were used, the shell would not perform any variable substitutions and the line would have been interpreted as

```
sed 's/XXX/$i/g' form | mail Jack
```

Clearly, this is not what should be sent to Jack, because it will start off like

```
Dear $i,
```

One problem remains. What happens if we issue the following command:

```
% sendform
```

We get the error message `empty list`. We need to ensure that this will not happen. To avoid this message, we use the `if` statement to make `sendform` look like

```
if ($#argv == 0) then
      echo "Usage: $0 user(s)"
      exit 1
endif
```

```
foreach i ($*)
      sed "s/XXX/$i/g" form | mail $i
      end
```

The script now informs the user that the program was used incorrectly and that it requires the specification of the user or users to whom to send the message. The `if` checks to see if the number of arguments to the shell script (given by the command `$#argv`) is 0. If so, the lines between `then` and `end` are executed. Thus, when there are no arguments, the `echo` and `exit` commands are executed. The `$0` refers to the zero argument to the shell script, which is the name of the shell script. Other arguments can be accessed by number also. For example, to get the first argument if available, the shell variable `$1` could be used.

The shell script as it stands requires that the form letter be named `form`. Now, let us suppose that we want the form letter name to be the first argument. For example, suppose we wanted to send our friends another form letter stored in `info`. We would like to be able to do this easily, like

```
% sendform info Jack John Mary
```

The script to do this is the following:

```
if ( $#argv < 2 ) then
      echo "Usage: $0 letter user(s)"
      exit 1
endif

set form=$1
shift
if ( ! -f $form || ! -r $form ) then
      echo "$form does not exist or is not readable."
      exit 1
endif

foreach i ($*)
      sed "s/XXX/$i/g" $form | mail $i
      end
```

The `if` statement is updated to reflect the fact that there must be at least two arguments (the form and one person). The next statement stores the name of the form letter in a variable named `$form`. This, together with the `shift` statement, allow the use of the `$*` in the familiar `foreach` statement. The `shift` statement adjusts the arguments so that the first argument disappears (we saved it in `$form`) and `$2` becomes `$1`, and so on. Next we check to see if the file stored in `$form` exists, is a plain file, and is readable. Here we use two of the file query operators (`-f` and `-r`) shown in Table 1.5. The `-f` tests to see if the file exists and if it is a file that is normal. The `-r` tests to see if the user has the capability to read the file. The `!` negates the results of the test. The `||` is the relational operator or, which returns TRUE if either one or both of the expressions are TRUE. Thus we could read the `if` expression as, "If the file contained in the variable form is not a plain file or is not readable, then report an error and exit." The logical operators are presented in Table 1.6, and the relational operators are presented in Table 1.7. Note that some operators require the use of parentheses to avoid confusion with other meanings (such as command substitution and pipes).

Flag	Meaning
d	File is a directory
e	File exists
f	File is a normal file
r	Readable file
w	Writable file
x	Executable file
z	Zero length file

Table 1.5 File query operators in csh

Operator	Meaning	Examples	Result
`||`	OR	`(1 == 1 || 1 == 2)`	1
		`(1 == 2 || 1 == 3)`	0
`&&`	AND	`(1 == 1 && 1 == 2)`	0
		`(1 < 2 && 4 > 3)`	1
`!`	NOT	`! (1 == 1)`	0

Table 1.6 Logical operators in csh

Operator	Meaning	Examples	Result
==	Equal	1 == 1	1
!=	Not equal	1 != 1	0
>	Greater than	1 > 2	0
>=	Greater than or equal	1 >= 1	1
<	Less than	1 < 2	1
<=	Less than or equal	3 <= 1	0

Table 1.7 Relational operators in csh

Another useful construct is the while statement. The while statement allows repeated testing of a condition. Suppose we want to have the computer notify us when someone logs in. The following program, sleuth, could be created:

```
#!/bin/csh
while ( 'u | fgrep -c $1' == 0 )
     sleep 300
end
echo " "
echo "$1 is IN"
echo " "
```

The program keeps looping until the first argument to the script logs in. This is tested by using the u command to see who is on the system and then piping that to fgrep, which counts the number of times the requested user is on. If the result is 0, the loop continues. Because we do not want to waste system resources by continually running the command, we have the script sleep for five minutes (300 seconds) each time the user is not found to be on the system.

Shells can be made interactive, allowing the user to input data while the shell is executing instead of as a command line argument. For example, if we wanted to make sleuth interactive:

```
#!/bin/csh
echo -n "Whom do you seek? "
set usr=$<
while ( 'grep -c "^${usr}:" /etc/passwd' == 0 )
     echo "$usr is not in the password file."
     echo -n "Whom do you seek? "
     set usr=$<
end
```

```
while ( 'u | grep -c $usr' == 0 )
    sleep 300
end
echo " "
echo "$usr is IN"
echo " "
```

The echo command's -n option is used so that a newline is not added after the text is printed. This allows the user to input his or her response on the same line:

```
Whom do you seek? briner
```

The next line ensures that the user did not mistype the user's login name, by checking to see if the user is in the password file. The grep command takes advantage of the -s option, which merely tests to see if a match is made. If a match is made, the error variable is set to 0; if a match is not made, it is set to 1. If we use the yellow pages system, we would need to use:

```
ypcat passwd | grep -s "$usr:"
```

The while loop then is continued as long as the user fails to enter a person who is not allowed on the system. The only way to get out of this loop is for the user to enter a user who is not allowed on the system or for the user to interrupt the command with a control-C.

Another enhancement to the sleuth program is to have the program kill itself after a certain number of tries. This means that we need csh to be able to count. To perform arithmetic with a variable in csh, set is not used; instead, @ is used:

```
set count=1
@ count=$count + 1
```

If instead we had tried using set:

```
set count=$count+1
```

We would have set $count to the value 1+1, not 2. Also, one should be careful to add spaces after the @ and around the +. The parsing capabilities of the shell are limited. In general, it is best to put spaces around operators. To avoid shell interpretation of some symbols (like |), it is best to add parenthesis also. For those familiar with C programming, the following commands are possible (see also Table 1.8):

```
@ count++
@ count += 1
```

Operator	Meaning	Defining	Result of echo $a
+	Addition	@ a = 1 + 1	2
-	Subtraction	@ a = 2 - 1	1
*	Multiplication	@ a = 2 * 2	4
/	Division	@ a = 7 / 3	2
%	Modulo	@ a = 7 % 3	1
|	OR	@ a = (4 | 5)	5
^	Exclusive OR	@ a = (4 ^ 5)	1
&	AND	@ a = (4 & 5)	4
~	Complement	@ a = (~15)	−16

Table 1.8 Arithmetic operators in csh

The final version of the sleuth program is given below. We have
added some more extensions beyond those for ensuring that the program would not wait more than an hour for the person sought to login.
MAXATTEMPTS is set at the beginning so that it is easy to modify if you
want to wait more than an hour (12 five minute periods). The if statement allows the user to decide whether to use a command line option
to select the user being sought. If there are no arguments, an interactive decision is wanted. If there is an argument, the first argument is
taken to be the user needed. The first while statement then ensures
that the person is in the password table. The next while loop does the
checking to see if the person has logged in. The variable attempts
keeps track of the number of times the test is performed. If the number of attempts exceeds the constant MAXATTEMPTS, the user is
informed that the time has been exceeded and that the program is giving up:

```
#!/bin/csh
set MAXATTEMPTS=12

if ($#argv == 0) then
      echo -n "Whom do you seek? "
      set usr=$<
else
      set usr=$1
endif
```

```
while ( 'grep -c "^${usr}:" /etc/passwd' == 0 )
      echo "$usr is not in the password file."
      echo -n "Whom do you seek? "
      set usr=$<
end

@ attempts = 1
while ( 'u | grep -c $usr' == 0 )
      @ attempts = $attempts + 1
      if ( $attempts > $MAXATTEMPTS) then
            echo "Giving up on $usr"
            exit 1
            endif
      sleep 300
end

echo " "
echo "$usr is IN"
echo " "
```

The switch statement is frequently used in interpreting command line options. Switch allows the comparison of a variable with many options, and allows operations to be performed based upon a match. This allows much more compact code than a series of if statements. For example, suppose that we wanted to have a program that can convert text from uppercase to lowercase or vice versa and that can also rotate the text so that a becomes n, b becomes o, n becomes a, etc.

The program below begins by setting flags to keep track of how the user wants to convert the file. By default, no conversion is performed. Next, the command line arguments are scanned one by one. The while loop counts down from the number of arguments remaining to be processed. If there are no arguments, the loop is skipped. For each argument the switch is tested. If it is a -u, the output flag is set to u, for *uppercase*. If it is a -l, the output flag is set to l, for *lowercase*. If it is -r, the output flag is r, for *rotate*. If an argument is none of these, the default option is taken and an error is output. After the command line argument is processed, all the command line arguments are shifted, making the second argument become the first. The old first argument is thrown away. The while loop is then tested to see if there are more arguments. If there are, then more flags are set. Once there are no more arguments, the processing of standard input begins. If the output flag is set, tr is used to convert to the proper case. If not, cat is used. The selected command is then executed and output is stored in the file /tmp/convert, with the process number appended. After that, the command for rotation is set up. If no rotation is to occur, cat is used. Otherwise, tr performs the rotation of the characters. Finally, the temporary file used for case conversion is removed:

```csh
#!/bin/csh -f
#
# This program has the capabilities to convert
# standard input:
#   (1) convert upper to lower case
#   (2) convert lower to upper case
#   (3) rotate the alphabetic text by 13 to
#    provide some privacy.
#
# Usage: convert [-[lu]] [-r]

set output=n # by default do not convert case
set rotate=n # by default do not rotate the alphabet
    while ( $#argv )
        switch ($1)
            case -u:
                set output=u
                breaksw
            case -l:
                set output=l
                breaksw
            case -r:
                set rotate=y
                breaksw
            default:
                echo "The command $1 is not
                understood"
                breaksw
        endsw
        shift
        end

set command=cat
if ($output == u) set command=(tr 'a-z' 'A-Z')
if ($output == l) set command=(tr 'A-Z' 'a-z')
$command > /tmp/convert$$
if ($rotate == y) then
    set command=(tr 'a-zA-Z' 'n-za-mN-ZA-M')
else
    set command=cat
endif

$command < /tmp/convert$$
rm -rf /tmp/convert$$
```

The goto statement allows execution to jump to a location given by a label. While using goto is considered poor programming practice by many, it is very useful in error handling. Once an error is detected it is convenient to jump to an error handling routine, clean up any stray problems and exit. Related to the goto statement is the onintr command, which causes execution to go to a specified label when a control-C is entered by the user. This, too, allows the cleanup of any unfinished business.

In the example below, a number of files are to be converted to uppercase letters from lowercase letters. In the process of converting files, we must be careful that the user cannot interrupt the moving of files. If he or she interrupts at the wrong time, a file could get lost. Thus, we use the onintr command to help us ensure smooth processing of the files. The set processed="" line initializes processed so that the user can be informed about the files that have been processed. The first onintr tells the shell to go to the line marked done: should the user interrupt the processing. A foreach loop then goes through each file given as an argument and begins processing. The file is converted by tr, whose output is sent to a file called tmp, with the process number attached (e.g., tmp1234, if the shell process is 1234). Then we want to ensure that the user cannot loose his or her file by interrupting the next process. So, the onintr with a dash (-) is given. Until the onintr is restored, the user cannot interrupt. During this time the file is moved and the list of files that have been processed is updated. After the foreach is finished or an interrupt has occurred (when allowed), the temporary file is removed (the -f option indicates not to complain if the file is nonexistent). Finally, the files that have been processed are reported:

```
#!/bin/csh
#
# This program converts the argument files to
# uppercase. Care is taken to ensure that if the user
# interrupts the process, no data will be lost.
#
# Usage: translate file [...]
#
set processed=""
onintr done
```

```
foreach i ($*)
      tr 'a-z' 'A-Z' < $i > tmp$$
      onintr -
      set processed=($i $processed)
      mv tmp$$ $i
      onintr done
end

done:
      rm -f tmp$$
      if ( "$processed" == "" ) then
            echo "No files were processed"
      else
            echo "Processed: " $processed
      endif
```

As a final note, a shell script is series of commands which direct a shell to perform some task. When a shell script is executed, another shell is created, and the script run through that shell. Thus, any environment changes (for example, path, setenv, and aliases) will not effect the shell which executed the shell script.

To find more about the C-Shell, *The UNIX C Shell Field Guide* by Gail and Paul Anderson is an excellent resource (Prentice Hall, 1986).

1.7.2   The Bourne Shell (sh)

The Bourne shell was the original shell provided with UNIX. Many of the system programmer utilities are written in this shell. If you need more information on this shell, the book *UNIX Shell Programming* by Lowell Jay Arthur (John Wiley & Sons, 1990) is useful. A comparison of the Bourne shell and the C Shell is given in Table 1.9.

Below is the sleuth program written in sh:

```
#!/bin/sh
while ( [ 'u | fgrep -c $1' = "0" ] ) do
      sleep 300
done

echo " "
echo "$1 is IN"
echo " "
```

C Shell	Bourne Shell
| ```
set a="hello, world"
@ a = $b * $c
set a=$<
``` | ```
a="hello world"
a='expr $b * $c'
read a
``` |
| ```
if ( $a == 1) then
   ...
endif
``` | ```
if ([ $a -eq 1 ]) then
   ...
fi
``` |
| ```
if ($1 > 7 || $j <= 5) then
   ...
else
   ...
endif
``` | ```
if ([ $a -gt 7 -o $j -le 5 ]) then
   ...
else
   ...
fi
``` |
| ```
while ( ! -f lock)
   ...
end
``` | ```
while ( [ ! -f lock ] ) do
   ...
done
``` |
| ```
foreach i ( a b c ) do
   ...
end
``` | ```
for i in a b c do
   ...
done
``` |
| ```
switch ( $a )
   case -a:
      ...
      breaksw
   case -b:
      ...
      breaksw
   default:
      ...
endsw
``` | ```
case $a in
   -a)
      ... ;;
   -b)
      ...;;
   *)
      ... ;;
esac
``` |

Table 1.9 Equivalent Bourne shell operations

1.7.3 The Korn Shell (ksh)

The Korn Shell is a greatly extended version of the Bourne Shell, and is perhaps the best shell. However, it is not available in many releases of UNIX. ksh allows much better control of the subshells and pipelines than any of the other shells. It also allows easy editing of past commands using either vi or emacs editor commands. Aliases are fully supported, and much more customization is possible. For more information about the Korn Shell, *The KornShell Command and Programming Language* by Morris I. Bolsky and David G. Korn (Prentice-Hall, 1989) is the ultimate reference. A quick reference of equivalent operations to csh is given in Table 1.10.

C Shell	Korn Shell

```
set a="hello, world"          a="hello world"
@ a = $b * $c                 let a=$b*$c
set a=$<                      read a

if ( $a == 1) then            if [[ $a -eq 1 ]]; then
    ...                           ...;
endif                         fi

if ($1 > 7 || $j <= 5) then   if [[ $a -gt 7 || $j -le 5 ]] ; then
    ...                           ...;
else                          else
    ...                           ...;
endif                         fi

while ( ! -f lock)            while [[  ! -f lock ]] ; do
    ...                           ...;
end                           done

foreach i ( a b c ) do        for i in a b c; do
    ...                           ...;
end                           done

switch ( $a )                 case $a in
   case -a:                       -a)
      ...                             ... ;;
      breaksw                    -b)
   case -b:                             ...;;
      ...                       *)
      breaksw                        ... ;;
   default:                    esac
      ...
endsw
```

Table 1.10   Equivalent ksh shell operations

Below is the `sleuth` program written in `ksh`:

```
#!/usr/bin/ksh
while [ 'u | fgrep -c $1' = "0" ] ; do
      sleep 3
done

echo " "
echo "$1 is IN"
echo " "
```

1.7.4   Other Shells or Environments for Shell Scripting

Another shell that you should be aware of is `tcs,h` which is a public domain shell extension of `csh` that adds command line editing like `ksh`, command line completion, better prompt handling, and many other features.

While `make` is not a shell, it provides access and control of programs, performing almost exactly the same duties as a shell. `make` is limited to making decisions based on the existence and last modification times of files. For more information about `make` see Chapter 2.

`perl` is an interpreted language built in a flavor of C, and has the strengths of awk and sed. `perl` can work on binary files and long lined files, problems that cannot not be handled by sed or awk. `perl` is in the public domain, and is reported to run faster than sed or awk.

1.8   Advanced Tools

We have focused on tools for text and data manipulation. However, there are other important tools available on most UNIX systems for looking at or manipulating data.

1.8.1   Where Is a Calculator?

Dealing with large numbers is frequently a problem in scientific fields, and many pocket calculators do not have the precision needed to solve certain problems. Also, despite the fact that you may have a $6,000 (or $2 million) computer in front of you, you might not have a $10 calculator.

bc and dc allow basic arithmetic operations at infinite precision. They also allow use of different bases. bc is just a front end processor for dc, which is rather cumbersome. For brevity, we will discuss bc. bc allows arbitrary precision arithmetic to be performed. Most computer languages are limited to working with finite representations of numbers, causing roundoff errors. bc allows very large or small numbers to be calculated. If more precision is needed, the scale command allows more precision to be added to the calculation.

bc runs from the keyboard and allows the definition of functions. However, most of the time, you just need to do a quick calculation. To do this, you can add a couple of aliases to your .cshrc file if you use that C-shell:

```
alias calc 'echo "scale=5; \!*" | bc'
alias d2x 'echo "obase=16; \!*" | bc'
alias x2d '(echo "ibase=16" ; echo "\!*" | tr "a-z"
"A-Z") | bc'
```

The first line allows you to type in simple expressions with 5 significant digits after the decimal place:

```
% calc 5*17/5.44
15.62500
```

The second line allows conversion of decimal numbers to hexadecimal. To do this, we must first change the base of the output. In general the input and the output are in decimal. This is changed with the `ibase` and `obase` commands, respectively. Thus, to change to hexadecimal output, we use the command `obase=16`:

```
% d2x 60
3C
```

The third line converts hexadecimal to decimal numbers. Thus, it requires an `ibase` of 16. The `tr` command is necessary because `bc` accepts only uppercase letters for hexadecimal inputs:

```
% x2d ff
255
```

1.8.2 Creating Graphs

UNIX comes with a graphing program called `graph`, which when used with the UNIX command `plot` can plot a graph of the contents of a file with x and y points on a number of plotting devices.

A much better program is the public domain program `gnuplot`. This program can produce plots of a number of functions, as well as data read from a file. `gnuplot` supports color and three-dimensional plotting. It has the capability of producing output for a very large number of devices, including the text processing language, LaTeX.

1.8.3 Saving Space and Reducing Transmission Times

The amount of data generated in your work may be enormous. To reduce the volume, you may compress your information into a more compact form. The result is not directly readable, but is perfectly reversible when needed later. This allows disk space to be saved or transmission time to be reduced. In most cases, the time to compress and uncompress is negligible.

`compress` takes as an argument a file or files. It takes each file and performs the Lempel-Ziv compression algorithm. It then destroys the original file and produces a file with the same name, having a .Z appended. `compress` can compress standard input if a dash is used as the file name. Standard out is then in compressed format.

A file can be reverted to its original state with uncompress, or it can be sent to standard out with zcat. If you have no room to uncompress a file, zcat is indispensable. For example, if you just want to search your very large phone directory for Jack's phone number, you might use:

```
zcat phone.Z | fgrep Jack
```

An alias that might be useful is:

```
alias zmore "zcat \!* | more"
```

This alias allows you to look at a file before uncompressing by simply typing

```
zmore file.Z
```

When sending large files over long distances, it is usually faster to compress the file on the foreign machine, send the file via ftp (or rcp), and then uncompress the file locally.

When dealing with standard output over long distances, it may also be useful to compress standard output:

```
% rsh foreign_machine 'bigprogram | compress - ' | zcat
```

Now bigprogram is run on foreign_machine, and its output is compressed on foreign_machine and then sent to the local machine, where it is uncompressed by zcat locally.

pack, unpack, and pcat work similarly but use the Huffman minimum redundancy codes on a byte-by-byte basis. The difference between pack and compress will vary by file. Most people seem to use compress.

1.8.4 Data Security

UNIX security is not foolproof, as many breakins have shown. However, even if breakins are not of concern, perusal of your files by privileged users is possible. Even if you have marked a file as readable only by you, a privileged user can look at, modify, or destroy any file. If you want to assure that a user with root privileges cannot look at a file, you must encode the file.

The crypt program provides a reasonable level of data encryption and decryption using a 256-rotor enigma algorithm. This is not the same mechanism used to encode your password. To keep a file from being seen when you are not using it:

```
% crypt key < file > secret
```

If you do not want to put the key on the command line, you can just say

```
% crypt < file > secret
```

This will prompt the user for the key. In any case, do not leave the original file hanging around, or there is no use in encrypting it.

To decrypt the file, you simply reverse the process:

```
% crypt key < secret > file
```

Vi, ex, and ed editors have the capability of reading and writing crypt files. So the steps above do not need to be performed directly when using one of these editors.

Some operating systems provide another level of encryption based upon the National Bureau of Standards' Data Encryption Standard (DES) using either the Cipher Block Chaining or Electronic Code Book format with the des command. This provides a higher level of protection but is relatively slow.

Whichever mechanism you choose, be aware that while you are looking at a file or have a file that is in plain text, it is not protected.

1.9   Finding Programs to Avoid Programming

When you think that your problem cannot be solved using the UNIX tools discussed here, you should double check by using man and apropos (see Section 1.2). If that does not seem to help, you may want to seek the advice of others. If you have a news feed, check the news groups available. Is one in your field? If so send a request for help to the appropriate group. A reply could be yours within a few hours.

As a response, you will likely be mailed a program or told to ftp a file from a machine. ftp stands for file transfer program. It provides the ability to login to a remote machine using the Internet, and to transfer files. Many systems provide *anonymous ftp*, which allows restricted access to some files on a system. By convention, you login to these machines by giving the login name of anonymous and a password that is your internet address. Upon logging in, you can look at what is in the directories with the ls command and change directories with the cd command.

Once you find the file that you wish, you should set the type of transfer that is going to be made. Three modes are supported, ASCII, binary, and tenex. If the file is just text, then ASCII should be selected by typing ascii at the ftp prompt. Binary should be used to transfer executable programs. Tenex should be used to transfer files which come from machines that have different word sizes.

Having selected a file type, the file can then be transfered to your machine with the get command. get takes one or two operands. With one operand, the operand represents the remote name of the file and the local name. If the file is to be saved as something else on the local machine, a second operand should be provided.

If the file is large, it may be compressed. You can tell if it is compressed if it has the .Z postfix. The file can be uncompressed with uncompress (see Section 1.8.3):

```
uncompress file.Z
```

If the file name ends with .tar, the file is a tar archive which is composed of more than one file. The files can be extracted with the tar command. To get all the files, use

```
tar -xf file.tar
```

After all the files have been distracted, the file with the .tar extension can be removed.

If the file name ends in .tar.Z, the process of getting the files can be shortened to

```
zcat file.tar.Z | tar xBf -
```

Remember to delete the file after you have uncompressed it and extracted the needed files.

There are literally hundreds of repositories for commonly used (or wanted) programs. The most famous and useful are listed in Table 1.11.

Washington University in St. Louis provides a convenient information service. Besides being an ftp site, they export several NFS directories to everyone. If you have NFS you can simply modify your /etc/fstab to include lines like the ones below for an Ultrix system, as well as to create the necessary directories on the local system:

Address	Contents
uunet.uu.net	A very large repository
wuarchive.wustl.edu	A very large repository
prep.ai.mit.edu	gnu software sources
dartmouth.edu	gnuplot
cert.sei.cmu.edu	CERT advisories and virus information
tesla.ee.cornell.edu	tcsh
jpl-devvax.jpl.nasa.gov	perl
pilot.njin.net	List of ftp sites

Table 1.11   FTP sites

```
/archive@wuarchive.wustl.edu:/wuarchive:
     ro:0:0:nfs:bg,hard,intr,nosuid:
/archive/usenet@wuarchive.wustl.edu:/wuarchive/usenet:
     ro:0:0:nfs:bg,hard,intr,nosuid:
/archive/mirrors@wuarchive.wustl.edu:
     /wuarchive/mirrors:
     ro:0:0:nfs:bg,hard,intr,nosuid:
/archive/mirrors2@wuarchive.wustl.edu:
     /wuarchive/mirrors2:ro:0:0:
     nfs:bg,hard,intr,nosuid:
```

Now you can search a very large archive for information on many topics. You can view files as if they were on your local file system. Responses, of course, will be much slower than any NFS activity you have done before. Consider how far your requests like ls have to go.

If you do not have access to the Internet and ftp, mail may be your only option. Mail requires that you know from whom to request information. A common source for transfering files by mail is responses from news requests that you have made. There are some automatic mail services which provide files and information. For example, Argonne National Laboratories provides a set of numerical analysis programs. Also, Princeton University provides a mail ftp server. For more information about this server, send the one line HELP in a mail message to BITFTP@pucc.princeton.edu.

Electronic mail is one of the best ways to send mail between incompatible systems and networks. Because the transport mechanism is plain text and because many mail systems are picky about characters, care must be taken to ensure that the data is not modified while being sent. The program called uuencode (UNIX-to-UNIX encode) converts a file to a format containing just ASCII readable characters. At the receiving end, the file can be decoded with uudecode. If a directory or subdirectories is to be sent, the program shar can package the directory into a file that can then be unpackaged by running the shell on the file.

Another problem with sending files by mail is that some mailers are unable to handle large files (64K or larger, usually). The program split can automatically break files for you so that the size is less than some predetermined amount. Each file is sent sequentially and put back together by the receiver.

As a final note, be aware that by running the downloaded programs you may be endangering your system or your account. It is possible that the programs that you download may contain viruses or trojan horses. I prefer to get a program with sources, so that I can scan the sources to see if there is anything that looks suspicious.

2

UNIX Programming Environment

Anselmo A. Lastra

Since UNIX was originally designed as an operating system for program development, it should come as no surprise that there are many programming languages and software development utilities available. In this chapter we will examine some of these compilers and tools.

Since C is the most heavily used language for programming on UNIX and the C compiler is representative of others, we shall examine it in detail, including the assembly and linking stages, as well as tools for managing object code libraries. This will be followed by a discussion of make, a tool for automating compilation, dbx, an interactive debugger, and *SCCS*, a set of tools for managing source code. Finally, we will briefly examine other languages and integrated development environments.

2.1 The C Compiler

Most of the UNIX operating system is written in C, as are the vast majority of the utilities, usually including the C compiler itself. Though you may be using another programming language, such as Pascal or FORTRAN, the structure of the C compiler as detailed in this section will be useful, since the usage of the various compilers tends to be very similar.

The compiler is accessed via the command cc (see the man pages for cc(1)). However, as we shall see in this section, the process of compilation consists of a variety of programs controlled by the program cc.

2.1.1   History and Background

The first UNIX C compiler was for the PDP11 series of computers from Digital Equipment Corporation. This compiler is commonly referred to as the *Ritchie C compiler,* for Dennis M. Ritchie, its author. This compiler implemented the standard version of the C programming language defined in the book *The C Programming Language* (First Edition) by Brian W. Kernighan and Ritchie. Since the Ritchie C compiler was designed only for the PDP11, and was partially coded in assembly language, it did not survive the move by UNIX toward a variety of machine architectures.

The compiler that replaced the Ritchie compiler is referred to as the *Portable C Compiler,* or *pcc* for short. This compiler was developed by Stephen C. Johnson of AT&T Bell Laboratories. For portability, the compiler was totally written in C and very successfully separated the machine independent and machine-dependent portions of the compiler. This allowed retargeting of the compiler for new architectures by changing only the machine-dependent sections. The pcc compiler also used the YACC parser generator (see Section 2.8.5). The pcc compiler is still in use at many sites, though current versions of UNIX from hardware manufacturers have usually replaced pcc with proprietary C compilers.

Many of the new compilers are designed to accept a new version of C defined by a committee of the American National Standards Institute (ANSI). The new C standard (commonly referred to as *ANSI standard C*) addresses some issues of machine independence, and specifies some standard libraries for input/output and auxiliary functions. However, the change most visible to the programmer is in function specification. In old C, the list of function parameters followed the parentheses after the function name, such as this:

```
int
strlen()
char *string;
{
    ...
}
```

In ANSI C, the arguments to functions are contained within the parentheses in a manner analogous to that of the function call:

```
int
strlen(char *string)
{
...
}
```

Furthermore, whereas the old standard allowed function declarations only to specify the return value, the ANSI standard allows *function prototypes* that also include the types of arguments to functions. This makes it possible for the compiler to check for consistency, and eliminates many simple, but very annoying bugs that commonly occurred before the function prototypes were available. For example, an old function declaration would be:

```
int strlen();
```

whereas an ANSI standard declaration would be:

```
int strlen(char *);
```

A new edition of the Kernighan and Ritchie book, *The C Programming Language,* continues to be a working reference for the C language. The ANSI standard specification is available in a document from the American National Standards Institute.

Many of the compilers available from hardware vendors incorporate the changes specified by the ANSI standard. There is also a significant, publicly available compiler that implements the ANSI standard, the GNU C compiler, which is available from the Free Software Foundation. This compiler, known as *gcc,* currently generates code for many different machine architectures, and is designed to be easily retargetable. It is used as the standard compiler by at least one manufacturer, the NeXT corporation.

2.1.2 Basic Use of the C Compiler.

The simplest invocation of the C compiler is obtained by typing the following to the shell:

```
% cc prog.c
```

where `prog.c` is the name of a file containing the C program. The suffix `.c` is necessary because the program `cc` uses the file suffix to determine the compilation needs. This line instructs the C compiler to compile and link the code contained in `prog.c`. The executable result

Flag	Description
-o	Specify name of resulting object file
-O	Optimize program
-c	Compile only—do not link
-l	Include specified library
-g	Compile for use with a debugger
-I	Directories in which to search for include files
-D	Define—equivalent to #define
-U	Undefine
-E	Execute C preprocessor only
-S	Generate assembly language file
-s	Strip the load module
-p	Compile for profiling

Table 2.1   Common C compiler command flags

is, by default, placed in a file named a.out. Assuming no compilation errors, the resulting program may be executed by typing

```
% a.out
```

to the shell.

Many tasks may be accomplished with this simple usage; however, we normally would like to specify options to the C compiler. This is done by using flags on the command line. A set of commonly used flags is shown in Table 2.1. Often used is the -o flag, which specifies the name of the resulting executable file. For example, we could have specified that the program in the previous example be named prog as follows:

```
% cc -o prog prog.c
```

The normal UNIX convention is that files containing executable programs have no extension (with the notable exception of a.out), while files containing items such as C code have a suffix of a period followed by one or more letters. Some of the common suffixes pertinent to pro-

Suffix	File type
.c	C code
.p	Pascal code
.f	FORTRAN code
.C	C++ code
.y	YACC code
.s	Assembler
.o	Object file
.a	Library file

Table 2.2   Common file suffixes

gram development are detailed in Table 2.2. We will be using some of this information in the rest of the chapter.

Since most programs of any significant size are separated into modules contained in multiple source files, cc compiles the C code in all of the files with a .c suffix that are specified on the command line. For example,

```
% cc -o prog file1.c file2.c file3.c
```

commands cc to compile the code contained in files file1.c, file2.c, and file3.c and to link the resulting code into an executable module in a file named prog.

Often you may want to specify that code should be compiled, but not linked into an executable program (see Section 2.4 on make for a reason to do this). This is accomplished with the -c flag. For example, you can compile the code in file prog.c into an object module as follows:

```
% cc -c prog.c
```

The suffix assigned to object files is .o. Thus, by default, the resulting object file is named prog.o.

The last command flag that we shall cover in this section on basic usage, is the -l flag. This is used to specify that a *library* be linked with the other code specified on the command line. The purpose and use of libraries is detailed in Section 2.2.3, but for now suffice it to say that a library is a file containing object code, usually specific to a particular specialized task. For example, a commonly used library contains code to perform floating point functions, such as square root and trigonometric functions (see the introduction to Section 3 of the UNIX Programmers manual, intro(3)).

The -l flag is followed by some text specifying the name of the library to be linked. (For example, the math library is named m.) To compile and link a program using mathematical functions, we could use a command line such as

```
% cc -o prog prog.c -lm
```

Other libraries often used are those containing code to manipulate displays. Some examples are libraries of X Window System code, such as -lX, -lXMenu, and -lXt, and libraries containing code to manipulate character displays, such as -ltermcap and -ltermlib.

2.1.3   Internals of the C Compiler.

For advanced usage of the C compiler, it is important to understand in some detail what the compiler is doing. This allows you to control the steps of the compilation, and to examine some of the intermediate results.

In most UNIX implementations, the program cc does not perform the actual compilation. Its function is really that of dispatcher, starting and controlling other programs to perform the functions that were specified on the command line. It is instructive to examine the possible flow of control of a compilation. This is diagrammed in Figure 2.1. Note that all of these steps may not be performed in all compilations, and some manufacturer's compilers may not follow these conventions.

Let us examine the compilation steps briefly:

Preprocessor   The preprocessor has historically been implemented as a separate step. It processes all of the lines, such as macros and file inclusion, preceded by a #. Common ones are #define, #include, and #ifdef. The preprocessor implements the functions requested by all of these directives, and outputs a file with no preprocessor directives. It strips all comments from the source file since comments contribute nothing to the compilation. Often the preprocessor program is named /lib/cpp. Due to its importance and utility, the preprocessor is examined in more detail in Section 2.1.4.

Compiler   This is the actual compilation step. Input to this step is the C program with the macros expanded, and #include files included. Many of the modern compilers consist of one program, often called /lib/ccom. Historically, the compiler has been implemented in two steps. This was due to memory limitations on the original target

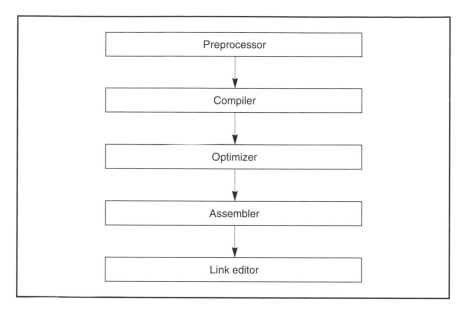

Figure 2.1   Stages of C compilation

machine, the PDP11. The two passes of the compiler were typically named `/lib/c0` and `/lib/c1`. The output of the compilation step is in the assembly language of the target machine or, perhaps, an intermediate language for the optimizer.

Optimizer   As its name suggests, the optimizer is meant to make the resulting assembly code more optimal in some sense. Often the function of the optimizer is to make the code execute faster, though sometimes it also makes the resulting code smaller in size. Especially in newer architectures, such as reduced instruction set (RISC) machine architectures, use of the optimizer results in programs with significantly faster execution times. Some vendors implement the optimizer as a separate program from the compiler; others package the optimizer and the compiler into one step.

Since debugging with a source level debugger (see Section 2.5) may be difficult or impossible when the optimizer is used, optimization is often desirable after the program has been debugged. The output of the optimization step is usually in assembly language. The optimizer is often named `/lib/c2`.

Assembler   The assembler accepts as input the assembly language output of the compilation step and generates object code of the target machine. The assembler is often named `/bin/as`. Usage of the assembler, especially in stand-alone fashion is detailed in Section 2.2.1.

Link Editor   The link editor, or linker (also historically known as a linking loader) takes as input *object modules* and *libraries* (see Section 2.2.3), and produces an executable module. Its function is detailed in Section 2.2.2. The linker is often named /bin/ld.

The C compiler executes some or all of these steps based on the suffixes of the files (see Table 2.2), and on the flags given as arguments. For example, this command

```
% cc file.o
```

will call only the linking step of the cc, not the compiler or the assembler, while this command

```
% cc file.s
```

will call the assembler and the linker. Of course, a command such as

```
% cc file.c
```

causes cc to call the compiler, assembler, and linker since the .c suffix signifies a file containing C language code.

2.1.4   The C Preprocessor

The C preprocessor provides three basic types of functions: file inclusion, macro substitution, and conditional inclusion. To lower the volume of data sent to the compiler, the preprocessor strips all comments from the source code. The preprocessor, usually called *cpp,* is often used for other languages, such as Pascal and FORTRAN.

The most commonly used function of the preprocessor is file inclusion via the statements

```
#include <filename>
```

or

```
#include "filename"
```

The function of these statements is to cause the preprocessor to copy the file filename into the character stream passed on to the compiler. In other words, the contents of the file are substituted for the #include statement.

The two different forms of the statement, quotation marks or less-than and greater-than symbols, affect the file system path that is searched for in the file. When the filename is bracketed by < and >, the standard directories are searched first. On the list of standard directories, the first one is usually /usr/include. This directory holds the standard include files for UNIX, such as stdio.h. On most implementations this is the only directory on the standard list.

If the filename is quoted, the directory where the source program is located is searched first. If filename is not found there, the standard list is searched. To allow customizing of the search path for #include, a compiler flag, -I, is provided. A directory following this flag is searched before the standard path.

For example, executing this command line

```
% cc -I/usr/local/include source.c
```

when the file source.c includes the line

```
#include "afile.h"
```

causes the preprocessor to search for afile.h in the following directories: the current directory, /usr/local/include, and, finally, the standard directories.

Another common use for the preprocessor is macro substitution, specifically to implement the #define directive. Often #define is used to substitute a constant for a mnemonic token, such as

```
#define BUFFER_SIZE 512
```

However, it may also be used to implement more complex macros such as

```
#define MAX(a, b) ((a) < (b) ? (a):(b))
```

Finally, the preprocessor interprets constructs such as #if and #ifdef that include code selectively. A simple example is

```
#ifdef SUNOS
#define LOOK_AND_FEEL "OpenLook"
#else
#define LOOK_AND_FEEL "Motif"
#endif
```

Control of the preprocessor macro definitions may be excerpted from the command line to the C compiler via two flags, -D and -U. The -D flag is used to create a definition for a macro. An example is:

```
% cc -DSUNOS prog.c
```

This flag sets the value of *SUNOS* to 1, much as the following line within the program would have:

```
#define SUNOS 1
```

To set a macro to an arbitrary value, an equal sign and a string may follow -D. For example:

```
% cc -DBUFFER_SIZE=512 prog.c
```

is equivalent to

```
#define BUFFER_SIZE 512
```

The -U flag is used to remove any initial definition of a macro. It is equivalent to the #undef directive. In practice this flag has limited utility because the only definitions that may be removed are those pre-defined by the compiler. These tend to define such things as the machine type and manufacturer of the machine.

It is sometimes useful to be able to examine the output of the pre-processor. In particular, when debugging the effect of a #define macro, it would be very handy to examine its effects. This may be done with the -E flag of the C compiler. This flag directs the compiler to run only the preprocessor and to direct the result to the standard output. For example, the command line

```
% cc -E prog.c
```

would expand macros, include files, and interpret the conditional inclusion directives on the code contained in the file prog.c. Most preprocessors will also strip comments from the code.

2.1.5 Advanced C Compiler Topics

The C compilers available from various vendors will often interpret many more flags than we can cover in this book. Often they are specific to the particular machines on which the compiler runs. Here are some examples of various categories of flags that may be important to you:

Floating Point Options   Some machines have different standard and optional floating point accelerators. Flags to the compiler are often provided to specify which accelerator is in use.

Memory Options You may be able to specify the type of memory model for which to compile. This is often necessary on some architectures such as the Intel 80X86 family.

Levels of Optimization Optimizers perform many functions. Some compilers allow you to select which optimizations you wish the compiler to perform. For example, on a Cray computer you may specify automatic vectorization, and even some parallelization.

Levels of ANSI Compatibility Some compilers allow you to select how strict the ANSI compatibility should be. For example, should all functions be required to have prototypes or do you prefer the compiler to be lenient about ANSI compliance?

Another topic that may be of concern is where the intermediate results of the compilation are being kept. Though one can think of the stages of the compilation as joined by pipes, they seldom are. This is for reasons of efficiency. Rather, the intermediate results are exchanged as files, usually in the /tmp directory.

If disk space on the file system containing /tmp is tight, one may not be able to compile very large programs. Some vendors provide flags to the C compiler to allow the user to specify the directory in which to put temporary files, or to specify that pipes should be used instead of intermediate files.

2.2 Assembling and Linking Programs

The information in this section is not necessary for occasional programming. However, it will be useful for creating complicated programs and for creating libraries of routines. We will discuss the assembler, linker, and object code libraries for use during the linking operation.

2.2.1 as

The assembler (usually known as /bin/as—see man pages for as(1)) is not often used by itself since the C language provides operators to perform most any function necessary. Even UNIX device drivers are almost always written in C. One operation that is occasionally important, though, is to examine the assembly language output of the compiler. A flag, -S, is provided for this purpose. A command such as this:

```
% cc -S prog.c
```

produces a file, prog.s, containing the assembly language resulting from the compilation. The assembler and loader are not executed.

If you find it necessary to use the assembler as directly to compile your assembly language programs, you should examine the manual page for it. Often the manual will describe assembler flags and directives specific to your machine's architecture.

2.2.2   ld

The link editor, usually the program /bin/ld, combines object code modules and resolves external references, such as global variables and subroutines. The resulting file, by default named a.out, may be executable if no errors occur during linking. The C compiler may call the linker as the final step of the compilation process. For a command line to cc such as this:

```
% cc -o prog prog.c
```

the call to the linker generated by cc may look something like this:

```
ld -o prog /lib/crt0.o prog.o -lc
```

The flag -o signifies the same thing for ld as it did for cc. The file prog.o is the output of the assembler. The other file named on the command line is /lib/crt0.o. The code in this file is responsible for initialization of a C program and for cleaning up upon exit. Normally it calls the subroutine main(), and on return from main() calls the subroutine exit(). There may be several versions of start-up files similar to crt0.o to perform various functions, such as profiling (see Section 2.6.1).

The flag -lc commands the linker to link the C library with the code. (Libraries are described in detail in the next section.) The C library contains commonly used subroutines and is normally linked in by cc. The flag -l is interpreted by the link editor as a command to include a file from one of the standard directories containing libraries. The name of the file is that specified after the -l, bracketed by the prefix lib and the suffix .a. For example, a flag such as -lfile commands the linker to search the standard directories (commonly /lib and /usr/lib, perhaps also /usr/local/lib) for the file named libfile.a. Some linkers allow you to expand the number of directories searched for in libraries by specifying the path in an environment variable such as LD_LIBRARY_PATH. This function may also be provided by a linker flag, -L, followed by a directory name.

A quirk of some linkers is that the complete symbol tables of the libraries are not saved, only the symbols that are necessary. Consider the problem that may be caused by this behavior. Suppose that two libraries are specified on the command line to the linker. The first library defines a symbol that is not used by the object files, but is used by some code in the second library. Since the linker did not save the complete symbol table of the first library, the symbol required by the second library is considered undefined, thus generating an error message. This behavior mandates that the user specify on the command line the names of the libraries in a particular order, left to right, with uses of a symbol in a library preceding its definition in a later library. Sometimes a library may have to be specified twice on the command line because of cross-referenced symbols between two libraries.

The link editor, as well as the assembler, tags the type of the object file being produced with a special code, known as the *magic number* (see the man pages for `magic(5)`). Knowing what a magic number is may keep you from scratching your head in bafflement at some of the more cryptic UNIX error messages. The magic number specifies traits of an object file, such as whether the code is relocatable, etc.

Another way to extract the type of the file, is with the program `file` (see the man pages for `file(1)`). This program examines files in order to try to determine the type of file. Part of that examination, if the file happens to be a binary file, is the magic number. `file` acts as a translator from magic number to English, thus saving the programmer from having to examine the magic number directly.

2.2.3 Libraries

The word *library* is defined as a collection of some objects, usually books. In computer science, the word usually signifies a *subroutine library,* a collection of subroutines or functions. Subroutine libraries are useful for reasons similar to why libraries of books are useful: they create a convenient and integrated package from a large number of subroutines.

A good example is the C library. It is composed of hundreds of subroutines. It is natural that as a programmer one would prefer to deal with these diverse subroutines individually or in small groups, not as one massive unit. However, as a user of the package, one prefers to deal with the subroutines as one entity, a library.

The archiver `ar` (see Sections 2.3.5 and 2.3.6) allows a programmer to concatenate files into one larger file that contains a table of contents describing which files are contained in the library and how they are packaged. The link editor is thus provided with one unit rather than hundreds.

Some UNIX systems are using shared libraries in order to save space. With this scheme, common code, such as the C library, is not linked with programs until run time, thus saving much disk space.

Furthermore, at run time only one copy of common read-only memory need be maintained, even for use by multiple programs. One can think of the shared library concept as linking just before running.

2.2.4   Object File Formats

The exact format of object files and of executable files (see *a.out(5)*) is often machine or vendor dependent, but we can discuss a specific implementation that is representative of most others. This format is known as the Common Object File Format (COFF) defined by AT&T for System V. COFF specifies the following as components of an object file:

- File header
- System header
- Section headers
- Data
- Relocation information
- Line numbers
- Symbol table
- String table

To allow programs to extract the information, the file and system headers specify the sizes of the other components. The file header also contains the magic number and specifies the sizes of the sections of data. Normally there are three data sections: read-only program text, initialized data, and uninitialized data (set to 0 before a program is run). The section headers contain more information about the sections of data, including pointers to the relocation tables.

Following the data, the relocation information contains an entry for each relocation reference in the data. This entry in turn provides a pointer to a symbol in the symbol table. The symbol table defines the type of symbol, and may contain a short name, or a reference into the string table for a longer name. The line number table is included for debugging with a symbolic debugger such as dbx (see Section 2.5.1). It associates the object code to the line number of high level language code.

There are some symbols that are often used in object files. They are _etext, which indicates the end of the read-only text region of object code; _edata, which indicates the end of the initialized data; and _end, which indicates the end of the uninitialized data.

2.3   Support Tools

Much of the usability of the UNIX system for programming is due to the variety of support tools available. Many of the simpler tools are described in this section. Some tools, such as `make`, are described in separate sections due to their complexity.

2.3.1   lint

The program `lint` (see man pages for `lint(1)`) is a very pedantic inspector of C code. It checks for nonportable constructs, inconsistencies in subroutine arguments, unreachable code, etc. The type checking of subroutine arguments is especially useful for old C, less so for ANSI C. Often the use of `lint` to clean up code results in the elimination of bugs.

Probably the biggest problem with `lint` is the volume of output. You are likely to be overwhelmed, especially on large C files. Some warnings may be safely overlooked, but at least `lint` provides a way for you to decide what sections of code may cause problems, now or in the future.

Some constructs, such as `longjmp()`, always cause `lint` to complain. In order to remove these warning messages, you may bracket sections of your program with

```
#ifndef lint
  ...code to be excluded...
#endif
```

since `lint` always defines the symbol `lint` before running the C preprocessor.

2.3.2   nm

The program `nm` (see man pages for `nm(1)`) lists the symbol table of object files, or library archive files. The name of the program results from calling the symbol table the *name list*. The output of `nm` consists of three columns. The first is the value of the symbol, if any. The second column is one letter describing the type of symbol. This is likely to be one of: `U` for *undefined*, `T` for a symbol in the *text* segment, `D` for a symbol in the *initialized data* segment, `B` for a symbol in the *uninitialized data* segment (referred to as the `bss` segment for very uninteresting historical reasons), etc. Refer to the manual page for `nm` on your machine for the specific types. The third column is the name of the symbol table entry, for example, the name of a variable or a function.

Many of the options to nm deal with the ordering and contents of the output. For example, some of the options allow you to specify that only global symbols are to be displayed, or only undefined symbols. Other options allow you to specify to nm how the output list should be sorted, such as alphabetically by name, in order of appearance, numerically by value, etc.

One instance where nm is particularly useful is when the link editor reports an undefined symbol, but the programmer has no idea in which file it may have occurred. It may possibly even exist in a library. Running nm on each file, perhaps with the output piped to grep, should reveal the culprit.

2.3.3 size

The program size (see the man pages for size(1)) prints the size, in bytes, of the three components of an object file: text (program code), initialized data, and uninitialized data (labeled bss). The sizes of the individual components are given in decimal. The total is given in both decimal and hex.

2.3.4 strip

The utility strip (see the man pages for strip(1)) removes the symbol tables from object files. This is useful for saving space, but prevents the use of a symbolic debugger, such as dbx (see Section 2.5.1). The -s option to the C compiler accomplishes the same goal.

2.3.5 ar

The library archiver ar (see the man pages for ar(1)) serves to concatenate a group of files into a single archive. It may be used for any type of file; however, it is usually used only for object files to create subroutine libraries. Other archivers, such as tar and cpio, are commonly used for general purpose archiving of files.

Historically, the arguments to ar did not follow the standard UNIX format of preceding flags with a dash. Some versions of UNIX have altered ar to conform to that standard. Refer to the manual page for ar on your system to see which format you should use. Our illustrations will use the traditional format. You may need to preface a flag with a dash. The template for using ar is

```
% ar key archive file1 file2 ...
```

where archive is the name of the archive file, and file1, etc., are the names of the files to be included in the library. The function to be performed is detailed by key, which is one or more letters. Of special interest to us are the keys c (create), r (replace), and t (list table of contents). There are other keys to replace or move files within an existing archive, but in practice an archive is just rebuilt when one of its members needs replacing. The command

```
% ar rc libxxx.a file1.o file2.o file3.o
```

creates a new archive named libxxx.a containing the code in the files file1.o, file2.o, and file3.o. To list the contents of an archive, use the following command

```
% ar t libxxx.a
```

More information may be obtained by using the key v (for verbose) as follows:

```
% ar tv libxxx.a
```

The table of contents of an archive lists only the names of the files archived and some auxiliary information about them. Since the linker needs the symbol table information contained within the files, it must extract this information from each of the archived files. To speed up this operation, a modified archive created by the program ranlib was designed. This archive is described in the next section.

2.3.6 ranlib

The program ranlib (see the man pages for ranlib(1)) modifies an archive created by ar to add a table of contents of the symbol tables of the component files. This table of contents is archived as the first file and is named ___.SYMDEF. To create the table of contents, use ranlib as follows:

```
% ranlib libxxx.a
```

This creates, or updates, the table of contents for the subroutine library libxxx.a.

The linker ld examines the date of creation of the table of contents and compares it to the date of modification of the library file (see Section 2.2.3). If the date of modification is newer than that of the table of contents, a warning message is printed. It may be that the new date has not been caused by any change in the library, but only by some action, such as copying the archive file. To suppress the warning message, `ranlib` must be run again on the library.

An option to `ranlib`, `-t`, is provided that *touches* the archive. In other words, it resets the creation date of the table of contents. This is useful when it is known that the archive has not changed, but has only been copied.

2.3.7   Pretty Printers

Many programs to beautify C source code exist on UNIX systems. Some, such as `cb` (see the man pages for `cb(1)`), which stands for *C beautifier,* are meant to make code easier to work with by applying uniform style rules. These consist mainly of indentation.

Other programs, such as `vgrind` (see the man pages for `vgrind(1)`), are meant to produce attractive printed output. For example, `vgrind` annotates program code with `troff` commands for printing. It attempts to make source code more readable by printing key words in boldface, comments in italic, etc.

2.3.8   Cross-Reference Programs

In large pieces of code, it becomes difficult to find the location of symbol definitions and references. There exist programs to create indexes of variable and function names, and locations in the source code. A common one is `ctags` (see the man pages for `ctags(1)`), which creates a tag table meant to be used by editors such as `vi`.

2.4   Make

The utility `make` (see the man pages for `make(1)`) reads a file, referred to as the `makefile`, that describes the dependencies between source, object, and executable files. By default, `make` searches first for the file named `Makefile`. If that is not found, the second possible name is `makefile`. If neither of these files is found and the user has not specified an alternative name (see Section 2.4.6), an error is signaled. The `makefile` provides recipes for updating programs when the source code files have been changed. `make` has to rank as one of the most successful and useful of the UNIX programs. It not only serves to provide the updating service for which it was designed, but since it specifies exactly how programs are made, the `makefile` also functions as a document describing the component parts that make up program modules. Most of the UNIX utilities, as well as the UNIX kernel, have `makefile` associated with their source code.

2.4.1 Basic Use

The easiest way to describe the structure of a makefile is by example. Consider a C program named prog, consisting of three source files: main.c, io.c, and misc.c. A makefile describing this program could be:

```
prog:
        cc -o prog main.c io.c misc.c
```

The first line states that the target, the file prog, depends on the three source files. If the modification date of the file prog is older than that of any of the source files, prog needs to be updated. The second line (*which must begin with a tab, not spaces*) describes what to do in order to update prog. This line, referred to as a *command*, should be a valid shell command (see the man pages for sh(1)).

This sample makefile is far from ideal. Note that the file prog does not directly depend on the C source files; it actually depends on the object files (.o suffix) which depend on the C files. The way we've set up our makefile, we recompile all of the source files even when only one has changed. We can make the description more accurate and avoid this extra effort by using the following makefile:

```
prog: main.o io.o misc.o
cc -o prog main.o io.o misc.o
```

Note that we have not provided a recipe for generating the .o files. This is because make has some built-in rules for common cases, such as compiling C files (more on this topic in the section on implicit rules). We can provide an explicit rule if we wish. One for generating main.o from main.c might look like

```
main.o: main.c
        cc -c main.c
```

Suppose that there's also one include file, globals.h, included by main.c and io.c, but not by misc.c. One can visually describe the dependencies between the files as a graph such as the one in Figure 2.2. The makefile describing these dependencies is:

```
prog: main.o io.o misc.o
        cc -o prog main.o io.o misc.o

main.o: globals.h
io.o: globals.h
```

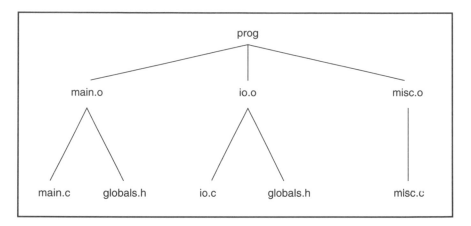

Figure 2.2 Stages of C compilation

This set of dependencies says, for example, that if the file globals.h is modified, the two object files main.o and io.o must be updated. A built-in rule describes how to make object files, such as main.o and io.o, from the source files, in this case main.c and io.c. Finally, as stated in the first line of the makefile, the executable program prog depends on the recompiled modules main.o and io.o; thus it must be relinked. The instructions for doing this are given by the second line of the makefile.

As in program source code, it's good practice to comment makefiles generously. A comment is preceded by the character #, and continues to the end of a line.

This section has covered most of what you need to know to use makefiles. However, macros, described in the next section, are useful both to simplify the content of the makefiles, and to help maintain consistency.

2.4.2 Macros

A macro is used to substitute a string for a name. It is defined by specifying a name, followed by an equal sign and the value to substitute for the name. For example,

```
FILES = main.o io.o misc.o
```

defines the macro FILES as consisting of the string listing the three object files. There are several ways to use a macro. If the name of the macro is only one character long, use a dollar sign and the name. If it is longer, the name must be bracketed by parentheses or curly braces. For example,

```
$(FILES)
```

or

```
${FILES}
```

are equivalent uses of the FILES macro. We could now rewrite our makefile example as follows:

```
FILES = main.o io.o misc.o

prog: ${FILES}
      cc -o prog ${FILES}

main.o: globals.h
io.o: globals.h
```

Some macros are defined dynamically as make is executing. They are especially useful for creating explicit rules (see Section 2.4.5). Some of these macros are:

- $@   Name of the target
- $?   Names of all dependencies newer than the target
- $<   Name of one dependence, generated by the recursive descent that make executes through the target/dependence graph. See Section 2.4.1.
- $*   Current target stripped of any suffix

The advantage to using the macro is that only one list of files needs to be updated. This lessens the chance of error. Macros may also be defined on the command line to make. See Section 2.4.6.

2.4.3   Targets and Commands

The syntax for target/command rules is

```
target [more targets] : [:] [dependents] [ ; commands]
[<TAB> commands]
```

Items inside brackets are optional. Names of multiple targets, separated by spaces, may be provided. These are followed by a single or double colon. Next comes an optional list of dependencies. If the target is out of date relative to the dependencies, the dependencies are, in turn, made targets. The target line may optionally end with a semicolon and a command, though this is not common usage. Other command lines must begin with a tab character. A noncomment line that does not begin with a tab ends the target specification. In practice, this is usually a blank line. If necessary, single commands or dependencies may be made to span multiple lines by terminating the lines with a backslash character.

The difference between a target followed by a single or double colon deals with the treatment of the dependencies. If a target appears on more than one single colon line, all of the dependencies are lumped onto one dependencies list. Only one of the single colon target lines should have a list of commands. A warning is issued if multiple target lines contain commands.

Multiple double colon targets are treated as completely separate entities. The dependencies associated with the target are examined individually. If the dependents on a particular rule are out of date with respect to the target, that rule is activated, the dependents are made new targets, and the commands associated with the rule are executed. Since rules are not combined, multiple rules for the same target may each have commands.

On some implementations of make, a target need not be a simple file name. There is some provision for name expansion. The character wildcard % may be used once in a target name. It expands to any sequence of zero or more characters. The percent character may be used in the dependencies list and is replaced by the same sequence of characters matched in the target. This pattern matching feature may be used to replace an implicit rule as follows:

```
%.o: %.c
    cc -c $<
```

This rule matches any file with a .o suffix and examines the modification date of a matching .c file. If necessary, the command is executed using dynamic macro substitution to expand the macro $< to the name of the dependent file. For a more conventional way to accomplish the same task, see Section 2.4.5.

It is important to understand the order in which make interprets target rules. The initial targets may be specified as command line arguments to make. Alternatively, a target may be set using the special target .DEFAULT: . For example,

```
.DEFAULT: prog
```

would make `prog` the initial target. If none of the above is specified, `make` chooses the first target in the `makefile`.

For each target, the dependencies are examined in turn. If a dependent file has a modification date newer than the target, it is made a new target. `make` recursively examines each new target. To update a target, once its dependents have been updated, any commands associated with the target are executed. If no commands are listed for the target, a search for an explicit or implicit rule is made. If none exists, any commands associated with the `.DEFAULT:` target are executed. If there are no commands, `make` signals an error and stops.

Each command line is printed and passed to a shell (by default a Bourne shell) for execution. Note that since each line is interpreted by a different execution of the shell, a sequence of commands may not have the effect that you, at first glance, think it should. This is especially true of commands that change the state of the shell, such as a `cd` command. If a sequence of commands must be executed by one shell, place them on one line, separated by semicolons. Recall that a backslash may be used to extend command lines. To change the default shell, set the shell macro to the full pathname of the shell you wish to use. This macro is not imported from the environment.

`make` normally halts if a nonzero exit code is returned by any of the commands. In order to prevent this, a hyphen may be placed at the beginning of a command line (following the tab). To globally prevent command errors from causing `make` to halt, the special target `.IGNORE:` may be declared. Note that this may be dangerous.

To prevent `make` from printing a command line as it is being executed, place an at sign @ at the beginning of the command line. To prevent the text of all commands from printing, place the target `.SILENT:` in the `makefile`.

2.4.4 Implicit Suffix Rules

To simplify the usage of `make`, a number of rules are built into the program (or read into it from a default start-up file). This frees the programmer from having to specify common rules in every `makefile`. The rules are based on file suffixes. Among the implicit rules are:

From	To	Action
`.c`	`.o`	Compile C code to object code
`.f`	`.o`	Fortran code to object file
`.p`	`.o`	Pascal code to object code
`.y`	`.c`	Yacc code to C code
`.l`	`.c`	Lex code to C code
`.s`	`.o`	Assembler to object code

To provide for simple modification, these rules use macros that may be specified by the programmer. Useful ones are:

CC	Name of the C compiler (cc by default)
CFLAGS	Flags to the C compiler
FC	Name of FORTRAN compiler (f77 by default)
FFLAGS	Flags to the FORTRAN compiler
PC	Name of the Pascal compiler (pc by default)
PFLAGS	Flags to the Pascal compiler

For example, we may choose to use the optimizer for our C compilations by declaring the macro

```
CFLAGS = -O
```

Older implementations of make use an internal table to store the implicit rules. Some newer versions, however, place them in a file. Check the manual page for make on your machine. If the implicit rules are in a file, it may be worth scanning them to see what rules are provided by default.

2.4.5   Adding Suffix Rules

Since it is unlikely that the implicit rules will cover all needs, a method for adding suffix rules has been provided. The list of suffixes of interest are declared in a special target named .SUFFIXES. For example, the list of suffixes for the table detailed above would be listed as

```
.SUFFIXES: .c .o .f .p .y .l .s
```

The suffixes are searched in the order in which they appear in the .SUFFIXES list. To change a rule with existing suffixes, one must provide a target consisting of the two suffixes. For example, a rule for compiling C files might look like this:

```
.c.o:
     $(CC)  -c  $(CFLAGS)  $<
```

This rule describes the process for updating a file with a .o suffix from a file with a .c suffix. In other words, it describes how to compile a file containing C code into one containing object code. The process is specified by the commands, in this case a call to the C compiler with the flag -c that instructs the compiler not to call the linker (see Section 2.1.2).

To add a rule with new suffixes, specify the set of new suffixes using the .SUFFIXES target. For example, to add a rule for compiling C++ code, one might place the following in the makefile:

```
.SUFFIXES: .C

.C.o:
    CC -c ${CFLAGS} $<
```

Suffixes accumulate. This works to your advantage if you are adding a suffix such as the .C suffix above. If you want to change the order of search of the suffixes, you must first reset the suffix list with a null .SUFFIXES target and then place new suffixes on the list. For example,

```
.SUFFIXES:
.SUFFIXES: .C .o
```

would result in a set of suffixes containing just the two suffixes, .C and .o.

2.4.6 Command Line Flags

As we mentioned above, targets may be specified on the command file. Macros may also be specified on the command line. The specification is equivalent to that of macros within the makefile. For example, a CFLAGS macro may be declared to include code profiling and optimization on our example program, prog, as follows:

```
% make "CFLAGS = -O -p" prog
```

Note that we have quoted the macro specification to inhibit interpretation by the shell.

There are also many useful flags to make. Some of the more important ones are

- -n Print commands, but do not execute them. This option cancels the effect of the @ sign directive.

- -d This is debug mode. It causes make to print out detailed information on its actions as it is executing.

- -i This is analogous to the .IGNORE target. It causes make to continue execution regardless of the return code of commands.

- -s This is the silent mode. This option is equivalent to the
  .SILENT target in suppressing printing of command lines.

- -f This overrides the default names of the makefile. It looks
  for rules in the file named in the argument after the flag
  instead of in the files makefile or Makefile.

- -r This ignores the built-in rules.

2.5   Debuggers

Debuggers are support tools that allow a programmer to interactively
execute a program and examine the state of the program. An early
UNIX debugger was adb, an assembly language debugger. This is still
available on most versions of UNIX, but has been replaced for normal
use by source language debuggers meant to work with a higher level
language, such as C, Fortran, or Pascal. There are many debuggers
available, but all share roughly the same features. In this section we
will give an overview of dbx (see the man pages for dbx(1)), the most
common source level debugger.

In order to use a source level debugger, you must instruct most compilers to append extra information to object files. This is accomplished
for the C compiler, cc, by using the -g flag. A restriction is that most
debuggers will not correctly debug code that has been optimized, such
as with the -O flag to cc. Many C compilers will issue a warning message to that effect if you specify both the -g and -O flags.

2.5.1   Starting dbx

To use dbx, type

```
% dbx [program_name]
```

If no program name is provided, the default name a.out will be used.
dbx will return with a command prompt, usually (dbx).

It is possible that you are using dbx to examine the state of a program that has crashed and generated a *core file* (see the man pages for
core(5)). The core file is a memory image of the process that crashed.
Some of the possible reasons for a core file to be generated are memory
faults, illegal instructions, etc. (see the man pages for sigvec(2)).
Regardless of the reason, the last part of the error message will say
something like *core dumped*. If there is a file named core in the current directory, dbx will automatically read it. You may use the same
commands that are described below, such as those to list the contents

of variables, to examine the state of the program as it was when it crashed.

Some help is available by using the command help. To exit dbx, use the command quit.

2.5.2 Listing Source in dbx

The basic command for listing lines from the source code files is list. There are two variations of this command

```
(dbx) list [starting line] [, ending line]
```

will list lines of a source file starting at the specified line. If no ending line is specified, only one line is listed. When no starting line is specified, the next ten lines are listed. To list the beginning of a specified function, use

```
(dbx) list function_name
```

The current source file may be searched for a matching text string in the same manner as a text editor such as vi. Type

```
(dbx) / regular expression
```

to search forward, and

```
(dbx) ? regular_expression
```

to search backward. To change the current source file, use

```
(dbx) file [filename]
```

If a filename is not specified, the name of the current file is listed. Files are searched for in the current directory. To change the directory in which to search for source files, type

```
(dbx) use directory_list
```

2.5.3 Examining and Setting Program State

One of the best features of dbx is the ability to print out the result of complex expressions. The command

```
(dbx) print expression [, expression]
```

will print the value of the argument or arguments. An expression may be any legal C expression, though often the argument consists just of the name of a variable. The value of an expression may be assigned to a variable within the program by using the command

```
(dbx) assign variable = expression
```

Part of the state of a program, of course, is the state of the stack and of the program counter. The command where will print out this information as procedure names and line numbers. A list of the active variables may be obtained with the command dump, though this list may be too long to be of practical use. An optional argument to dump is the name of a function which will limit the variables listed to those local to that function.

2.5.4   Break Points and Tracing

A common strategy for debugging is to execute a program until a specified point (a *breakpoint*) is reached. The user can then examine the state of the program, or execute the program one line at a time. To set a breakpoint, use the command stop. There are several variations of this command

```
(dbx) stop at line number
```

will set a breakpoint at the specified source code line, while

```
(dbx) stop in function
```

will set one at the beginning of the specified function. One may also command dbx to stop, not at a particular place, but rather when a specified condition occurs. For example

```
(dbx) stop variable
```

will break when the value of variable changes.

A function related to breakpoints is trace. The effect is similar, except that instead of returning dbx to command mode, the trace function will just print some tracing information and continue execution. The variations are similar to those for the stop command. For example, assuming that i is a variable in the program,

```
(dbx) trace i
```

will print the value of the variable i whenever it changes.

Both the `stop` and `trace` commands may be made conditional by amending them with an `if` statement. For example

```
(dbx) stop at 34 if j > 1000
```

will only stop at line 34 when the variable `j` is greater than one thousand. The conditional `stop` and `trace` commands provide a rich repertoire of debugging possibilities. You may find, however, that the use of some constructs may slow execution drastically.

Each use of a `trace` or `stop` command is associated with a unique number. This number may be used to remove the effect of the trace or breakpoint with the `delete` command. To see the command numbers of the active breakpoints and traces, use the `status` command.

2.5.5 Running a Program

You may run a program as follows

```
(dbx) run [argument_list]
```

where the `argument_list` may include I/O redirection with the `>` and `<` symbols. Presumably you have set up breakpoints and trace locations before you run a program. To continue from a breakpoint, use the `cont` command.

It is also possible to execute a program line by line. Two commands are available for this, `step` and `next`. Each will execute one line of code. The difference is that if there is a subroutine call on that line, `step` will stop at the beginning of the subroutine, whereas `next` will completely execute all of the code called by that line before stopping.

2.5.6 Auxiliary Functions

You may customize the user interface to `dbx` by using the `alias` command. This will associate one name with another. For example,

```
(dbx) alias r run
```

will enable `r` to be used as an abbreviation for run. When `dbx` starts executing, it will search for a file named `.dbxinit`, first in the current directory, then in the user's home directory. If this file is found, its contents are executed. The `.dbxinit` file is a convenient place to execute any `alias` commands, and to set any default breakpoints. Many programmers maintain a .dbxinit file in their home directories to customize dbx to reflect their needs and preferences.

A file of dbx commands may be read by using the source command. This allows batch-style debugging, if desired.

2.5.7   Other debuggers

In functionality, dbx is representative of many source level debuggers. One that is commonly available is gdb from the GNU project. A different user interface is provided by the debuggers using a workstation's windowing system. These programs usually contain a display of the source code, complete with scrollbars, and a set of buttons detailing many of the available commands. Selection of breakpoint locations and of variables is made with the mouse. Often such a debugger is actually just a user interface program that communicates with a command line oriented debugger, such as dbx, in order to do the actual debugging. The windowing debugger thus adds no new functionality, but the use of the mouse and the graphical interface provide a very useful function and may make the debugger easier to use, especially for the casual user.

2.6   Performance Analysis

The simplest way to analyze the performance of a program is, of course, to measure the time it takes to run. Both the program /bin/time (see the man pages for time (1)) and the built-in time command of the csh will display data on the wall clock time and the CPU time consumed by the execution of a program. For example, to measure how long the program a.out takes to execute, we might type

```
% /bin/time a.out
```

The response might be

```
10.5 real      8.9 user     0.3 sys
```

This states that the wall clock time consumed was 10.5 seconds. Of that time, 8.9 was spent running the program itself, while 0.3 seconds were consumed by the kernel on the program's behalf.

Simply timing the program, however, doesn't provide much information to the programmer. What the programmer needs to know is where in the program the time is being spent. This information is provided by utilities known as profilers.

2.6.1 prof

The original profiler supplied with the UNIX system is called prof (see the man pages for prof(1)). It provides a count of the number of times each subroutine in a program has been called, along with the time spent in the subroutine. In order to use prof to profile the execution of a program, compile the program with the -p flag to cc. This flag instructs the compiler to include profiling code in the executable program.

When the program to be profiled exits, it will create a file named mon.out. This file contains the raw timing information. The data contained in the mon.out file are interpreted by prof to generate a report. An argument to prof is the name of the program. Consider the following example (characters typed by the user are printed in bold and comments are in italics):

```
% cc -g -o prog prog.c
% prog
                    ...running prog generates file mon.out
% prof prog
 %time   cumsecs   #call   ms/call   name
  73.4     2.15      25     86.00    _calc1
  26.3     2.92     100      7.70    _calc2
   0.0     2.93      25      0.00    __doprnt
   0.0     2.93       1      0.00    _exit
   0.0     2.93       1      0.00    _main
   0.0     2.93      25      0.00    _printf
                    ...more times
```

The columns in the execution profile are the percentage of time spent in each subroutine, cumulative seconds spent in the subroutine, the number of calls, average milliseconds per call (calculated by prof) and the name of the subroutine. Obviously, the function calc1 is a good candidate for optimization efforts since most of the time is spent executing it.

The timing information generated by this profiling is gathered statistically. The program is interrupted regularly (at a machine dependent rate, say every 1/60th of a second). At that time, the program counter is examined and the location of the instruction being executed is tallied in a histogram. This is essentially the information that is saved in the mon.out file. Something to keep in mind when using prof is that programs that run for very short periods of time are unlikely to record very accurate results. Therefore, when profiling a program, it is crucial to include amounts of data representative of those encountered during normal executions of the program.

2.6.2   Other Analysis Tools

Some manufacturers provide other analysis tools, including other pro-filers. One of these is gprof. It works in a fashion similar to prof, but also displays a *call graph* of the execution. The call graph shows how much time was spent in each subroutine, just as prof did, but subdivides these times based on the calling subroutine. This becomes useful if there is a utility subroutine that is called from several places in a program and the programmer wishes to see what the usage patterns are. On machines with fine-grained clocks, nonstatistical profilers that actually measure the time spent in subroutines, or executing lines of code, are sometimes provided.

A similar function to call graph profiling, but without timing, is provided by utilities that display the control flow of a program. There are two types, static and dynamic. A static analysis is mostly useful in visualizing the flow of an unfamiliar program by showing the sequence of subroutine calls. An example of a program that does this is ftref on the Cray Y-MP. A dynamic analyzer shows the actual code executed (an example is the tcov utility on products from Sun). This is useful when testing to determine *code coverage*. When testing a program, one may wish to know whether test data actually exercised all code in a program, including seldom used code, such as error recovery routines.

2.7   SCCS

A frequent task that must be performed to maintain software systems is to track changes made to the code over time. It is often important to know not only what changes were made, but also when they were made and who made them. In an environment where more than one programmer is working on a project, it may also be necessary to coordinate access to program code in order to prevent two people from making changes to the same piece of code at the same time. All of these needs are addressed by the Source Code Control System, known as SCCS.

2.7.1   Creating an SCCS File

The most common use for SCCS (see the man pages for sccs(1)) is to maintain a change history for a set of source files. Normally these source files are kept together in one directory. By default, SCCS will keep the change history in files on a subdirectory named SCCS. Before submitting your files to SCCS control, you must create this subdirectory. Failure to do this results in an error message from SCCS. Once the subdirectory has been created, you may place individual files under the control of *SCCS* by using the command `create`. Assuming that one of your source files is named `prog.c`, use of the command

```
% sccs create prog.c
```

will initialize an edit history for the file. Note that the program called is `sccs`. The function of this program is similar to that of `cc`. It acts as a front end for other programs that perform the actual work.

The `create` command writes a file in the SCCS subdirectory that contains some initialization information, and your code. The name of this file is the same as that of the original, prefixed by the characters "`s.`" In our example, the file created is named `SCCS/s.prog.c`. This file, for obvious reasons, is called the *s-file*. In case of an error, *SCCS* saves a copy of the original file prefixed by a comma. When you have assured yourself that the *SCCS* file is correct, you may remove this backup.

Execution of `create` results in some output. If you tried `create` before reading the rest of this section, part of that output will be the message

```
No id keywords (cm 7)
```

This message is to warn you that there was no keyword in the source code file for *SCCS* to replace with the new file ID. For more information on keywords, please refer to Section 2.7.6, but for basic usage of *SCCS*, place the following line near the beginning of your source files before using `create`:

```
static char SccsID[] = "%W% %G%";
```

This line will be replaced by *SCCS* with a line similar to the following:

```
static char SccsID[] = "@(#)prog.c 1.1 02/29/91";
```

This line details the program name, `prog.c`, the version number, `1.1`, and the date the file was created, `02/29/91`. The string, `@(#)`, is placed in the ID string in order to make identification and retrieval easy (see Section 2.7.5).

The function `sccs help` will provide brief information about commands, or about error messages. Unfortunately, it provides information only about the basic commands. No information is available on complex commands, such as `create`, which are composed of subcommands executed by the program `sccs`. The help function is more useful for providing an expanded version of the error messages. Each error message from *SCCS* is followed by a code in parentheses. Use this as an argument to the help function. For example:

```
% sccs help cm7
```

provides more information about the *No id keywords* error discussed above.

2.7.2   Checking Out For Compilation

A result of the `create` command is that a copy of the original file, with an *SCCS* ID, exists in the main directory, but without write permission. This, of course, is to try to prevent it from being edited. This file is not meant to be changed, and any changes made to it may be lost. The purpose of this file is for reading, printing, and compiling.

Since this file was created from the s-file, it may be replaced on demand by SCCS. In fact, you may delete it to save space and obtain a new copy with the command

```
% sccs get prog.c
```

`make` and `sscs` are particularly suited for use together since `make` contains rules for dealing with *s.files*. When a file is not present, `make` will execute an SCCS `get` command to obtain a new copy.

2.7.3   Editing

To check out a file for editing use the SCCS `edit` command. For example,

```
% sccs edit prog.c
```

will create a writable version of the file `prog.c`, and SCCS will mark the file as being checked out. Another attempt to check out the file, before checking it back in, will result in an error message.

When a file is checked out for editing, a new version number is created for it. This is referred to as a *delta,* since SCCS creates files by making all of the incremental changes to the original. The first version number of a file is 1.1. The next version will be 1.2. Subsequent check in/out cycles will result in incremental changes to the number following the decimal point. This format for the version number is the familiar major release/minor release format.

Once any desired changes have been made, the file should be checked in. This is accomplished by using the command `delta`. The reason it is referred to as *delta* is that it causes the changes between the old and new versions to be saved. When you issue the command, such as

```
% sccs delta prog.c
```

the `sccs` program will prompt you for comments. Here is where you should enter a brief summary of the changes that were made. If your comments will extend beyond one line, end all but the last line with a backslash \. When you have completed typing the comments, *SCCS* will report the version number of the file, and the number of lines changed and deleted. The original file, in this example `prog.c`, will be removed.

Since it is common to follow `delta` with `get`, an abbreviated version of the two commands exists. The `delget` command will perform a `delta` followed by a `get`. A similar abbreviated command is `deledit`, which performs a `delta` followed by an `edit` to allow you to continue making changes.

2.7.4 Correcting Errors

SCCS provides many ways to fix errors, and allows you to "back out" of an edit session if you decide that you've made a mistake. The command

```
% sccs unedit prog.c
```

will remove the copy of the file `prog.c` that has been checked out for editing, and execute a `get` command to obtain a read-only version of the file `prog.c`.

If you find yourself uncertain about what changes have been made to a file that has been checked out for editing, use the `sccs diff` command. It will run the `diff` program on the current version, and the previous version of the source file.

Sometimes you check in a file only to find that you've made a small spelling error, or perhaps made a mistake in your changes. If you would like to replace the last edited version with a new one, you may use the `fix` command as follows:

```
% sccs fix -rx.y prog.c
```

where `x.y` is the version number to check out. That version will be checked out for editing, but the version number will not be incremented. Thus when you check in the new revision, the version number will have been incremented only by a total of one for the two editing sessions. A record of the `fix` is maintained in the SCCS history.

If you prefer to completely remove the history log for `delta`, the `rmdel` command may be used. It also must be used with the latest version number. For example,

```
% sccs rmdel -r1.5 prog.c
```

will remove all traces of the last changes to `prog.c`, assuming that the latest version number was 1.5.

Since the comments solicited during a check-in operation, or `delta`, are often entered interactively, it is common to forget something. The command `cdc` allows you to add text to the comment after a version of a file has been checked in. Assuming that the last version was numbered 1.5,

```
% sccs cdc -r1.5 prog.c
```

will prompt you for comments. The new comment line or lines will be added to the ones previously entered.

2.7.5   File Status

There are many commands available for checking the status of a file, and for examining the edit history of a file. A simple one is the `-g` flag to the `get` function. It provides the latest version number of a file. For example,

```
% sccs get -g prog.c
```

will print the latest version number for the file `prog.c`. You may use this information, along with that obtained from the program `what`. It searches a file, ASCII or binary, for the token `@(#)` which was placed in the source file by `sccs`, and extracts the string following that token. You may use this to see the version numbers of the source files that were used to create an executable program. Try

```
% what /bin/ls
```

to see the version number of the source file used to make the program `ls` (assuming that your computer vendor uses `sccs` for source control).

It is often useful to see the comments attached to the edit history of a file. The function `prt` provides this information. For example,

```
% sccs prt prog.c
```

will print a record of the change history of the file `prog.c`, along with the comments associated with the changes. More information is provided by the function `print`. Following the edit history and comments, the file is printed. At the beginning of each line of the file, the version number when that line was inserted is printed. This provides a convenient display of the history of individual portions of the file.

Finally, the function `info` displays a list of the files that are checked out for editing along with associated information, such as who checked out the file. The function `tell`, provides just a simple list of the files that are checked out. It is well suited for use within shell scripts.

2.7.6 Advanced Usage

The `edit`/`delta` pairs change the minor revision level of the version number. To change the major revision, use the flag `-r` of the `edit` function. For example,

```
% sccs edit -r2 prog.c
```

will check out `prog.c` for editing and will assign it the version number 2.1. Since it is often useful to change the major revision number for all of the files in a project, the command

```
% sccs edit -r2 SCCS
```

will check all of the files out and update the major revision level to 2. You may use the same format to refer to all files collectively for other functions such as `delta` and `get`. For example,

```
% sccs delta SCCS
```

will check all files in.

In Section 2.7.1, we introduced the concept of keywords. They are tags that `sccs` replaces with particular information. For example, we suggested that you place the following line in each of your source files:

```
static char SccsID[] = "%W% %G%";
```

`sccs` replaces the `%W%` with the string `@(#)` followed by the file name and the version number. The keyword `%G%` is replaced by the date of the last delta. Table 2.3 lists the keywords recognized by `sccs`.

The *SCCS* system saves a large amount of information about changes made to files under its control. Rather than providing a

Keyword	Replaced by
%Z%	@(#)
%M%	File name
%I%	Version number
%G%	Date of last delta
%R%	Major revision number
%W%	Abbreviated version of %Z%%M%\T%I%

Table 2.3   SSCS keywords

program to print out all of that information, a report generating function, prs, is supplied. For example,

```
% sccs prs -d"Last changes to :M: were made by :P:" prog.c
```

will print out a string such as

```
Last changes to prog.c were made by aal
```

by substituting information from the *s-file* for keywords in the string
given as an argument. The list of keywords for prs is too long for us to
include in this book. Display the man page for sccs-prs to see the
list.

   SCCS is capable of more complex functions, such as maintaining
several branches of changes, and providing for such things as "frozen"
releases. See the man page for the function sccs-admin for more
details on advanced usage of *SCCS*.

2.7.7   RCS

SCCS is not the only program for source revision control. A similar
program exists named *RCS* (Revision Control System). The functionality is basically the same as that of SCCS. The choice of program
depends mainly on what is available on your system.

2.8 Other Languages

There are compilers and interpreters available for many languages that run on UNIX systems. They are produced by the hardware vendors, third party companies, and such institutions as universities and government laboratories. It is beyond the scope of this book to cover these products fully. In this section we will try to provide an overview of the major languages that are available.

2.8.1 FORTRAN

Since this is a major language in the scientific computing field, most computer manufacturers offer a FORTRAN 77 compiler. In fact, many companies lavish extensive resources on their Fortran compilers. This is especially true for high performance machines often used in scientific computing. Third-party vendors also supply Fortran compilers for many computers.

The main strength of FORTRAN lies in its extensive use. There is a large body of software written in FORTRAN, especially for numeric processing. Most UNIX C compilers and systems allow a programmer to link object files generated by compilers for different languages. To do this, one must use the correct function calling style. It is often easy to write a main program in C, and call functions written in FORTRAN.

2.8.2 Pascal

A large market exists for Pascal in education. As with FORTRAN, the large market prompts most manufacturers to include a Pascal compiler in their product offerings. The language MODULA-2 is replacing Pascal in some educational settings.

2.8.3 C++

This object-oriented extension to C is experiencing rapid growth in the marketplace. There are several compilers available. AT&T offers a preprocessor that translates C++ to C, which is then compiled by the regular C compiler. Many vendors offer their own version. There is also a publicly available compiler, g++, from the GNU project. Other object-oriented languages such as Objective C and Smalltalk are available for some UNIX systems.

2.8.4 Lisp and Related Languages

There are a variety of dialects of Lisp. Manufacturers and third party vendors tend to offer versions of Common Lisp. Related languages, such as `scheme` are available in the public domain.

2.8.5   LEX and YACC

The languages LEX and YACC are used, in combination with C code, to recognize structured input to a program. The original use of LEX and YACC was to generate a parser for a compiler. They are also very useful for programs that interpret any similar input, such as command languages, or structured data. LEX and YACC are too complex to be described fully here. This introductory section is intended only to illustrate their use.

Here's an example of YACC code to recognize a simple expression:

```
expr  :    expr PLUS expr
      |    expr MINUS expr
      |    NUMBER
      ;
```

This says that an expression (expr) can be an expression plus an expression, an expression minus an expression, or a number. The tokens (a token is considered to be the basic unit of input) PLUS, MINUS, and NUMBER are recognized by LEX. A fragment of C code is normally included by the programmer with the YACC code for expr. The C code is executed when input matches the YACC template.

LEX code to recognize the necessary tokens might be written as:

```
\+          return(PLUS);
\-          return(MINUS);
[0-9]+      return(NUMBER);
```

This instructs LEX to generate code to recognize the plus and minus signs as PLUS and MINUS, respectively, and an instance of one or more digits from 0 through 9 as a NUMBER. One would normally use more elaborate LEX and YACC rules than these, to recognize negative numbers for instance.

LEX and YACC are useful not only for writing compilers, but also for interpreting structured commands or data. They are well worth using for any task where the structure of the input is nontrivial. The advantages of LEX and YACC over writing C code to interpret the input are ease of use, readability, and maintainability.

2.8.6   Integrated Environments

Integrated software development environments are becoming available for UNIX. These systems package editing, compiling and debugging into one environment, with a windowing point-and-click user interface. The features are similar to those popular on Macintoshes and PCs. These packages are commercial products that do not usually come bundled with UNIX systems.

An example is ObjectCenter by CenterLine Software. It can execute a program as a combination of C++ source code (there's a C version as well), object files, and libraries. The debugger is similar to dbx, but uses a menu-driven interface. There is a graphical browser that allows the programmer to examine complex data structures and to easily follow pointers. A built-in C++ interpreter, and an incremental linker allow for fast changes, potentially resulting in a shorter development cycle.

2.9 Conclusions

More detailed information on the programs described in this chapter may be obtained by reading the manuals supplied by the vendor of your UNIX software. Similar information on the equivalent GNU software is available from the Free Software Foundation. The best way to obtain an introduction to their software is via ftp to prep.ai.mit.edu. USENET news is an excellent way to learn and to participate in discussions about UNIX programming tools.

UNIX was originally written for programmers and continues to be an excellent platform for program development. More tools are being added to the existing suite, by commercial vendors, universities, and by the GNU project. A prudent programmer should actively seek out new tools, evaluate them, and add to his or her toolkit those that will increase productivity.

3

The X Window System

Jon Mauney

The X Window System has become the *de facto* standard for graphi-cal/window interfaces on UNIX workstations. X was developed at the Massachusetts Institute of Technology, building on (and drastically changing) an earlier experimental window system from Stanford called W. The X Window System is constantly evolving. The first wide-spread release, version 10, was in 1985. After X10 was released, a major redesign effort was begun, creating some significant improve-ments and some incompatible changes to the protocol. The result was X version 11, first released in 1987. Subsequent releases of X11 have been compatible, adding new features, fixing bugs, and improving per-formance. Release 5 of version 11 of the X Window System, or X11R5 as it is usually known, was released in October 1991. Notable features in X11R5 are support for internationalization, scalable fonts, a net-work font server, device-independent color specification, and improved security. X11R6, released in June 1994, includes support for graphical embedding, multithread execution, and several extensions.

As X became the basis of more and more commercial workstation offerings, it outgrew the university development project that had started it. Vendors, however, preferred to have X controlled by the neutral party, MIT, rather than by any commercial operation. Therefore the X Consortium was formed. The Consortium continues to support and develop the X Window System, with contributions both of money and of software from vendors and with control retained by a neutral organization.

The X Window System has been phenomenally successful, surpassing both older systems such as SunView, and newer ones such as NeWS and NextStep, which some people feel are technically superior. The widespread adoption of X is due to factors similar to those that led to the early popularity of UNIX: a fairly elegant design, great flexibility, portability, and easy availability of source code.

X was designed at the outset to have good support for networked workstations, and to be portable to a variety of CPU and display architectures. X is a layered system, and the lowest layer, the X11 protocol, is low level indeed. It is modeled on a network packet-transmission system, sending messages between applications and the display; the ability to remotely display information across a network is thus built in at the lowest level of X.

Using the X11 protocol directly (or through the procedural interface Xlib) is a very cumbersome way to build applications. Because X provides support for essentially any workstation hardware, there are many options that must be specified on output requests, and many possibilities that must be considered for input events. Application programmers will usually use a higher level toolkit.

3.1   Mechanism Versus Policy

Any windowing workstation system must provide answers to the following questions:

- How is the screen divided into multiple windows?

- How are the positions of windows determined?

- How are the windows drawn on the screen?

- How is text written into a window?

- How are graphics drawn into a window?

- Can a window change size, and if so, how are the contents affected?

- Can windows overlap, and if so, how is the overlapping area handled? How is the stacking order determined?

- How is keyboard input handled? That is, can multiple applications be informed from the same keystroke? If not, how is it determined which application receives the information?

- How are mouse motion and mouse button inputs handled?

- Can portions of one window be selected and then copied into another window?

Some of these questions are in the realm of *policy*: Should something be allowed? Other questions are more concrete: How is something to be accomplished? The X Window System has a stated goal to provide "mechanism, not policy," which means that the *how* is answered in a way general enough to support any reasonable answer to the question of *should*. For example, X allows windows to overlap, and provides a mechanism for describing which window will be fully visible and which will be obscured. But, the mechanism for deciding which window *should* be visible is not a part of X; a policy requiring that windows never overlap is also easily implemented.

Of course, it is not actually possible to avoid making policy decisions, and any usable X-Window workstation will be chock-full of such decisions. The point is simply that the basic X system does not enforce any particular policy. Thus a variety of look-and-feel styles can all be offered on the same underlying system, and new policies can be tried at any time. Policies in X are, in fact, dictated by a set of conventions, and by higher level toolkits.

Just as the typical X user will happily click the mouse buttons without worrying about how an X application is coded, so will many X application programmers accomplish their goals by using window components called *widgets,* chosen from a prebuilt widget library such as Motif or OPEN LOOK, without knowing what is going on at lower levels of the system. But understanding all the layers of X is very useful when trying to implement something not directly provided by a widget set or an interface builder.

3.2   Layers of X Software

The basic definition of X is the network protocol. But while it is possible to build programs that create message packets and write them into a network connection (or *socket*), the X protocol is not really a suitable programming interface. The next layer of X is called Xlib. It is primarily a C library implementing the X protocol requests in a procedure call interface. Thus, XOpenDisplay initializes the socket connection, and XDrawLine sends a DrawLine request through the socket. The C programmer can then think in terms of the familiar function call and

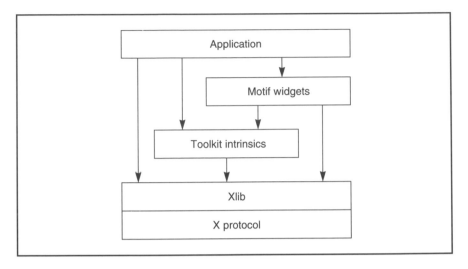

Figure 3.1   Layers of software in an X application

parameter model, and need not worry about the format of packets. Xlib also provides many "convenience functions" that do not correspond to protocol requests.

The Xlib programming interface is very flexible, but also very low level. A higher level interface is needed for effective programming. X includes a basic toolkit, consisting of functions called the Xt Intrinsics, for an object-oriented programming interface. The Intrinsics, however, are still a basic technology; they supply the means to develop a full toolkit of widgets, but do not enforce any particular policy or user interface style.

Figure 3.1 shows the layers of software in a typical application built using components called the Motif widget set. The application calls not only the Motif layer, but also uses the Toolkit and Xlib directly for certain basic operations.

The stated goal of X—providing "mechanism, not policy"—is a good one for the base technology, but it is untenable in building real-life applications. There are two reasons why policy is required. The more obvious is the desire for standardization of user interfaces. That the middle mouse button is given a particular meaning is a policy that must be stated somewhere. Such policy is dictated by user interface style guidelines such as Motif and OPEN LOOK, and implemented by applications built using the associated toolkits.

A less obvious need for policy is in the interaction among applications and between an application and the window manager. If two or more clients are going to coexist on a single display, there must be some basic rules of conduct, and those rules constitute policy. This policy is set out in a parallel document to the X protocol specification, known as the Inter-Client Communication Conventions Manual, or ICCCM. The conventions cover such things as information the application window should supply to the window manager, the ways in which an application will be notified when its window is iconified, and rules about taking control of the keyboard or mouse.

3.3   The Window Manager

The X Window System was designed for a multitasking environment; it is expected that several applications will be active, competing for the shared resources of display screen, keyboard, and mouse. Allocation of the shared resources is a policy decision, the kind of thing X tries to avoid dictating. Some policies are set out in the ICCCM, to which applications should adhere voluntarily. Most policies are enforced by a special program called the *window manager*. A few policies are unavoidably built into the X server.

Mouse activity is handled by the server. Mouse events are generally reported to the window in which the mouse cursor currently resides; an application may *grab* the mouse, ensuring that all events will be reported to that application regardless of the mouse position, but grabs are intended to be temporary, in compliance with the ICCCM.

Within a given application, there exists a hierarchy of windows— every window, except the root window, is created as a child of some other window. A child window is totally dependent on its parent for visibility on the screen; a window is visible only to the extent that all of its ancestors are visible. If the parent is not visible, either because it is covered by some other window or because it is not mapped (i.e., designated as being visible on the screen), then the child is not visible. If the boundaries of the child extend beyond the boundaries of the parent, for example if the child is larger than the parent, then the child is *clipped,* meaning that only the part of the child that lies within the boundaries of the parent can be seen. The position coordinates of the child window are relative to the upper-left corner of the parent.

Figure 3.2 shows the window hierarchy of the simple application in Program 3.1, which is shown and described in Section 3.6. The application has a main window, which is a child of the Root Window of the display; the main window in turn has three children, A, B, and C.

Since windows may overlap, like papers on a desktop, there must be some way of determining the stacking order. Information on the size, position, and stacking of windows is maintained by the server, but these functions are left under control of the applications.

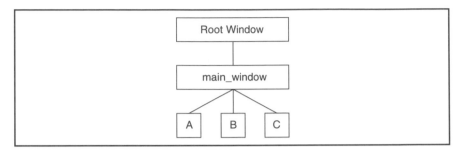

Figure 3.2   Window hierarchy of sample program

The X protocol provides requests for setting and changing the size, position, and stacking of windows, and within an application any configuration requests are honored without question—it is purely an internal matter for the application. But the top level window of an application is a child of the Root Window that covers the entire screen, and applications must compete with each other for use of the screen space. Some sort of policy must be imposed.

In X, policy on the sharing of screen resources is determined by the window manager. As far as the X server is concerned, the window manager is just another client. There are protocol requests that are provided specifically for the use of the window manager, and only one window manager may run on the display at any time, but users may switch window managers at will and any programmer who so desires can write a new window manager to support whatever policy is needed.

All changes to the Root Window and its immediate children are intercepted by the window manager. That is, whenever a new top level window is created, or tries to change its size or position, the change will not be made by the server immediately. Instead, the request is forwarded to the window manager, which will determine whether the request should be honored. The window manager may deny the request entirely; more likely, it will modify the request before sending it back to the server to be completed. Thus the window manager can ensure that the size and position of windows always conform to its policy. For example, a window manager may enforce a *tiling* policy, in which application windows are not allowed to overlap; if an application tries to make its window larger, other applications might be made smaller, and the original size request might be scaled back because there is not sufficient room to honor the request.

The most obvious intervention of the window manager occurs when the application's top level window is first created and mapped. The

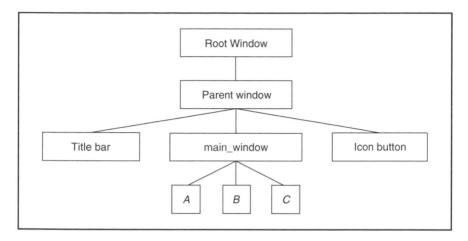

Figure 3.3 Window hierarchy after reparenting

window does not actually appear until the window manager has approved the size and position. In many cases, the window manager will create a new window, and *reparent* the application window so that it is a child of that new window instead of the Root Window. In this way, the window manager can more easily control the size and position of the application. If the new parent is moved, then the application window moves automatically, since its coordinates are always relative to the parent. Similarly, the window manager can *iconify* a window—remove the window from the screen, replacing it with a small *icon* window, thus freeing some screen space—simply by unmapping the parent; the application window becomes invisible if its parent is not visible. Figure 3.3 shows the window hierarchy of the sample application after reparenting by a hypothetical window manager. The manager has not only added a new parent between the Root Window and the application's main window, it has also created two more children for the new parent. These children provide a descriptive title on the window and a control button to allow the user to iconify the window. (A real window manager will add even more controls, to allow resizing, menus, etc.)

The window manager can create a certain amount of uniformity among applications by allowing the user to change the position, size, and stacking of application windows, and by iconifying and deiconifying windows. All applications will behave the same in this regard because the controls are provided by the window manager. Furthermore, the applications don't have to contain any code to provide such controls, since the window manager will take care of it.

On the other hand, applications must be built with the understanding that they have no control over size, position, stacking, and iconification. Requests for a particular position on the screen may be denied. The window may be enlarged, shrunk, or iconified at any time. In fact, the window may even be destroyed at any time: the window manager may provide the user with a command to close the window, and since the window manager owns the parent upon which the application is dependent, the window manager has the power to essentially pull the rug out from under an application at any time.

Clearly, a high degree of cooperation is required between the window manager and the applications. An application must be prepared for all the things the window manager can do to it. The window manager, in turn, must not take action without due cause, and must give fair warning before taking drastic actions such as closing the top level window. Such cooperation is a policy question that must be common to all client programs. Guidelines for cooperation are set out in a section of the ICCCM.

3.4 X Networking

At its base, X is a network protocol between an X server and its client applications. The X protocol specifies the format of request and reply packets, and the actions of the server in response to those requests. The network nature of this protocol is a key to the flexibility of X. Since the protocol merely specifies the format of data being sent via a standard interprocess communication (IPC) mechanism, it makes no demands upon the way in which client applications are coded. Clients may be written in any language and may run on any operating system, as long as the IPC mechanism is supported. They need not meet any special linkage conventions nor include any specific libraries.

An X client merely opens the appropriate network socket—corresponding to the display upon which it wishes to appear—and writes X-protocol packets into that socket. The X server for the display accepts packets on the same socket and responds to the requests. In a common workstation environment, the application and the server are separate processes running on the same CPU. But the application might well be running on a remote machine, perhaps a specialized server down the hall, perhaps a machine at another institution on the other side of the country.

Figure 3.4 shows a typical situation. The X server is a process on the workstation controlling input from the keyboard and mouse and output to the CRT display monitor. Applications 1 and 2 are running on the local machine, and communicate with the server by a UNIX-

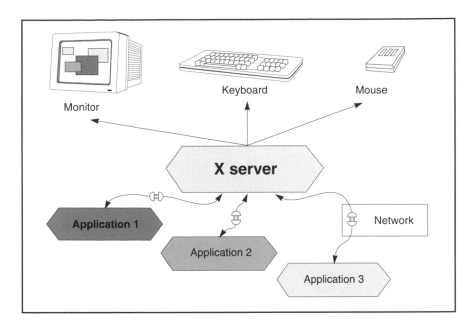

Figure 3.4   X Window System server and applications

domain socket. Application 3 is running on a remote host and communicates by a network connection.

The network transparency of X brings tremendous flexibility to the system. In fact, a properly compiled X application can be executed on a compute server, say a supercomputer, that doesn't run an X server and doesn't even have any of the X libraries stored on its disks. At the extreme, the X-terminal products are stripped-down workstations dedicated to running just the X server—all other processes must be run on some other host. It is also easy to use X's network capability to write multiuser applications: a single application process can open windows on several workstations, displaying information to and accepting input from all the users.

On the face of it, X does not have a redirection capability comparable to the UNIX pipe. An X application opens a connection directly to a display, writing its graphic output on that display and accepting keyboard and mouse input from the display. It is not possible, in general, for another application on the same display to filter these input and output events. But the network connection provides a way in which such filters can be written. Suppose for example, that we wish to demonstrate the use of an X application, and to record the session so that it can be played back later. We can write a pseudo-server that will intercept all the events as follows: The pseudo-server listens on a socket corresponding to a display that is not actually in use; everything received on that socket is both recorded into a file and sent along another socket to a real X server and display. The application is directed to connect to the nonexistent display. As far as the application is concerned, it is communicating with a normal server.

3.5   The X11 Protocol

The X protocol defines the interaction between an X client and the server. It specifies the data format of requests and responses, but not the transport mechanism to be used. If the client and server are both running on the same host, then shared memory or some other local communication method might be used. If the client and server are on distinct hosts, then a network connection is needed. Any network transport can be used, as long as it guarantees that data arrive in the order sent, and as long as both the client and server support the method.

The most commonly used network for X connections is probably TCP/IP. The X server listens on a well-known port; since a host may support more than one display, the port for display N is 6000 + N. A client merely needs to open a socket to the desired host and port, and to begin using the protocol.

The data packets in the X protocol have a simple format, designed to be highly machine independent. As part of the initial exchange in the protocol the client defines the byte order of multibyte data. All values exchanged in the X protocol are integers; in the few cases where real numbers are needed, they are transmitted as two integers—a numerator and denominator forming a rational number.

Figure 3.5 shows the general format of packets in the X protocol. Requests from client to server have a variable-length format. A request begins with a 4-byte header, containing an 8-bit opcode, a 16-bit length field, and an 8-bit data field. This header may be followed by zero or more additional bytes, as specified by the length.

Most of the requests from client to server are one-way messages. The X protocol is asynchronous; the server guarantees to perform actions in the order requested, but for efficiency reasons does not normally acknowledge a request or send an indication that a request has been completed. A few of the protocol codes are requests for information from the server; a reply containing the requested information will be sent from server to client. Naturally, these round-trip requests are more costly and are avoided by skilled programmers.

Packets sent from the server are of three types: reply, event, and error. Packets from the server generally are 32 bytes long; not all of

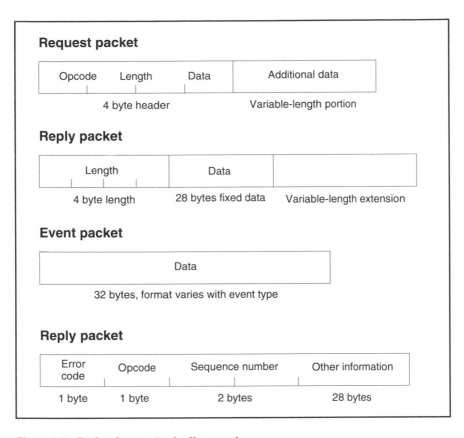

Figure 3.5   Packet formats in the X protocol

the bytes are necessarily used. A reply sent in response to a request from a client contains a 32-bit length field. The reply will be 32 bytes, and possibly more, as specified by the length field. The contents of the reply depend on the type of the corresponding request.

Most of the information sent from the server to the client is in the form of *events*. Whenever some activity occurs on the display—a key is pressed, the mouse is moved, etc.—the server may need to report that fact to one or more clients. The server sends event information to all clients that have registered an interest in that particular kind of event. Events are 32 bytes; the contents depend on the type of the event.

Since X is an asynchronous protocol, a client does not receive a return status from most requests. The client will send the request, and then proceed under the assumption that the request will be

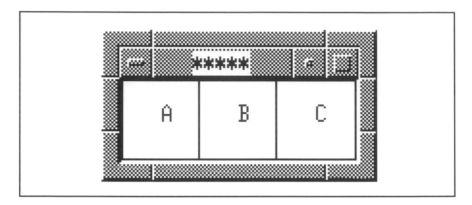

Figure 3.6   Window drawn by sample Xlib program

performed. If the server finds that the request is erroneous, it sends an error packet back to the client. An error report is 32 bytes, containing a 1-byte error code, the opcode and sequence number of the failed request, and possibly other information, depending on the request. It is left up to the client to determine how to respond to the error.

3.6   Basic X Programming: Xlib

A simple X-Window program using Xlib functions is shown in Program 3.1. Figure 3.6 shows the windows created by this program. The program opens a main window, subdivides it into three "buttons" labeled *A*, *B*, and *C*, and accepts mouse-button clicks in the three screen buttons. Typing a q on the keyboard terminates the program. Line 17 in the program starts things off by opening the connection to the X server. The argument to XOpenDisplay indicates the workstation on which to display the window. In this case, the argument is the null string, which on UNIX systems means to use the value of the DISPLAY variable in the environment. XOpenDisplay will return NULL if the connection cannot be opened for any reason.

Lines 22 and 23 determine the proper values for black and white pixels on the display device. These values will be used to set the drawing colors in the application windows.

The next step is to create a window. XCreateSimpleWindow is the simpler of the two Xlib calls that create a window. Line 24 creates the main window for our application. Arguments specify the display, the parent window of the new window, the *x*- and *y*-coordinates of the new window, its height and width, the width and color of the border, and the background color of the window. Other attributes of the new

```
 1: #include <stdio.h>
 2: #include <X11/Xlib.h>
 3:
 4: main()
 5: {
 6:    Display *disp;
 7:    Font fd;
 8:    Window main_win, A, B, C;
 9:    GC gc;
10:     XEvent event;
11:     char buffer[10];
12:     int height=40;
13:     int button_width = 40;
14:     int width=button_width*3;
15:     int len, quit, black, white;
16:
17:     disp = XOpenDisplay("");
18:     if (disp == NULL) {
19:       fprintf(stderr, "cannot open display\n");
20:       exit(1);
21:     }
22:     black = BlackPixel(disp,DefaultScreen(disp));
23:     white = WhitePixel(disp,DefaultScreen(disp));
24:     main_win = XCreateSimpleWindow(disp,DefaultRootWindow(disp),
25:       0,0, width+2, height+2, 4, black, white);
26:     A = XCreateSimpleWindow(disp,main_win, 0,0,
27:       button_width, height, 1, black, white);
28:     B = XCreateSimpleWindow(disp,main_win, button_width, 0,
29:       button_width, height, 1, black, white);
30:     C = XCreateSimpleWindow(disp,main_win, 2*button_width, 0,
31:       button_width, height, 1, black, white);
32:
33:     XSelectInput(disp,main_win, KeyPressMask);
34:     XSelectInput(disp, A, ButtonPressMask | ExposureMask);
35:     XSelectInput(disp, B, ButtonPressMask | ExposureMask);
36:     XSelectInput(disp, C, ButtonPressMask | ExposureMask);
37:
38:     XMapRaised(disp,A);
39:     XMapRaised(disp,B);
40:     XMapRaised(disp,C);
41:     XMapRaised(disp,main_win);
42:     gc = DefaultGC(disp,DefaultScreen(disp));
43:     quit = 0;
44:     while(!quit) {
45:       XNextEvent(disp, &event);
46:       switch(event.type) {
47:         case Expose:
48:            XDrawString(disp,A,gc, button_width/2, height/2, "A",1);
49:            XDrawString(disp,B,gc, button_width/2, height/2, "B",1);
50:            XDrawString(disp,C,gc, button_width/2, height/2, "C",1);
51:            break;
```

Program 3.1   Sample application using Xlib

```
52:        case ButtonPress:
53:            if (event.xbutton.window == A)
54:                printf("A was selected\n");
55:            else if (event.xbutton.window == B)
56:                printf("B was selected\n");
57:            else printf("C was selected\n");
58:            break;
59:        case KeyPress:
60:            len = XLookupString(&event, buffer, 10, 0, 0);
61:            if (len == 1 && buffer[0] == 'q')
62:                quit = 1;
63:            break;
64:        case MappingNotify:
65:            XRefreshKeyboardMapping(&event);
66:            break;
67:        default:
68:            printf(stderr,"unexpected event type:%d\n",event.type);
69:            break;
70:        }
71:    }
72:    XCloseDisplay(disp);
73: }
```

Program 3.1 (continued)   Sample application using Xlib

window are left unspecified or are inherited from the parent window. The newly created window is not yet visible on the screen.

Lines 26 through 31 create three more windows as children of the first window. Subwindows are dependent on the parent window—the position of a subwindow is specified relative to the parent, the visible portion of a subwindow is limited by the boundaries of the parent, and making a parent window invisible will likewise remove the children. Thus the window hierarchy can be a powerful organizing tool. In this case we choose the height, width, and position of the three children to divide the parent window into three sections. Figure 3.2 shows the hierarchy of windows created by the application.

The Xlib function XSelectInput informs the server as to which of the many possible events relating to the window should be reported back to the application. This information is indicated by building a mask with the bitwise OR of a number of predefined event masks. In the parent window (line 33) we are interested in keys being pressed and the window becoming visible. In the three children (lines 34–36) we are interested only in the mouse buttons being pressed.

Windows in X may be *mapped* or *unmapped*. An unmapped window has no manifestation on the screen. When a window is first created, it is unmapped; it is convenient to set the attributes of a window while it is unmapped, so that when it is first displayed, it has its proper appearance. Likewise, it is useful to call XSelectInput while the window is unmapped, so that the window can start receiving input events as soon as it appears on the screen; this applies especially to the all-important Expose event, discussed below. A window will be visible only if it has been explicitly mapped, if its parent window is mapped, and if no other window covers it.

The call to XMapRaised instructs the server to map the window, and to place it at the top of the stacking order, so that the window will be fully visible, not obscured by other windows. We map the children in lines 38–40, before mapping the parent in line 41. This approach ensures that all windows will be drawn at once.

All drawing actions performed in a window are done relative to a *graphics context* (GC) which keeps information on drawing colors, line styles, etc. In line 42 we simply ask for a default GC. In a complex application there may be many GCs, each representing a distinct drawing style that will be used. If we wished to print text using a different type face or style, that information would be stored in a GC. If we wished to draw dots larger than a single pixel, the size would be stored in a GC.

The sample program enters the *event loop*, the heart of the program, at line 44. A window program cannot control all of its destiny, since it must share the screen with other applications, and since the user may decide to use the mouse or keyboard at unpredictable times. Therefore the properly written X program has a loop in which it simply accepts the next event as reported by the server, and deals with that event as appropriate. The event loop is essentially an infinite loop, exiting only when the application terminates.

XNextEvent (line 45) is the Xlib call that retrieves the event from the event queue. The event structure is a union of the various kinds of information that might be provided by different events, and the *type field* distinguishes the event type. The switch statement on line 46 separates the four event types we expect to receive.

The *Expose* event (line 47) occurs whenever a part of a window that was not visible becomes visible, such as when a window once covered by another window is exposed, or when a newly created window is first mapped. It is left up to the X application to redraw the contents of an exposed window; although a given server *may* keep track of the contents of an obscured window, it is not required to, and such service may be provided and then revoked as the server runs out of memory. In this example, we choose the simple approach of redrawing the labels of all three buttons, even though it may be that only one has been obscured and then exposed. The event structure provides information on exactly which parts of which windows need redrawing, but we ignore it.

In this application, as with any well-designed X application, nothing is written into the window until the first Expose event is received. After the call to XMapRaised, we still don't know for sure that the window actually appears on the screen, since the map request may be intercepted and delayed by the window manager. Therefore the only safe way to draw the initial contents of the window is to wait for the first Expose event.

Text is written into a window with the request XDrawString, which takes as arguments the display and window, the GC that controls drawing parameters, the x- and y-coordinates of the beginning of the string, the string itself, and the length of the string. Xlib does not use the C convention of null-terminated strings.

The *ButtonPress* event (line 52) is reported to a window whenever a mouse button is depressed while the mouse cursor is within that window. (There is a corresponding *ButtonRelease* event that this application ignores.) The window identifier contained in the event structure reveals which screen button was chosen.

A *Keypress event* (line 59) is reported to a window whenever a key is depressed while that window receives input focus. Since there are multiple windows on a display and only one keyboard, there must be a policy determining which window will receive keyboard input. The window which will receive input is said to have the *focus*, and movement of focus is determined by the window manager.

X allows for the keyboard to be customized, changing the meanings of keys and even binding a single keystroke to expand into a string of characters. To make use of this keyboard mapping, we pass the Key-Press event, which contains information on the physical key that was pressed, to the convenience routine XLookupString (line 60), which translates the KeyPress to an ascii string. In this program we simply check whether the key translates to the single letter q, and if so exit the program.

The keyboard mapping may be changed at any time by user command. Such a change results in a *MappingNotify* event, which cannot be masked out by the application. A call to XRefreshKeyboardMapping updates the tables within the application.

As mentioned, the application leaves the event loop only when ready to quit, so outside the loop it simply remains to clean up by closing the display connection, and to exit.

Our sample program leaves quite a lot out. The border that is added to the window by the window manager has a space for the name of the window to be displayed. As you can see in Figure 3.6, the name is shown as **** because the application doesn't provide a window name, nor does it provide several other hints that smooth the interaction between window manager and application. A well-designed application will allow the user to stretch or shrink the main window, adjusting the subwindows and contents to fit; this example ignores such changes.

In a more realistic application, it would be desirable to use a typeface that is more attractive than the default font, and to choose the type size to fill the button window. Doing so involves opening an X-Window entity called a *font*, storing it in the GC, and computing the proper position of the labels, based on the size information extracted from the font. Of course, the font size should change if the window size is changed.

All of this points up some of the drawbacks of writing an application using Xlib. Xlib is a very low level interface, requiring quite a lot of application code to get anything done. Because X was designed to be flexible, there are myriad details that an X application must specify. Quite a lot of code will be replicated many times within an application and from one application to another: the code to create a window, select input, and map the window, to open a font and draw text, to adjust to a new size for the parent window, to figure out how much of a window has been exposed and how to redraw it, etc.

A higher level programming model is really needed for effective applications programming in X. To that end, the X Consortium has specified another layer of software above Xlib: a toolkit of facilities called the Xt Intrinsics. The Intrinsics do not form a complete application programming interface. Instead, they form a basic toolkit that supports yet another layer, a widget set.

3.7   The Toolkit and Widget Programming

There are several facilities that a window-programming interface must provide. One is a way of describing what is desired on the display—a button labeled *A*, a scrollbar with its initial position in the middle, a menu with a certain set of choices. Another requirement is a library of code that will manage the displayed items and respond to standard situations, such as resizing and exposure events. Third, there must be some way to invoke application-specific code as needed.

It is difficult to provide these capabilities in a standard procedure-call model of programming: It is easy enough for a procedure to set up a window and all its attributes, but after the procedure returns, how is that window linked to future actions? The object-oriented programming model, on the other hand, is well suited to such needs, and indeed most of the evolution of object-oriented systems has occurred in conjunction with windowing systems. Unfortunately, the language chosen for implementation of Xlib—C—is not object-oriented, nor was there a widely available object-oriented language for the X team to

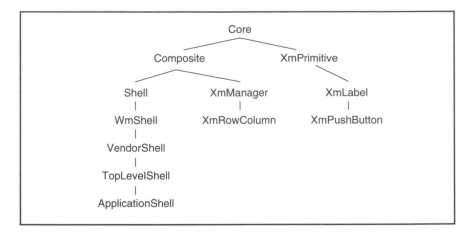

Figure 3.7   Widget class hierarchy

build on. Instead, the Intrinsics provide a mechanism for following an object-oriented style in C, using window-oriented objects called *widgets*.

A widget is a window, plus data defining the contents of the window, and code defining the behavior of the window. As in other object-oriented systems, there are widget *classes*, which provide the code and define the general structure of the widgets, and widget *instances*, which are the actual windows and the data specific to those windows. Classes are organized into a hierarchy, with child classes inheriting behavior from the parent class. Figure 3.7 shows the class hierarchy of the widget classes used in the following example.

In practice, a widget class definition consists primarily of a large structure declaration. The structure contains, first, all of the structure of the parent class—this is the mechanism of inheritance—and then the data specific to the class and pointers to the code defining the behavior of the class. Information-hiding is implemented simply by providing two class definitions: one containing "public" definitions and one containing "private" definitions.

The Intrinsics provide functions for creating and managing widget instances, and a main event loop that accepts X events, determines which widget instance the event belongs to, and calls the code associated with that event and widget. The widget's response to an event might be based purely on code supplied with the class definition, such as redrawing the contents of a window after an Expose event. Or the response may be to call some application-specific function. Functions called from the main loop in response to some activity in a widget are

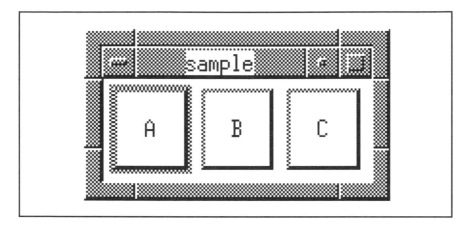

Figure 3.8   Window drawn by sample Motif program

known as *callback* functions, and these callbacks are the way that the general widget library interfaces with application-specific code.

The Intrinsics do not, however, provide a set of widgets suitable for use in building an application; again, the goal is "mechanism, not policy." The Xt toolkit provides a mechanism for building widgets. A given widget set will implement a particular look-and-feel—a policy.

Program 3.2 shows the sample program rewritten using the Xt Intrinsics and the Motif widget set. Figure 3.8 shows the resulting window; among the benefits of a good widget set is windows that have more visual appeal, such as the shaded borders provided by Motif. The #include directives in lines 3–5 bring in the basic Motif definitions, <Xm.h>, and the specific definitions for the two widget classes used in this example, <RowColumn.h> and <PushB.h>.

Function pushed, defined in lines 7–12, is a callback function, to be called when a screen button is pushed; as before, it simply prints the fact that it was called. The parameter client_data indicates which of the buttons was chosen. Function quit (lines 13–17) is to be called when the user types the letter q, as before.

The main function declares a variable context of type XtAppContext. This variable will hold global data used by the Intrinsics. The AppContext was added to release 4 of X11, to allow the Intrinsics to function as a shared library. Main also declares several widget variables. All widgets are of the same type as far as the C program is concerned.

The first line of executable code (line 32) calls XtAppInitialize, which initializes the Intrinsics, processes options, and creates a shell widget, which in this case is assigned to the variable `toplevel`. The shell widget will be the parent of the other widgets used in this program, much as `main_win` was used in the Xlib version. The shell widget also handles all interaction between the application and the window manager.

Lines 34–37 create a *RowColumn* widget. The RowColumn widget class is an example of a manager widget, one whose primary duty is to manage the screen arrangement of other widgets. Specific characteristics of the widget are passed in an argument array, initialized by calls to `XtSetArg`. In line 35 we indicate that the RowColumn widget should arrange its subwidgets horizontally. `XmNorientation` and `XmHORIZONTAL` are names that are `#defined` in the Motif header files; the use of these names makes it easier to detect misspellings of

```
1:      #include <stdio.h>
2:
3:      #include <Xm/Xm.h>
4:      #include <Xm/RowColumn.h>
5:      #include <Xm/PushB.h>
6:
7:      void pushed(w, client_data, call_data)
8:          Widget w;
9:          XtPointer client_data, call_data;
10:     {
11:         printf("%s was selected\n",client_data);
12:     }
13:     void quit()
14:     {
15:         printf("quit\n");
16:         exit(0);
17:     }
18:     XtActionsRec actions[] = {
19:         {"quit", quit}};
20:     char *my_translations = " <Key> Q: quit()";
21:
22:     main(argc, argv)
23:         int argc;
24:         char **argv;
25:     {
26:         XtAppContext context;
27:         Widget toplevel;
28:         Widget rc, pb_a, pb_b, pb_c;
29:         Arg args[10];
30:         int num_args;
31:
```

Program 3.2   Sample application using Motif widgets

```
32:        toplevel = XtAppInitialize(&context, "sample", NULL,
33:                    0, &argc, argv, NULL, NULL, 0);
34:        num_args = 0;
35:        XtSetArg(args[num_args], XmNorientation, XmHORIZONTAL);
                    num_args++;
36:        rc = XtCreateManagedWidget("row",xmRowColumnWidgetClass,
37:                    toplevel, args, num_args);
38:        pb_a = XtCreateManagedWidget(" A ",xmPushButtonWidgetClass,
39:                    rc, NULL, 0);
40:          pb_b = XtCreateManagedWidget(" B ",xmPushButtonWidgetClass,
41:                    rc, NULL, 0);
42:          pb_c = XtCreateManagedWidget(" C ",xmPushButtonWidgetClass,
43:                    rc, NULL, 0);
44:        XtAddCallback(pb_a, XmNactivateCallback, pushed, "A");
45:        XtAddCallback(pb_b, XmNactivateCallback, pushed, "B");
46:        XtAddCallback(pb_c, XmNactivateCallback, pushed, "C");
47:
48:        num_args = 0;
49:          XtSetArg(args[num_args],XtNinput,TRUE); num_args++;
50:        XtSetValues(toplevel,args,num_args);
51:
52:        XtAppAddActions( context, actions, XtNumber(actions));
53:        XtOverrideTranslations( pb_c,
54:          XtParseTranslationTable (my_translations));
55:        XtOverrideTranslations( pb_b,
56:          XtParseTranslationTable (my_translations));
57:        XtOverrideTranslations( pb_a,
58:          XtParseTranslationTable (my_translations));
59:
60:        XtRealizeWidget(toplevel);
61:
62:        XtAppMainLoop(context);
63:  }
```

Program 3.2 (continued)   Sample application using Motif widgets

option values. Lines 36–37 call `XtCreateManagedWidget` to create the widget.

Lines 38 through 43 create three push-button widgets as children of the RowColumn widget. The RowColumn will arrange its children in a row in the order in which they are created.

After the widgets are created, we can define the callback functions (lines 44–46). The Motif push-button widget will call the *activate* callback when the mouse button is pressed and released while the mouse is within the button area. The Intrinsic function `XtAddCallback` takes four parameters: the widget, the kind of callback, the function to be called, and a parameter to be passed to the function. In this example, a single callback function `pushed` is used for all three window buttons. The parameter to `pushed` will be *A*, *B*, or *C*, depending on which button was activated.

Next we define the *translations*—actions to be taken in response to other events. In this case we define that function `quit` is to be called if the `q` key is pressed. The definition occurs in two parts: On line 52, `XtAppAddActions` sets the association between the abstract action *quit* and the C function `quit`. On lines 53 through 58, `XtOverride-Translations` sets the correspondence between the event of the `q` key being pressed and the abstract action *quit*, for each of the three push buttons.

Finally the widgets are *realized* on line 60, causing the actual windows to be created and drawn on the screen, and the main loop is entered on line 62. `XtAppMainLoop` is similar to the infinite loop used in the Xlib example. It simply loops forever, checking for the next event and reacting to it. The main loop in the Intrinsics handles all possible events, using its tables to determine which widget the event belongs to and calling the associated callback functions and other code.

The toolkit version of this example is shorter than the Xlib version, but it does more. The RowColumn widget will adjust the spacing of the push buttons if the size of the whole window is changed. The push buttons will change color to indicate they have been pressed. The Intrinsics will process user-specified options that can select particular colors for the background, typefaces for the labels, etc. All of this additional functionality comes built into the Intrinsics and the widget set. Of course, it is only our source code that is reduced in size; the translated executable program will be quite large because it will include the entire Xt and Motif libraries.

3.8   User Interface Language

Another, higher level way to write Motif programs is to use the Motif User Interface Language, or UIL. Readers who have studied the Motif example carefully may have noticed that widgets are all created using the same Intrinsics function: `XtCreateManagedWidget` (`XtCreate-Widget` could also have be used); the kind of widget to create is specified as a parameter to this function. That is, information about the widgets is built into the program in the form of data, not as code. This is a very important point. First, it is part of the reason why even a small Motif source program produces a huge executable program (in the absence of shared libraries): the usual techniques for linking in only those library functions that will be called do not work. Which widgets are created, and therefore which widget functions are called, depends on data, and so all library code must be linked in.

```
 1:    module sample
 2:    version = '1.1'
 3:    names=case_insensitive
 4:
 5:    procedure
 6:      pushed(string);
 7:
 8:    object
 9:      main_window: XmRowColumn {
10:        arguments {
11:          XmNorientation = XmHORIZONTAL;
12:        };
13:        controls {
14:            XmPushButton {
15:            arguments { XmNlabelString = " A "; };
16:            callbacks {
17:            XmNactivateCallback = procedure pushed("A");
18:            };
19:            };
20:            XmPushButton {
21:            arguments { XmNlabelString = " B "; };
22:            callbacks {
23:            XmNactivateCallback = procedure pushed("B");
24:            };
25:            };
26:            XmPushButton {
27:            arguments { XmNlabelString = " C "; };
28:            callbacks {
29:            XmNactivateCallback = procedure pushed("C");
30:            };
31:            };
32:        };
33:      };
34:    end module;
```

Program 3.3   Sample UIL specification

A more useful consequence is the ability to write very flexible window programs, and to change the look of the program without recompiling it. An example of this approach is distributed along with Motif, and it works as follows:

The programmer specifies the widget structure of the application in a special language, called UIL. The UIL specification defines the widget hierarchy, any special options for the widgets, and the callback functions. A UIL specification for our example application is shown in Program 3.3. The UIL specification is translated into a more concise form by the UIL compiler, producing a User Interface Definition (UID) file.

```
1:      #include <stdio.h>
2:      #include <Mrm/MrmAppl.h>
3:      #include <Mrm/MrmPublic.h>
4:
5:      char *uid_files[]={"sample.uid"};
6:      void pushed();
7:      static MrmRegisterArg reglist[] = {
8:        {"PUSHED", (caddr_t) pushed}
9:        };
10:
11:     main(argc, argv)
12:       int argc;
13:       char ** argv;
14:     {
15:        MrmHierarchy hid;
16:        Widget top_level, main_widget;
17:        MrmType dummy;
18:
19:        MrmInitialize();
20:        top_level = XtInitialize("sample", "sample",
21:                    NULL, 0, &argc, argv);
22:        MrmRegisterNames(reglist, 1);
23:        if ( MrmOpenHierarchy(1, uid_files, NULL, &hid)
24:           != MrmSUCCESS)
25:              printf("open hierarchy failed\n");
26:        if ( MrmFetchWidget(hid, "MAIN_WINDOW", top_level,
27:                      &main_widget,&dummy)
28:           != MrmSUCCESS)
29:              printf("fetch widget failed\n");
30:        XtManageChild(main_widget);
31:        XtRealizeWidget(top_level);
32:        XtMainLoop();
33:     }
34:     void pushed(w, s, c)
35:        Widget w;
36:        char *s;
37:        void *c;
38:     {
39:        printf("%s was selected\n", s);
40:     }
```

Program 3.4   Main program for UIL

All of the real code of the application, including callbacks, must of course be programmed in C in the usual way. The main body of the application calls library functions to read in one or more UID files and to create the widgets thus specified. The main program for our example application using UIL is shown in Program 3.4.

Once the application has been built using UIL, the look can easily be changed by modifying the UIL definition. Rerunning the UIL compiler is much faster than recompiling and relinking even a small C module, so UIL is ideal for prototyping the application. It is also possible to have the same program present different interfaces to different groups of users—different languages for different countries, or different menu choices for novices versus experts—simply by selecting from several different UID files.

3.9 Other Toolkits

The previous examples have shown three possible approaches that a programmer might take to produce a X client application: using the Xlib routines directly, using the Xt Intrinsics and the Motif widget set, and using the special-purpose language UIL. There are numerous other options.

Motif is by no means the only widget set available. The standard source distribution of X includes sample widgets, called the Athena widgets. The major competitor to Motif is OPEN LOOK, developed by AT&T and Sun, and there is a set of OPEN LOOK widgets commercially available.

Programmers may also use other toolkits, not based on the Intrinsics. XView is an X toolkit that provides the OPEN LOOK look and feel with a programmatic interface derived from Sun's earlier SunView product. Interviews is a toolkit based on C++, written at Stanford University and freely available.

There are many proprietary toolkits on the market. Most of these offer an advantage to the commercial software developer of being independent of the target window system. Applications can be developed using the proprietary program interface; by changing a compile-time switch the application can be built to run on Microsoft Windows, OS/2 Presentation Manager, X with Motif look and feel, or X with OPEN LOOK look and feel.

Finally, for many programmers, the toolkit of choice is none of the above. Instead of using a text editor to write procedure calls to the appropriate library, the programmer will build window-based applications using a window-based program builder. The programmer can choose the various screen components—menus, push buttons, dialog boxes—from a palette, and use the mouse to drag them to the correct place, resize, reshape, etc., as in draw or paint applications. When the screen layout is completed, the interface builder generates C (or UIL) source code with the necessary toolkit procedure calls to produce the interface. The rest of the application—callback functions and any non-windowing code—is written using normal tools. The source code produced by the builder is compiled and linked with the rest of the application code.

3.10   Selected References

There are many books on X, mostly concerned with applications programming. An extensive bibliography is available on-line along with the software contributed to the X distribution. The bibliography is available for anonymous FTP from `export.lcs.mit.edu` in file `pub/Xbibliography`.

The following list merely highlights the range of topics covered by books on X.

Robert Scheifler, James Gettys, and Ron Newman, *X Window System*, Third Edition, Digital Press, 1992. The standard reference on the X protocol, Xlib, and the ICCCM. The third edition covers X11R5. The authors of the book are the authors of X.

P. J. Asente and R. R. Swick, *X Window System Toolkit*, Digital Press, 1990. A companion to *X Window System*, this is the standard reference for the Xt Intrinsics.

Elias Israel and Erik Fortune, *The X Window System Server*, Digital Press, 1992. A technical reference to the internals of the X server.

Open Software Foundation, *OSF/Motif Series*, Englewood Cliffs: Prentice Hall, 1992. A five-volume set of references and guides to Motif.

UNIX System Laboratory, *OPEN LOOK Release 4 Graphical User Interface: Programmer's Guide*, Englewood Cliffs: Prentice Hall, 1991. A guide to using the OPEN LOOK Interface Toolkit, a competing widget set to Motif.

The Definitive Guides to the X Window System, Sebastopol, CA: O'Reilly and Associates, 1988–1992. A long multivolume series, covering all aspects of X, from end users to administrators, from Motif to OPEN LOOK to three-dimensional graphics.

S. Kobara, *Visual Design With OSF/Motif*, Reading: Addison-Wesley, 1991. This book is concerned not with how to program in Motif, but rather how to design Motif applications that look good.

J. D. Smith, *Object-oriented Programming with the X Window System Toolkits*, John Wiley & Sons, 1991. Discusses the object-oriented style of the Xt Intrinsics, both using existing widgets and creating new widget classes.

D. Young, *Object-Oriented Programming with C++ and OSF/Motif*, Englewood Cliffs: Prentice Hall, 1992. One of the few books to tackle the problem of meshing the pseudo object-oriented Motif toolkit with the object-oriented language C++.

N. Mansfield, *The X Window System: A User's Guide*, Reading: Addison-Wesley, 1991. As the title says, a guide for end users, not programmers.

UNIX Internals

Dean Brock

Most users of UNIX believe that the word *UNIX* refers to a collection of powerful, mysterious, and sometime frustrating commands like `ls`, `grep`, and `vi`. However, to the UNIX geek, the term *UNIX* refers to the UNIX operating system, or kernel. The UNIX operating system is the foundation of all the utilities of UNIX. Its synonym, *kernel,* suggests the central role the operating system plays in UNIX. The most reverent UNIX users call it simply *the system.*

The kernel is both the slave and master of all UNIX applications. For example, the command `more` lists a file by ordering the kernel to provide the file's contents. However, it is the kernel which determines when `more` can run and decides if `more`, or more precisely the user running `more`, is really allowed to read the contents of the file.

The kernel is positioned between the user applications and the hardware as shown in Figure 4.1. In certain instances, applications have direct access to the hardware. For example, the application can multiply two integers with a single machine instruction. However, other facilities of the computer are protected from direct manipulation by user applications. For example, a user application cannot directly command the disk to write blocks of data. If this were possible, applications written by malicious or careless users could damage the structure of the UNIX file system. An application is not even allowed complete control over when it runs. If it were, it could "hog" the resources of the processor and prevent other jobs from performing their work.

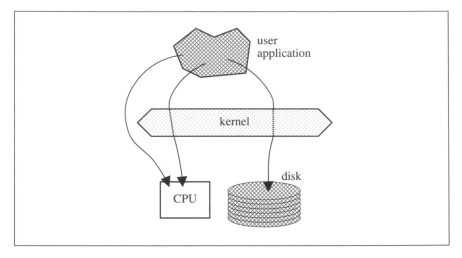

Figure 4.1   Kernel as an interface

The top layer of the operating system is the *system call interface*. To the programmer, this is a collection of about 100 special functions. These are the functions described in Section 2 of the UNIX manual. They are named *system calls* because they are invocations of the UNIX operating system. One system call is rmdir, which removes a directory. A simple program using rmdir to remove a directory called remove.me is shown in Figure 4.2. You are probably familiar with the UNIX command rmdir, documented in Section 1 of the manual. This command is nothing more than a C program that performs the system call rmdir and then determines if the call succeeds.

Oddly enough, UNIX programmers rarely make direct use of system calls. Generally, they use friendlier C library routines, such as

```
#include <stdio.h>

main()
   {
    if (rmdir("remove.me"))
       fputs("remove.me not removed\n", stderr) ;
    else
       fputs("remove.me removed\n", stout) ;
   }
```

Figure 4.2   A simple system call

`fprintf`, which do the dirty work of speaking to the kernel via system calls, such as `write`. System calls are UNIX's lowest-level application programmer's interface (API). Unfortunately, there are minor variations of this API between the various flavors of UNIX. These differences are especially noticeable in programming tarpits like controlling a terminal.

POSIX, IEEE's *Portable Operating System Interface for Computing Environments*, is one attempt to create a universal UNIX-like system call interface sanctioned by the American National Standard Institute and similar organizations. POSIX is sufficiently portable that even non-UNIX operating systems such as OS/2, Windows NT, and VMS can hide their considerable blemishes beneath a POSIX interface. If you must make system calls, it's a good idea to stick to the POSIX interface. Read Lewine's book, *POSIX Programmer's Guide*, for more information about programming with POSIX.

The kernel is a large program, weighing in at several megabytes of compiled code. The operating system on your UNIX computer is probably stored in a file called `/vmunix`, `/unix`, or `/kernel/unix`. Almost all of the kernel is written in ordinary C. A few routines are written in low level assembly or machine code. In general, assembly coded routines form a thin veneer that covers the upper and lower surfaces of the kernel. The purpose of this chapter is to discuss the structure of the kernel. As you might suspect, UNIX kernels vary from vendor to vendor; however, almost all versions incorporate structure, concepts, and even C statements derived from early versions of UNIX written at Bell Labs and enhancements provided by the Computer Systems Research Group of the University of California at Berkeley. Consequently, there are many similarities among widely used UNIX operating system kernels. Significant vendor-written additions, such as Sun's Network File System, find their way into the products of other vendors by cross-licensing agreements.

The kernel has complete control of the hardware. It can execute privileged machine instructions that are forbidden in user-written applications. The operating system achieves this power by executing in a special mode we'll call *kernel* mode but which also goes by the names *monitor, supervisor,* or *system* mode. Modern computers are designed to support at least two modes of execution in order to run multiuser operating systems such as UNIX. We'll call the other mode of operation *user* mode, because it is the mode in which all user-written applications run. Almost all the important control programs, such as the line printer spooler or *daemon*, are executed in user mode. The power of these daemons (and yes, that is the correct spelling) is derived from their *user id,* which is usually 0, the number identifying *superuser* or *root*. The kernel has some very special rules for dealing with system calls made by applications running under the user id of the superuser. We'll see a few of these later in this chapter. There are a couple of daemons which actually execute in kernel mode, but because these daemons execute code that is compiled into the kernel, it's best to consider them an integral part of the operating system. We'll return to these oddities in a little while.

One of the privileges of system mode is the ability to switch into user mode. The kernel can schedule an application, or process, to run by switching into user mode and then branching to compiled code of that application. The application switches into kernel mode when it makes a system call. At the machine level, this is accomplished by executing a special *trap* instruction, which may be called a *monitor call* or *supervisor call* by some computer manufacturers. Because the trap instruction is also an automatic branch to compiled code of the kernel, the user application loses control of the machine when it executes the trap, and thus the user code is denied execution in the privileged state.

Underneath the operating system is the hardware. We've already mentioned that the operating system has privileged access to the instructions needed to schedule user applications. The kernel also has direct access to devices attached to the processor. One of the important services provided by the kernel is hiding all the nasty little details of handling devices from user-written programs. For example, an application doesn't need to know how to position the heads of a disk in order to read data. It only needs to open a file. We'll discuss device handling in detail in this chapter. It isn't easy. The UNIX kernel, unlike the MS/DOS "kernel," doesn't just order the disk to read a block of data and wait for the disk controller to respond. Rather, the system directs an I/O request to the controller and then finds some other useful work to perform. When the disk has completed its assignment, it *interrupts* the kernel which then forwards the disk's data to the appropriate user application.

We'll look at the components of the average UNIX kernel in the remainder of this chapter. First, we study the control of running applications, or *processes*. We'll pay particular attention to the problems of executing several processes "simultaneously." Then we'll see how the kernel manages memory and actually provides applications with more memory than is physically present in the computer. Devices and files are next. Here, the UNIX file system is dissected. UNIX's networking capability is a significant reason for its popularity. The implementation of the popular TCP/IP protocol suite is the next-to-last topic of the chapter. The chapter ends with a discussion of the steps required to get a UNIX system up and running when it is powered on.

You will not find the details of the UNIX kernel in this chapter. You'll have to buy a source code license or get your hands on one of those public domain versions of UNIX to make a really close inspection. I've tried to cover those aspects of the kernel that you're most likely to encounter as a user or system administrator. Many of the important data structures of the kernel are presented in this chapter. If you have a working UNIX system, you can view many of these structures using system "debugging" commands such as `pstat`, `ps`, or `crash`. Most UNIX systems have a directory, usually `/usr/include/sys`, which contains C definitions of the data structures used by the kernel. If you want a more interactive reading of this chapter, you should log into your UNIX system and check out your possibilities for examining the kernel as you read.

4.1   Processes

The universal definition of a process is a *program in execution*. A UNIX application, loaded and running, is a UNIX process. There are many components to the process. Many of these parts go by special names in the UNIX system. The compiled code of the process is the *text*. The local variables, those declared within a function, are stored on the *stack*. The remaining storage, external variables and dynamic data obtained by calling `malloc()`, are simply called *data*. The programmer is well aware of these three components of the process. In fact, data and compiled code are often the only characteristics of a process that concern your average C programmer.

However, the kernel must keep up with many other features of the process. For example, the kernel must know the program counter (PC) of a process, so that the process can be resumed after it is stopped. The kernel must also know the identity of the user running the process, the files opened by the process, and many other details. As a result, the process is divided into two halves. The user half consists of memory that can be directly accessed or changed by the user's program. This includes the previously discussed text, stack, and data areas, and in some versions of UNIX, shared memory segments attached to several processes. The other half consists of a couple of data structures used by the kernel to manage the process. These data structures may be accessed only by the kernel and are the focus of our discussion of the internals of process management.

In the "traditional" implementation of UNIX, there are two kernel data structures for each process. The first is the *process table entry*, also known as the *proc structure* or *proc area*. The process table is an array with one entry for each possible process. Each entry contains fields that hold the values of certain crucial features of the process.

Typically these include the following, along with many, many other values:

- Process id
- Process credentials
  - User id—real, effective, and saved
  - Group ids
- Related process
  - Parent process id
  - Pointer to list of child processes
- Scheduling information
  - Priority
  - System usage
  - "Nice" value
- Signal information
  - Blocked and handled signals
  - Pending signals
- State of the process—running, waiting, etc.

The file `/usr/include/sys/proc.h` gives a complete definition of the `proc` structure on most versions of UNIX.

The second kernel data structure for managing the process is the *user area*. A user area is allocated for each newly created process. The user area contains process data the kernel must "know" when the process is active. An inactive process may be completely unloaded from memory and *swapped* to disk. The user area may be swapped along with all information—text, data, and stack—used by the process when it executes in user mode. The separation of process-related kernel structure into the process table entry and the user area allows the kernel to store some of its knowledge of inactive processes on disk. In general, the process table entry contains the minimal information needed to determine which process gets the next chance to run. Our previous list of process table entry fields may seem a bit excessive for these purposes, but many of these fields qualify by unexpected means. For example, a signal can start a process; consequently, the signal information must be contained in the process table entry.

The user area contains many fields. Typically it contains copies of arguments passed to the kernel by system calls, memory management information, and statistics related to system resource utilization. One of its most important components is the *file descriptor table*, an array used to record files opened by the process. In some versions of UNIX, the user area ends with the process' *kernel stack*. When the process makes a system call and executes in kernel mode, it uses its own personal kernel stack to hold the local variables of the kernel's C routines. You should be able to find a definition of the C data structure for your computer's user area in the file `/usr/include/sys/user.h`. When executing a system call, the kernel variable `u` is set to refer to the user area of the calling process, so that `u.u_ofile` (or something similar) refers to the file descriptions of the current process. Consequently, the user area is sometimes called the *u area* or *u dot area*.

Some versions of UNIX have made radical changes to the traditional UNIX process. One change is kernel support for *threads* or *lightweight processes*. A thread is similar to a process in that it has a program counter and stack, but several threads may execute within a single process and share certain resources of the process, such as open files. OSF/1 is an example of a UNIX operating system which supports multithreaded processes. The OSF/1 kernel is a marriage of the Mach microkernel developed at Carnegie Mellon University and a traditional UNIX kernel. In OSF/1, the user area has been divided into two separate structures: a *utask* structure for the entire process and a *uthread* structure for each thread. Additionally, the Mach-inspired routines of OSF/1 use their own task (process) and thread structures to schedule threads and manage virtual memory. Consequently, the proc and user areas of OSF/1 are quite a bit different than those you'll find in many other versions of UNIX.

Many UNIX system calls can be satisfied merely by accessing fields of the proc and user areas. For example, `get_pid` (get process id), requires nothing more than getting into kernel mode and retrieving the `p_pid` field from the process table entry of the executing process. A process invokes a system call via a *wrapper* routine. The wrapper is a machine-specific procedure that packs the system call arguments for shipment into the kernel, transfers into kernel mode by executing a special hardware trap instruction, and unpacks the results returned by the kernel into the system call return value, and when appropriate, an error variable `errno`.

When a process enters kernel mode to execute a system call, the kernel executes that call until the call completes, the kernel decides to *block* to wait for an event, such as the completion of a disk operation, or an interrupt occurs. In the case of system call completion, the kernel will check to see if the running process has exceeded its *time slice* or *quantum*. If it hasn't, the process reenters user mode. The kernel will return arguments to the user process by placing return values in machine registers, or perhaps on the user stack. To the process, the system call appears pretty much like any other procedure call. However, if the process has exceeded its quantum and there are other processes which are ready-to-run, one of those processes will be given the CPU for its own quantum.

In the case of blocking, the kernel inserts the process into a queue of *sleeping* processes. The process *sleeps* on a specific event, represented by a *wait channel*. Usually the wait channel is the address of the data structure associated with the expected event. For example, if a process is waiting for a data block to be read from a disk, the wait channel should be the address of the buffer that will eventually contain the block. The ps command lists the wait channels on which processes are napping. You'll have to read the man page for your system to see exactly how to do this.

Not all events are associated with external I/O. For example, one process may wait for another to terminate or to write a character to a pipe. The kernel must be carefully written to control process sleep. It must make sure that sleeping processes really do receive the appropriate wakeup calls. Also, some forms of sleep are *interruptible* in that the process may be awakened before the event really occurs. In general, a process enters an interruptible sleep when there is no guarantee that the awaited event will occur in a timely fashion. Waiting for terminal input is an example of an interruptible sleep. It may be necessary to awaken the process before the event really occurs. A process entering interruptible sleep must check the reasons it was awakened when it is rescheduled. Other sorts of sleep, e.g., waiting for disk I/O, are noninterruptible. The use of the word *interruptible* is a bit misleading here. It does not mean that the hardware is not allowed to interrupt the system, but only that the process sleep may be terminated early. Using ps on your system, you should be able to recognize noninterruptible sleepers by examining either the PRI field or the STAT field.

In the case of the *real* hardware interrupt, the kernel is diverted from the task of completing the system call. The interrupt is the hardware's way of getting the attention of the operating system. The kernel executes a handler appropriate for the interrupt. Handlers run briefly. Usually, they set a bit or two, and occasionally, they initiate new I/O operations. For example, assume a disk interrupt handler has been invoked to oversee the completion of a read operation. The handler will locate processes waiting for the newly arrived data by examining the wait channel of sleeping processes. Processes waiting for the data are marked as ready-to-run. They will be restarted at a later moment. Once one disk operation is finished, the handler may be able to start another.

The handler executes on its own stack, independent of the process that was executing when the interrupt was delivered. Because processes may be interrupted, the kernel must be carefully written to prevent processes from interfering with each other. Suppose the following C statement occurs within the kernel:

```
num_procs++ ;
```

The intent of the statement is to count the number of processes that have been created by the kernel. Translated into machine language, the single C statement expands to several machine instructions similar to:

```
LOAD            ACC,num_procs
INCREMENT       ACC
STORE           ACC,num_procs
```

There is a danger that between the time one process loads the value of num_procs into the accumulator ACC, increments the accumulator, and stores the result back in num_procs, an interrupt will occur. Should a second process be scheduled after the interrupt, it could charge through this same section of code with the eventual result that num_procs will be incremented once rather than twice. The consequences of this race ending in a "tie" aren't serious, but the UNIX kernel must be designed to avoid situations where two processes or a process and an interrupt handler interfere with each other while executing within the kernel.

Within the traditional UNIX kernel, there are three ways of arbitrating ties. First, the kernel can disable specific interrupts for brief periods to ensure that a crucial section of code is executed as an atomic unit. Second, data structures can be protected by *busy* fields. The first process to use the structure sets the busy field. Late arrivals will test the busy field, and seeing it set, sleep upon the event of the data structure being freed. The temporary owner of the structure will awaken the sleepers when it is done with the structure. Finally, most UNIX kernels are *nonpreemptible* in the sense that if an interrupt occurs while the CPU is performing a system call in kernel mode, the interrupt handler returns the CPU to the process executing the system call. Nonpreemptibility severely restricts the opportunities in which two processes may race within the kernel. In fact, for practical purposes, processes race only with interrupt handlers.

However, nonpreemptibility has its costs. It can delay important processes from useful work in user mode while some other process completes a time-consuming system call such as fork or exit. In some kernels, this cost is reduced by building *preemption points* in the kernel where processes performing a system call may volunteer to yield the CPU. True multiprocessing, where the computer contains several processors, is the ultimate foe of the nonpreemptible kernel. The "benefits" of nonpreemptibility are lost if more than one processor can simultaneously execute in kernel mode. Preemptible UNIX kernels, such as symmetric multiprocessing (SMP) versions of System V and OSF/1, have required additional mechanisms for controlling concurrency. OSF/1 has borrowed *locks* from Mach. Kernel data structures are protected by locks which processes hold while manipulating the data structure. Locks resemble the previously discussed fields but are designed for use within SMP kernels.

4.2 Signals

Let's take a look at how signals are delivered and handled in UNIX to illustrate how the kernel controls processes. Signals are an interrupt mechanism for user processes. One process can send a signal to another using the kill system call. Signals are also generated for machine exceptions, e.g., the process dividing by 0, and terminal interrupts, e.g., the user typing a ^C.

A user process installs a signal handler, a function executed when the signal occurs, by calling the routine signal, which in turns calls the appropriate wrapper for the running version of UNIX. Executing within the kernel, the process modifies its process table entry to show that the signal is being handled and modifies its user area to contain the address of the handler. The process table field that keeps up with handled signals is usually called p_sigcaught. It is modified by executing a C statement similar to:

```
p->p_sigcaught |= 1 << signum
```

Because of the possibility that an interrupt handler may also want to modify this same field at the same time, this statement should be executed with either interrupts off or locks on. The address of the signal handler is usually stored at location u_signal[signum] within the user area. Note that the process table entry contains only the signal information necessary to determine if the process should be scheduled. All other information needed when the process is running is stored in the user area.

Invoking the signal handler is divided into two phases: posting and delivery. Posting consists of checking the proc structure to see if the signal is being handled, and if so, setting the appropriate bit of field p_sig of the process table entry to show that the signal is pending. If the target process is in an interruptible sleep, it will be awakened.

In kernel mode, processes can post a signal to other target process; however, processes must deliver their own signals. Just before a process makes a transition from kernel to user mode, it checks its process table entry. If a signal is pending, it arranges for the delivery of the signal. The mechanism for actually invoking the system handler from user mode is very machine dependent. It is accomplished by modifying the process' user stack so that it will execute a small section of *trampoline code* when it returns to user mode. The trampoline code is responsible for executing the signal handler and then bouncing back into the kernel. Many fields of the process table entry and user area will be modified to handle the signal. Signal delivery is one of the kernel's most challenging tasks.

4.3   Virtual Memory

Today's computers allow programs to address more memory than is physically available in the machine. This is accomplished with a mechanism called *virtual memory*, in which *virtual* addresses generated by the program are translated into *physical* addresses that point to *real* memory locations. The hardware used to accomplish this translation varies. In general, the virtual address spaces addressed by processes are divided into fixed size *pages*. The physical address space is also divided into pages, although many people reserve the term *page* for the divisions of virtual memory and the term *frame* for the divisions of physical memory. For clarity, we'll follow that convention in our discussion. Page sizes range from 512 to 16,384 bytes on modern CPUs. Each virtual address is divided into two parts, a page number and an offset within the page. A hardware address translation facility transforms the virtual page number into a physical frame number. These interactions of the various components of virtual memory are illustrated in Figure 4.3.

Because there are more virtual addresses than physical addresses, occasionally a process will attempt to address a virtual page that has no corresponding physical frame. When this occurs a *page fault* generates an interrupt and causes the processes to enter kernel mode. In the UNIX operating system, pages that are not in core, i.e., in physical frames, are stored in an area of the disk called the *swap space*. When a page fault occurs, the kernel must move the needed page from the swap space into a physical frame. The kernel must also run a *page replacement* algorithm that locates a victim frame to *page out* to disk to free up frames needed to page in recently addressed data.

The goal of good memory management is to minimize page faults. This requires a page replacement algorithm that has a knack for choosing victim frames unlikely to be accessed in the near future. The details of virtual memory management are best left to the classic operating system texts such as Silberschatz and Galvin's *Operating Systems Concepts* or Deitel's *Operating Systems*. The details of hardware

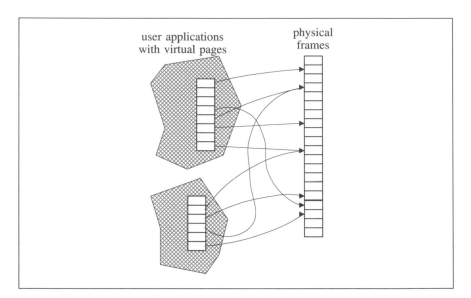

Figure 4.3   Virtual memory

address translation vary widely (and wildly) among various computer designs. You'll have to consult the hardware reference manual for your computer to extract information about your own system's peculiarities. Most UNIX users and system managers are blissfully ignorant of these details.

Early UNIX operating systems did not support virtual memory. Instead they divided memory into two parts, one part for the kernel and the rest for user programs. User programs would run only when they were completely loaded into physical memory. When it was necessary to run unloaded user programs, entire programs—with the possible exception of shared text or compiled code—were swapped to and from disks. Process 0 was the *swapper* or *swap daemon*, a kernel-only process in charge of this loading and unloading of user processes.

Release 4.0 of the Berkeley Standard Distribution, 4BSD, was the first version of UNIX to support true virtual memory. A new kernel-only process, the *page daemon*, ran as process 2. The page daemon is awakened at regular intervals, one-fourth of a second in older BSD implementations, to check the number of free frames in the system. If there are lots of free frames (in particular, if the number of free frames is greater than a threshold variable `lotsfree`), the page daemon goes back to sleep. Otherwise, the page daemon scans several physical frames and places inactive frames on the *free list*. The identification of inactive frames is a machine-dependent operation. Some computers provide significant hardware support to identify inactive frames. Some provide none; on these computers, the operating system must be creative.

When page faults occur, frames are taken from the free list and given to the process needing the memory. Thus one process *steals* pages from another. *Dirty* pages have been modified since they were loaded into memory. Before a dirty frame can be turned over to another process, the kernel must make sure that the contents of the frame are written to the swap area.

Under certain circumstances a system may be trying to run more processes than its limited memory can handle. When this happens, the system *thrashes* as processes continually steal pages from each other. When the page daemon notices that it is having a hard time finding inactive pages, it will ask its fellow kernel-only process, the swapper, to forcibly move entire processes out to disk.

Many ideas of 4BSD memory management, such as the threshold-driven page daemon, survive in recent versions of UNIX. However, several vendors have modified these algorithms to improve performance. Most of these modifications improve the ability of processes to share pages and will be described below. SunOS was the first UNIX to allow different processes to share libraries of commonly used routines. Such sharing significantly reduces the space used by executable problems on the disk and in memory.

The OSF/1 kernel seems to be the most radical departure from 4BSD. It uses a memory management strategy adopted from Mach. There is a threshold-driven page daemon, but now it maintains three pools of pages: active, inactive, and free. It also supports *external pagers*, user tasks which assume the responsibility of moving pages between memory and their more permanent location, which could be a disk drive or some exotic networked storage device.

In the System V flavor of UNIX, the virtual memory address space of a process is divided into *regions* of contiguous pages. The data structure used to manage regions is usually defined in the file `/usr/include/sys/region.h`. The previously mentioned text, data, and stack are each stored in their own regions. Shared memory segments also form regions. Each process has its own *per process region table*, or *pregion*, which points to its regions. Under certain circumstances, e.g., two processes executing the same text or accessing the same shared memory segment, two or more pregion entries point to one region. In OSF/1, the kernel uses *virtual memory objects* for a similar purpose.

The challenge of UNIX memory management is allowing different processes to efficiently share pages. The `fork` system call is the biggest creator of sharable memory in UNIX. The `fork` creates a new child process by "copying" the virtual memory of the parent process. Because `fork` is the only way to create a process, it is used frequently by UNIX programs. Every time you type a new UNIX command using a shell, the shell calls `fork` to create a new copy of itself. However, all these copied data are used only for a very short time. The newly created process soon makes the system call `execve` and completely replaces itself with the code and data of the program required to execute the command you typed.

All UNIX implementations easily handle sharing of read-only text regions. Efficient sharing of writable data and stack segments is more difficult. This requires the use of a technique called *copy-on-write*. In copy-on-write, two or more processes share a page in a read-only fashion until one process attempts to modify the page. At that time, the writing process causes a memory protection fault. The kernel diagnoses the protection fault as an attempt to modify a copy-on-write page and gives the writing process its own writable copy of the page which it may modify however it pleases. Today most commercial versions of UNIX support some form of copy-on-write.

In addition to allocating physical frames to processes, the kernel must also allocate sections of the swap area to provide the backing store needed for pages that cannot be stored in core. Usually, the swap area is stored on a contiguous section of a disk. It is also possible to spread the swap area over several disks so that system performance can be improved by scheduling multiple concurrent page swaps. Many versions of UNIX also support paging over a network connection for diskless workstations. In general, the location of the primary swap area will be built into the kernel while the locations of secondary swap areas are specified in system files.

It is possible for a UNIX system running many large processes to run out of swap space, resulting in an *insufficient memory* error. This error is often misinterpreted by the neophyte UNIX user to mean that more RAM is needed when, in fact, it is the swap space that is exhausted. The problem can be eliminated by allocating additional secondary swap areas. Most Unixes have a `pstat` or `swap` command which prints how much of the swap space is free. This command is useful for anticipating shortfalls in swap space. The `vmstat` command also prints all sorts of useful statistics about paging activity. Consult your man page for the details.

4.4   Devices

Physical devices such as disks and tapes attach to our computers in a modular fashion. You'd hope that our operating systems support similar plug-in attachment for the software needed to control these devices, and indeed they do. All contemporary operating systems (yes, even MS/DOS) provide a means of controlling devices through modules called *device drivers*.

The UNIX device driver is a collection of procedures. Each procedure is responsible for performing some operation on the device. All kernel code specific to the peculiarities of the device are hidden within the driver. For instance, there is only one part of the UNIX operating system that knows what it takes to read a sector from a SCSI disk: the SCSI disk device driver.

There are routines, or *entry points*, in the device driver for the I/O operations, like read and write, which are available at the user level. The entry points of these routines are stored in a *switch table*. Whenever the kernel must perform a particular operation on the device, it simply looks up the appropriate routine in the device's switch table and calls it. In addition, the device driver contains routines for probing the system to see if the device is present, for initializing the device, and for handling device interrupts.

In UNIX, there are two types of devices, *character* and *block*, and consequently, two types of device drivers and corresponding switch tables. The definitions of the structures which hold the switch table are usually found in /usr/include/sys/conf.h. Within the kernel, device drivers are known by numbers, actually indices into the global device switch tables. Because there are separate switch tables for character and block devices, it is possible for different character and block device drivers to share the same number.

Individual devices are known by two numbers. A *major* number identifies the device driver. A *minor* number identifies the specific device (e.g., the tape drive with SCSI ID 2), or a specific part of a device (e.g., the fourth partition of the third disk), or sometimes even a specific way of accessing the device (e.g., the second tape drive set to its highest output density). The device driver is expected to handle all devices of its type. User programs may access devices through device *special* files contained in the directory /dev and its subdirectories. By typing ls -l /dev you can obtain a listing of the many device special files of your computer. On my workstation, the entry

```
brw-------  1 root    system   8,3074 Jun 30 15:45 /dev/rz3c
```

identifies a block device (note the b in the first column) with major number 8 and minor number 3074. The entry

```
crw-rw----  1 root    system   0,   1 Jun 30 15:00 /dev/mouse
```

is for character device (c in the first column) with major number 0 and minor number 1. Device special files are created by the kernel in response to the mknod system call. See Chapter 5 on system administration for more information.

Block devices are usually reserved for disk partitions. The kernel reduces the number of disk I/O operations by saving recently read and written data blocks in an area of memory called the *buffer cache* or *buffer pool*. Whenever possible, disk I/O requests are satisfied using the buffer cache rather than the disk. Device drives for block devices transfer data to and from the buffer pool. Before actually initiating an I/O operation for a block device, the kernel checks the buffer pool to see if the desired data is already present in memory.

Disk partitions are actually accessible through both character and block device special files. The character, or *raw*, device is needed for low level operations such as formatting the disk or writing a new UNIX file system onto a disk partition. These devices are often given names starting with an r, such as /dev/rsd0c, to hint at their raw nature. The block device is needed for relatively high level operations such as file system backup.

Device drivers are not just for reading and writing. The device driver for a CD-ROM reader has an ioctl (I/O control) entry point that can be reached via the system call of the same name. Given the right CD and the right ioctl arguments, the device driver will order the CD-ROM to start playing MacArthur's Park through your earphones. (And *please*, use the earphones!)

There are also many useful *software* devices, sometimes also called *pseudo* devices. The kernel memory itself can be accessed via a software device known to users as /dev/kmem. Reads and writes of /dev/kmem are transformed into reads and writes of kernel memory by the software device driver. Programs such as ps and pstat open /dev/kmem to read the kernel variables needed to generate their reports. If you want to take an intimate look at a running kernel to test your knowledge of UNIX internals, run dbx using /dev/kmem as "core." The ultimate example of a do-nothing pseudo device is /dev/null, which looks like an empty file when read and like an infinite trash can when written.

This flexibility of the device driver interface has resulted in a few feature-laden devices. Terminal drivers are immense. They have been given the responsibility for echoing and editing user input and implementing the concept of a *control terminal*. When a process without a control terminal opens a terminal, the terminal driver assigns the opened terminal to be the control terminal of the process. The terminal driver also provides ioctl points that allow the process to change its control terminal. When special interrupt characters like ^C are typed on a terminal, the terminal driver posts the appropriate signal to all processes under that terminal's control. The terminal driver is also able to make distinctions between foreground and background processes. For example, the terminal controller can be asked to post a signal to any background process attempting to write to the terminal.

Obviously, there are many applications that don't really want the terminal driver to provide these services. Text editors really want to do their own editing and processing of interrupt characters without any interference from a terminal driver. Consequently, the terminal driver provides different levels of services, ranging from a *canonical* or *cooked mode*, with full editing, to a *raw mode*, with little processing. To further complicate matters, there are several different flavors of cooked terminals. Some applications prefer the "standard" and others prefer the "new." Often other choices, such as the System V and POSIX interfaces, are available. These choices are usually implemented in the form of *line disciplines*, collections of routines that are invoked by the terminal driver.

Because so many UNIX applications are dependent on services provided by the complex UNIX terminal driver, the kernel must include special pseudo terminal device drivers so that applications connected to a networked or windowed "terminal" session will behave properly.

In System V, *streams* may be used to extend the capabilities of ordinary device drivers. Streams are sequences of modules starting with a *stream head*, providing the user-level interface, and terminating in a driver, providing the hardware-level interface. Between the head and the driver, there may be *stream modules* which provide special services. Data written by the user application pass through the stream head and *downstream* through the stream modules to the driver. Data read by user applications are generated by the driver and pass *upstream*. Stream modules provide services by manipulating the passing data. For example, terminal line editing can be implemented as a stream module. BSD-based versions of UNIX have been slow to embrace streams; consequently, few applications use them in spite of the nifty modularization they allow. If you are interested in learning more about streams (or *STREAMS,* as the System V Release 3 version is capitalized), take a look at the *STREAMS Primer* or *STREAMS Programmer's Guide*.

If you're the sort of person who attaches unusual few-of-a-kind devices to your UNIX computer, someday you may need to write a device driver. Your UNIX vendor will produce the documentation needed to accomplish this job; however, you'd better read one of those many how-to books on the subject, such as Egan and Teixeira's *Writing a UNIX Device Driver*, before sitting down to write any C code.

4.5   Open File Management

UNIX has a rather simple view of files: a file is nothing more than a sequence of bytes. Consequently, the UNIX kernel doesn't have to worry about record formats. Those concerns are left to mainframe operating systems like IBM's MVS. However, UNIX does allow random access to any byte within a file. That's something the designers of MVS didn't worry about.

UNIX vendors have done so much experimenting with the implementation of virtual memory that it's difficult to name any kernel data structures for memory management that are common to all the UNIX internals we encounter these days. In contrast, the UNIX file system always revolves around three kernel data structures—the file descriptor tables, the file table, and the vnode table—which contain a fairly consistent collection of fields.

The user area of every UNIX process contains that process' file descriptor table. The file descriptor table is really quite simple. It's nothing more than an array of pointers to entries of the open file table. Each time a file is opened, the kernel will allocate an unused file descriptor for the file and return to the process the index of the newly allocated descriptor. System programmers refer to the returned index itself as the file descriptor, a double use of the word that can result in some confusion. Anyway, once the user process has obtained the file descriptor, it is used in subsequent I/O operations to identify the file.

An entry within the file table is also allocated with every successful open system call. File table entries contain the following fields:

- f_flag   How the file was opened, e.g., read-only, read-write
- f_offset   Present position within the file, i.e., how far into the file the reads and writes have progressed
- f_count   Reference count of the number of file descriptor tables that point to this file table entry
- f_type   Type of the file, e.g., regular file or socket
- f_data   Address of the appropriate vnode table entry or socket structure

Sockets are used in interprocess communication and will be discussed below. The reference count is needed because when the kernel performs a fork system call, it duplicates the file descriptors of parent processes for the newly created child processes, thus increasing the number of references to the file table entry. Each time a file is closed, the corresponding file descriptor is freed and the reference count of its file table entry is decremented. When the reference count reaches zero, the file table entry is freed. When child and parent processes share one file table entry, they share a common offset into the file. Reads performed by one advance the file offset for both.

The information needed to manage a UNIX file on disk is contained in its *inode* or *index node*. Originally, all the inodes of a disk were contained on one contiguous collection of sectors. The "identity" of the file was the index of its inode which, by the way, can be obtained using the `-i` option of the `ls` command. Information contained within the disk inode includes

- User id of file's owner

- Group id of file's group

- File *modes* or protection

- Size of file

- Type of file, e.g., regular file, directory, or block device special file

- Major and minor device numbers for device special files

- Map of file's data blocks

When a local file is opened for the first time, an incore *vnode* or *virtual node* is allocated that will hold the disk inode plus additional information such as the inode number and a reference count. The vnode is held in memory until its reference count reaches zero. Generally, that means the vnode remains allocated until all processes that have opened the file close it. When a remote file is opened via the Network File System, the vnode will contain an *nfsnode* rather than an inode. Vnodes are a relatively recent addition to UNIX. What we're calling vnodes were incore inodes before Sun Microsystems introduced the Virtual File System. You'll still find a few holdouts, so whenever you see the term *inode table*, think *vnode table*. In Ultrix internals, you may even hear about *gnodes* or *generic nodes*.

On each I/O operation, the kernel follows pointers from the *file descriptor* down to the appropriate vnode. It acquires the present file offset as it passes through the file table entry. When the kernel finds the file table entry, it can also check if the attempted I/O operation is consistent with the manner in which the file was opened. For example, an attempt to write to a file opened for reading will fail when the kernel looks at the file table entry and notes that the file was opened read-only. The relationship of these three table structures is given in Figure 4.4.

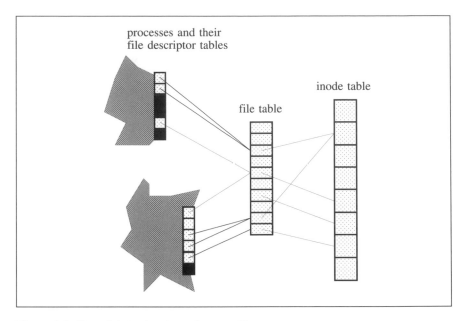

Figure 4.4   Kernel data structures for open files

Your system's definition of file table entries should be found in `/usr/include/sys/file.h`. The file most likely to contain your system's definition of a vnode is `/usr/include/sys/vnode.h`. If you type the command `pstat -f`, you should get a listing of the file table entries presently in use within your system. If you use the `-i` (for inode, of course) option of `pstat`, you'll be rewarded with a view of the vnode table. As a test of your understanding of the role of the file table entries and vnodes within the kernel, you might start a program that reads a very long file and try using the commands `ls -i`, `pstat -i`, and `pstat -f` to monitor how far into the file the program has read.

4.6   Virtual File Systems

In UNIX, the file system consists of the data structures and routines that transform the data blocks of disk partitions into the UNIX directory hierarchy. Early versions of UNIX supported only one file system, which is now called the System V File System. At Berkeley this file system was enhanced to yield a file structure very similar to those found on the disks of UNIX computers today. When Sun Microsystems implemented the Network File System, the kernel had to support two types of files systems: local and remote. This was accomplished by implementing the Virtual File System.

The Virtual File System (VFS) is the abstraction of all UNIX file systems. It provides a template that can be used to plug new file systems into UNIX. The file system is represented by a collection of about fifty procedures. Every vnode contains a pointer to a switch table of procedures used to perform operations on the file associated with the vnode. These modules perform operations such as creating and deleting files, looking up files within a directory, and reading and writing data to a file.

Now that UNIX has VFS, the task of adding new types of file systems is much easier. Consequently, in recent years we have seen UNIX kernels that can access files of a floppy disk formatted under the MS/DOS file system and a CD-ROM pressed according to the ISO 9660 specification. Below, you'll be introduced to a couple of very unconventional file systems, such as the *process* file system containing "files" consisting of images of the virtual memory of executing processes. If you can make any collection of information look like a UNIX file system (that is, have a root and a directory hierarchy), someone can write the procedures that transform it into a virtual file system.

The roots of file systems are attached to the larger UNIX directory hierarchy at *mount points*. Chapter 5, on system administration, explains how the system manager constructs an ASCII file, usually /etc/fstab, containing lines similar to

```
/dev/vg1/tryon   /backup/tryon   ufs rw 1 2
```

which specifies that a virtual file system of type ufs (UNIX file system), stored on device /dev/vg1/tryon is attached to the system's directory hierarchy at the mount point /backup/tryon. When the system is booted, the mount program makes the mount system call to order the kernel to add this file system to the directory hierarchy.

The kernel maintains an in-memory data structure called the *mount table* for all accessible file systems. The mechanism for maintaining mounted file systems is both simple and elegant. Let's study it using our example from the previous paragraph. Before the mount system call is made, a directory /backup/tryon must exist within the smaller directory hierarchy. This directory will be the *mount point*. The file system /backup/tryon has a root directory, or at least the illusion of a root directory created by the routines of the virtual file system. Mounting is the joining of the mount point directory and the file system's root directory. The system's directory hierarchy grows a new branch consisting of the newly mounted file system.

When the kernel executes the mount system call, it allocates two in-core vnodes, one for the mount point and one for the file system root, along with a mount table entry, or *mount structure*, which points

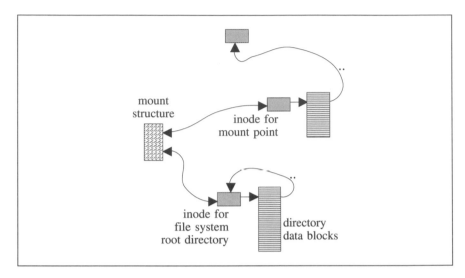

Figure 4.5   Reaching . . through a mount point

to the two vnodes. The kernel is able to distinguish the vnodes for mount points and file system roots from their mundane counterparts. When the kernel is moving down the directory hierarchy (away from the root) and encounters a mount point directory, it uses the mount structure to jump from the mount point vnode to the file system root vnode. When the kernel is moving toward the root following a trail of double dots (. .) similar to . . / . . / . . / . . and encounters a file system root, it crosses over to the mount point vnode. Figure 4.5 shows how the kernel ties these three structures together in versions of UNIX supporting virtual file systems. The mount structure also contains pointers to vital information needed to maintain the file system.

In the "good ole" days, things were a bit different. To conserve valuable memory, the in-core inodes didn't contain pointers back to the mount structure. Crossing a mount point involved searching the mount table looking for pointers aimed back at the mount point or root inodes. If you look hard enough, you can still find a couple of systems that still save memory the old-fashioned way.

4.7   Real File Systems

We now turn our attention to the problem of mapping a file system consisting of UNIX directories onto physical devices such as disks. First, let's review the structure of a disk as illustrated in Figure 4.6. The disk consists of several vertically aligned *platters* rotating on a

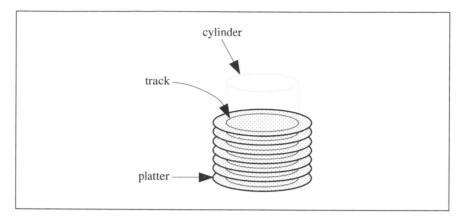

Figure 4.6 Abstract disk anatomy

common axis. An assembly of disk *heads* moves between the platters. The circle traced by the head on a surface is called a *track*. A *cylinder* is a collection of vertically aligned tracks. When the head is still, data can be read from or written to the surfaces of the platters. Data is written in *sectors*, which are 512 bytes on most recent disks.

It takes a long time for the disk heads to *seek* from one cylinder to the next. If a file is spread throughout the disk, user programs do nothing while the heads ramble from track to track. The smart operating system tries to keeps a file on a single cylinder or at least confine the file to a small neighborhood of cylinders. Mainframe operating systems like MVS tend to be smart when it comes to allocating data sectors for a file. However, they often rely on advice, such as estimates of file size from users in making these decisions. MS/DOS can be pretty dumb. It works fine when the disk is new, but in time it starts scattering files all over the disk. When it comes to file allocation, UNIX operating system kernels aren't dumb, but this certainly isn't an area in which they shine. Fortunately, they are getting smarter.

In our exposition of the disk-based UNIX file system, we will concentrate on the "new" or "fast" file system of the Berkeley Software Distribution. This file system format seems to be the most common one found on UNIX systems today. The UNIX file system is built using the data blocks of the entire disk or a *partition* of the disks. Partitions are large collections of adjacent cylinders. The UNIX operating system treats the partition as if it is a disk, just a bit smaller. The data blocks of the partition can be accessed directly though the appropriate device files. The `mkfs` command creates a new file system by writing to a partition's character device file.

The UNIX file system is really a varied collection of data indices. For each file, there is an *inode* that locates the data blocks of the file. For each directory, there is a *directory file* that locates the files of the directory. And for the file system, there are a *superblock* and several *cylinder group blocks* that keep up with other useful information, such as the location of unused data blocks. We're going to take a bottom-up look at the layout of the UNIX file system starting with the data blocks of the file.

To be written physically onto a disk, a file must be broken into sectors. However, because sectors are only about 512 bytes long, the kernel does not allocate disk space in units of sectors. Instead it breaks the file into data blocks of a significantly larger size, typically 8192 bytes. In addition to reducing bookkeeping costs, the larger allocation units allow the kernel to package several disk I/O operations into one. Of course, storing a 9000-byte file into 8192-byte data blocks leads to certain inefficiencies, in particular 7384 wasted bytes in the last block. To avoid this potential loss, the last "block" of small files can be broken into *fragments* of a much smaller size, usually 1024 bytes. So a file of 20,000 bytes would be stored in two 8192-byte data blocks and four 1024-byte fragments with only 480 precious bytes wasted in the last fragment. The last fragments of a file are allocated so that they are all contained within consecutive fragments of one of the larger data blocks. This rule might seem odd, but it simplifies the job of the kernel. It doesn't have to keep up with the location of four separate fragments, just the location of the first of the four. By the way, the sizes of blocks and fragments are not fixed by the operating system but can be specified by the system administrator when he or she creates a new file system.

We introduced the disk inode in Section 4.5. We mentioned that every disk file has an inode which contains several pieces of information, such as its access permissions and the identity of its owner. In this section, we will concentrate on only one aspect of the inode, its map of the file's data blocks. The inode itself isn't very large. On most versions of UNIX, it is only 256 bytes long and can store the locations of only a few data blocks. For larger files, a tree-structured data block directory is used. Let's use some real numbers to show how this is done. Assume that the block size is 8192 bytes and that the disk inode is big enough to hold the locations of the first twelve data blocks. We don't have to worry about the fragment size because all the fragments of the file are stored in one data block. As long as a file is less than 98,304 (12×8192) bytes long, the location of all its data blocks can be contained within the disk inode.

For longer files, the inode points to the location of a *single indirect* block. The indirect block points to additional data blocks of a file. If

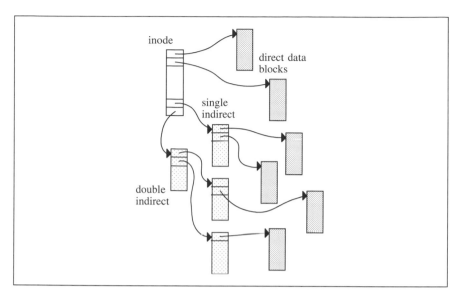

Figure 4.7 Inode as a data directory

four bytes are required to address a disk block, then the indirect block could hold the address of the next 2048 (8192/4) blocks of the file. With one indirect block, the kernel can manage files up to 16,875,520 (2060 × 8192) bytes long. However, there are a few disk hogs out there who create files that exceed the capacities of the single indirect block. For them, there is the *double indirect* block. The double indirect block is the root of a two-level data directory. It is a disk block that contains the addresses of several single indirect blocks which, in turn, contain the addresses of data blocks. The structure of the inode and its indirect blocks is illustrated in Figure 4.7. With double indirect blocks, files may now contain 4,188,172 (2048 × 2048 + 2048 + 12) blocks or 34,309,505,024 bytes. Unfortunately, the UNIX requirement that files be byte-addressable and the 32-bit words of most computers restrict our files to a mere 2,147,483,647 bytes.

Originally, the inodes of the file system were stored in contiguous sectors near the beginning of the partition. This led to rather serious performance problems. For example, executing the command:

```
grep fun *
```

which searches all the files of a directory would result in a great deal of disk head motion. For each file, the heads would move to the front of the partition to read the file's inode and then back into the center of the partition to read the file's data. In today's "fast" file systems, this problem is lessened by the use of *cylinder groups* of sixteen contiguous cylinders. Each cylinder group contains its own set of inodes and data blocks. For small files, the kernel attempts to allocate both the inode and the data blocks of the file within one cylinder group. For directories, the kernel tries to allocate all the inodes of the regular files, but not subdirectories, of the directory into one cylinder group. The result of these two allocation strategies is that, in general, all the inodes and data blocks associated with a directory and its files are contained in a small area of a disk.

Each cylinder group also contains a *cylinder group block* that records the free inodes and the free fragments of the group. These records are stored as bit maps. Checking if a particular inode or fragment is free is simply a matter of going to the appropriate bit and testing its value. Testing if an entire data block is free is accomplished by testing all the bits corresponding to the fragments of the data block. The kernel tries to allocate data blocks in such a way that when successive blocks of a file are read or written, the next block is just a short rotation of the platter away.

If you've ever created a file system using `newfs`, you've probably seen the messages `newfs` prints out giving the size of the cylinder groups and the number of groups within the partition before it starts writing to the disk. After the file system is created, you can use the `dumpfs` to see this same information.

Directories are nothing more than specially marked files which have one entry for each file of the directory. The entry contains the *component name* and inode number of the file. The kernel locates the file `/etc/passwd` by searching the directory file of the root for the component `etc` and its associated inode number. It then searches the directory file for `/etc` to find the component `passwd`. The inode number of the root directory is always 2. That simple convention gives the kernel a starting place for its inode search.

There is one more special disk: the *superblock*. The superblock contains all sorts of information that is needed to manage the file system. This includes:

- The number of blocks in the file system
- The size of data blocks
- The size of fragments
- The number of cylinder groups
- The size of cylinder groups
- The number of inodes within a cylinder group

Because the information contained within the superblock is so crucial to the management of the file system, the superblock is replicated within each cylinder group in such a way that it is stored on different platters throughout the partition. Your best bet for determining what is contained within the superblock and cylinder group blocks of your UNIX computer is to take a short break to login as root and try out the command dumpfs on a few systems. This will reinforce your knowledge of structures used to maintain the file system.

In recent versions of UNIX, several vendors have made some significant changes to the UNIX file system. One of these is the *journaled* file system used in AIX, the UNIX used in IBM's RS/6000 workstations. In AIX's journaled file system, the kernel maintains a transaction log of important changes made to a file system. The transaction log is actually written to a second *log* file system. For example, when a new directory is created, a record summarizing file system changes is written to the log. At first glance, it's not at all obvious that the journaled file system is such a great idea. After all, aren't you now writing to the disk twice, once when you write the log record and once more when you *really* modify the file system? The advantages are that the transaction log can be written sequentially, with very little head motion to the log disk, and that once the transaction record is written, the real disk updates, which are scattered all over the actual file system disk, can be written at leisure. Should the system crash before the actual updates are written, it's straightforward to update the file system to a consistent state using the information stored in the log.

AIX also introduced *logical volumes* to UNIX. In most versions of UNIX, a file system is confined to one disk or partition. Consequently, when designing the logical UNIX directory hierarchy, the system administrator must be sure to match file systems to available physical disks. Logical volumes can be thought of as logical disks. Several physical disks are joined into a *volume group*. The volume group can be partitioned into several logical volumes, each of which can hold a UNIX file system. The underlying physical data block of a logical volume may actually be spread across several disks. In fact, it is possible to *mirror* a logical volume so that each of its data blocks is stored on two different disks.

With the "standard" UNIX file system, it is possible for files, especially large files, to get scattered across the disk a bit too much. To lessen this problem, some UNIX vendors have introduced *extent-based* file systems, similar to those used in those proprietary mainframe operating systems. An extent is a large block of consecutive disk sectors. The file system attempts to allocate the file in a few large extents. In the best case, the file will be allocated in a single block of consecutive sectors. Because the UNIX operating system provides no system calls that set the maximum size of a file when the file it created, the implementation of extent-base file systems is a challenge. One extent-based file system for UNIX is Digital's recently introduced Polycenter Advanced File System for DEC OSF/1.

As we mentioned earlier in this section, not all file systems get their data from local disks. The most famous nondisk file system is NFS, the Network File System designed by Sun Microsystems. A great deal of the administration and a bit of the implementation of NFS is discussed in Chapter 7 on network administration. NFS follows the client–server paradigm. Servers *export* files. Clients *import* files. The server machine runs an NFS daemon which receives packets from clients requesting that I/O operations be performed on the server's local disk using one of the server's local file systems. Although the NFS daemon could be implemented as a user process, it is invariably implemented as a special kernel-only process just like the swapper and page daemons mentioned in Section 4.3.

The client side of NFS is exercised when a process makes a system call involving an imported file. Using the Sun Remote Procedure Call (RPC) protocol, the client kernel makes a request to the server. Because Sun RPC is inherently synchronous, that is, the client process makes an RPC and waits for the result, the client side of NFS is usually implemented with a gang of block I/O daemons which run as kernel-only processes on the client machine. Suppose a process has entered kernel mode making a system call involving an NFS file system and wants the service of a remote NFS daemon *but* does not want to hang around waiting for the response. In this case, the process gets one of the block I/O daemons to do the actual calling and waiting while the process goes back to its own important task of executing the user program.

4.8 Optimizing File Access

At this time, you might be wondering just why or how the kernel might issue a request for some data that aren't immediately needed by a user process. Well, it turns out that in addition to providing a mechanism for managing virtual file systems, the kernel has a few tricks to optimize the transfer of data from virtual file system to user process. First, the kernel maintains a *buffer cache* of recently read and written data blocks. In our discussion of virtual memory, we saw how the kernel tries to keep the active pages of a process in core and the inactive pages on disk. The kernel does something similar for the data blocks of the process using the buffer cache. When a user process writes some data, instead of blocking the user process until the data is actually written to a block of the local or perhaps remote disk, the kernel remembers the modified data in its in-core copy of the data block, stored in the buffer cache. At some later time, the data will really be written to disk. If the process modifies the data block twice before it is written to disk, the kernel saves an I/O operation. This technique may be called either *write-behind* or *delayed write* by UNIX gurus.

Write-behind has a cost. If the system crashes before the new data reaches the disk, the file update may be lost, even though a *real* user has been assured that the new data was saved. To lessen this possibility, the kernel supports a system call named sync which causes all modified, but unwritten, data blocks in the cache to be written through the appropriate virtual file system. The kernel also can also detect when a file is being written sequentially. Once a data block is completely filled with new data, the kernel realizes that the block may not be used for a very long time and schedules the writing of data blocks to free up some room in the buffer cache.

Important file system *meta data*, such as inodes and indirect blocks, are also stored in the data cache. The kernel must treat blocks containing meta data carefully. If the wrong piece of meta data is lost, files and entire directories may be lost. Usually, updated meta data are written immediately to disk. Even then, the kernel must be careful about the order in which meta data are written to the disk. Suppose a user deletes a file, thus freeing an inode. What should be written to the disk first, the updated inode or the updated directory entry? No matter which is written first, the file system will be inconsistent if the computer loses power between the two writes. An excellent discussion of how UNIX maintains file system consistency can be found in Bach's *The Design of the UNIX Operating System*. No UNIX file system, except possibly the journaled file system, is completely safe from unexpected crashes. Consequently, when UNIX boots it runs a program called fsck (for file system check) on its local disks. This program is able to repair minor file system inconsistences. Although fsck is not part of the kernel, it has a rather intimate relationship with it. fsck knows the order in which the kernel updates meta data, and it uses this information quite well when it must reconstruct a file system.

File system reads are optimizing using *read-ahead*. The kernel can be an obsequious piece of code when it comes to serving user processes. It never wants to keep a user process waiting. When it notices that a file is being read sequentially, it endeavors to get that next block of data into memory before the process even asks for it by reading ahead. This is why the kernel needs all those block I/O daemons for the Network File System.

Most UNIX kernels have a few other data structures that are used to keep file information in memory. There is a *directory name lookup* cache that speeds up the translation of a pathname into an inode number. The cache is indexed by a pair consisting of the inode number of a directory and a character string of a component within the directory to yield the inode number of the component. If you're lucky, you'll find the inode number of /usr/local/bin/emacs by four quick trips to the directory name lookup cache instead of a half dozen or more disk reads.

There is also a *file attribute cache* which remembers characteristics of recently accessed files. UNIX programs frequently look up file attributes, and consequently this cache has proven to make a big difference in the performance of the Network File System. Although caches make remote file access faster, they can lead to annoying inconsistences. For example, if you use an editor to change a file's data, chmod to change a file's access, or rm to disavow the file's existence while logged into an NFS server, clients may continue to hold onto their old view of the file. To reduce the occurrences of these problems, the Network File System uses timers to expire information.

The Network File System has some other imaginative solutions to the problems of maintaining traditional UNIX file semantics in a networked environment. For example, in UNIX when you unlink (remove) a file that is open, the kernel removes the file's name from the directory hierarchy but retains the file's data until the file is closed. If a user application running on an NFS client unlinks an open file, the client kernel instructs the server to rename the file to some rather odd name that is unlikely to be used by any user program. When the user application finally closes the file, the client kernel tells the server to really remove the recently renamed file. For a more detailed discussion of this and other subterfuges practiced by NFS, consult the article by Sandberg et al. in the Summer 1985 USENIX proceedings.

4.9   Networking

We're going to take a rather abstract look at the implementation of networking within the UNIX kernel. There are two reasons for this. First, the details of networking are found in the protocol definitions. These definitions specify the format and meaning of the packets transmitted between machines. There are many excellent *and lengthy* sources of information about protocols, and we do not need or wish to include yet another description of the seven layer OSI model in this chapter. The popular protocols for UNIX operating systems follow the ARPANET Reference Model. While this protocol stack is not as deep as the OSI model, a remote login between two UNIX computers connected by an Ethernet still involve four levels of protocols:

1. Application layer: data exchanged between the user programs

2. Transport layer: the Transmission Control Protocol (TCP)

3. Network layer: the Internet Protocol (IP)

4. Physical layer: the Ethernet hardware and cabling

The operating system is responsible for implementing the middle two layers of the stack. TCP manages the sessions that connect user programs on different machines. IP is able to route packets across many diverse physical networks. If you want to find out more about these protocols, take a look at the recently released book by Stevens entitled *TCP/IP Illustrated*.

The operating system must also provide an interface between the network layer and the physical layer. This interface is more or less a souped-up device driver and is sometimes referred to as the *link layer* in the BSD dialect. Finally, the operating system provides the interface between the application layer and the transport layer. In BSD-based UNIX, this is implemented as a collection of system calls using *sockets*. In System V UNIX, a special Transport Layer Interface (TLI) is defined.

The existence of both the TLI and the socket interface is the second reason why we are avoiding details in our discussion of networking. This is one area in which BSD and System V based implementations of UNIX can differ greatly. The layering that can be obtained using System V streams (or STREAMS, if you wish to shout) is very useful for implementing network protocols. Write a streams module for each protocol and just stack them up. The streams device driver interfaces with the hardware. The TLI is actually a programmer-friendly collection of routines that manipulate the streams head at the top of the stack.

Although the System V implementation should be commended for its use of an elegant kernel facility to implement networking, by the time it appeared many important network applications had already been written using the BSD socket interface. The socket interface continues to be the most popular choice for UNIX network programming, and for this reason, we will concentrate on it for the remainder of this section.

A *socket* is an endpoint of communication. When applications are connected by a TCP session or *stream* (an overused word in UNIX as you are beginning to notice), applications exchange messages by reading and writing sockets. To the programmer, the socket looks very similar to a file. The `socket` system call creates a new socket and returns a file descriptor that refers to the socket, similar to how the `open` call returns a file descriptor that refers to the file. Reads and writes to a socket have the same syntax as reads and writes to a file. Inside the kernel, the socket's file descriptor points to a file table entry, but now the file table entry points to a socket structure (struct socket) rather than a vnode.

The kernel's socket structure is where the applications and protocols meet. You should find the socket structure defined in the file /usr/include/sys/socketvar.h. The socket structure has many fields, such as pointers to queues for data waiting to be read by the applications, for data waiting to be transmitted by the protocols, and even for connections waiting to be accepted. The socket structure is also the beginning of a chain of kernel data structures used to implement the relevant network protocols.

Protocols are controlled through two major data structures, the *protocol switch table* and the *protocol control blocks*. The protocol switch table points to a dozen or so modules that implement the protocol. The kernel calls the appropriate modules as data pass up and down the protocol stack. The protocol control block (PCB) points to all the information required to manage the protocol. The format of the PCB varies according to the needs of the underlying protocol. For example, the TCP control block contains information required to generate acknowledgments for received data, while the IP control block points to information required to route messages to the appropriate hardware interfaces. Many protocols actually use two different kinds of control blocks, a single *perprotocol* PCB for global management of the protocol and several PCBs with specialized information for each connection.

At the bottom of the kernel's protocol chain is the network interface structure. This structure contains a switch table of procedures that are called to get data in and out of the hardware interface. The network interface structure also points to an output queue of messages waiting for their chance to appear on the external network.

Most kernel data structures, such as file table entries or disk data blocks, have a fixed size. This greatly simplifies memory allocation. However, the messages generated in networking have unpredictable sizes. Even worse, while going down the protocol stack, messages grow as each protocol places its own header on the front of the message, and while going up the stack, messages shrink. The efficient implementation of networking within the kernel required a new method of memory allocation. In BSD UNIX, the *mbuf*, or memory buffer, was introduced for this purpose. The mbuf is a rather intricate data structure which kernel programmers access through a well-designed set of routines. A single mbuf is small, less than 128 bytes longs, but an mbuf can point to a much larger data area, and several mbufs can be chained together to hold large messages. The mbuf is used throughout the kernel implementation of networking. Messages are passed between protocols in mbufs and most data structures, such as routing tables and protocol control blocks, are stored in mbufs.

4.10   Booting the Kernel

We end our survey of the UNIX kernel with a look at how the kernel starts. Booting the kernel starts with some very machine specific actions required to load an initial *bootstrap* program. Generally, a computer has a special console monitor which knows how to load a few thousand bytes of data by reading special *boot blocks* from a disk or by downloading a file from a network server. This bootstrap may be able to directly load the kernel into memory, or it may only load yet another bootstrap, such as the one stored in /ufsboot on systems running Solaris, which loads the kernel.

Once loaded, the kernel executes a special *cold start* routine that constructs the foundation needed to call the kernel's main C routine. The kernel then performs various initialization activities such as allocating memory, setting values, and threading pointers between its major data structures. Many other tasks must also be completed. The root file system must be mounted and the two initial kernel-only processes, the swapper and the page daemon, are created.

About this time, the kernel will also try to determine the status of the devices attached to the computer. This is done by executing special *probe* routines included with device drivers. As each device is discovered, the associated device driver is ordered to configure itself. As your UNIX computer boots, you should see the kernel print a brief message each time it discovers and configures a device.

The kernel probes only for devices whose drivers have been linked into the kernel by the system administrator. There are a few versions of UNIX, such as NeXTSTEP and Solaris, that actually support the loading of additional modules into a running kernel. On these systems, the loading and initialization of a device driver can be deferred long after the kernel boots.

The first true user process run by the kernel is process number 1, init. The init process is ultimately responsible for all other aspects of system installation, such as mounting file systems and starting network daemons. Unlike the other two initial processes, the swapper and the page daemon, init does have a user side. Most UNIX kernels have a clever way to start init. Hidden inside the kernel is code for a program that makes a single system call:

```
execve("/etc/init", init, boot arguments ... );
```

which, *if* executed in user mode, replaces the code of the user program with the code stored in /etc/init. The kernel loads the one system call program into a text area allocated for process 1 and marks process 1 as runnable. Once /etc/init is loaded, it finishes the job of bringing the system into multiuser mode.

There are some significant differences between the BSD and System V versions of init. The BSD init executes the shell script stored in /etc/rc to complete the boot, while the System V init executes a series of programs specified in /etc/inittab. However, this isn't our concern. This is an *internals* chapter, and now we're talking about a user-mode process. Turn to Chapters 5 and 7 to follow the further adventures of our number 1 process.

4.11 Learning More

This chapter provides you with some basic and useful knowledge of the UNIX kernel. The books and articles listed below contain more detailed knowledge of the kernel of UNIX and many other operating systems.

If you want to do your own kernel "hacking" and don't work for one of the major UNIX vendors, you should load Linux onto your Intel-based personal computer. Linux is a public domain implementation of UNIX that is freely available on the Internet. There are also several USENET newsgroups in which the Linux kernel hackers share their wares. This is the closest a mortal can get to a real UNIX kernel.

AT&T, *STREAMS Primer*, Englewood Cliffs: Prentice Hall, 1987.

AT&T, *STREAMS Programmer's Reference Guide*, Englewood Cliffs: Prentice Hall, 1989.

M. J. Bach, *The Design of the UNIX Operating System*, Englewood Cliffs: Prentice Hall, 1986.

H. M. Deitel, *An Introduction to Operating Systems*, Second Edition, Reading: Addison-Wesley, 1990.

J. I. Egan, T. J. Teixeira, *Writing a UNIX Device Driver*, New York: Wiley, 1988.

R. A. Gingell, Joseph P. Moran, and William A. Shannon, "Virtual Memory Architecture in SunOS," *USENIX Conference Proceedings,* Berkeley: USENIX Association, Summer 1987.

S. J. Leffler, Marshall Kirk McKusick, Michael J. Karels, and John S. Quarterman, *The Design and Implementation of the 4.3BSD UNIX Operating System*. Reading: Addison-Wesley, 1989.

D. Lewine, *POSIX Programmer's Guide*, Sebastopol, CA: O'Reilly & Associates, 1991.

R. Sandberg, D. Goldman, S. Kleiman, D. Walsh, and B. Lyon, "Design and implementation of the Sun Network File System," *USENIX Conference Proceedings,* Berkeley: USENIX Association, Summer 1985.

A. Silberschatz, and Peter B. Galvin, *Operating System Concepts*, Reading: Addison-Wesley, 1994.

W. R. Stevens, *TCP/IP Illustrated, Volume 1: The Protocols*, Reading: Addison-Wesley, 1993.

5

UNIX System Administration

Lynne Cohen Duncan

By this point, you've seen the flexibility and features of UNIX. You, or the organization you work for, may be planning to purchase one or more UNIX systems. UNIX machines are gaining popularity, not only in the academic arena, but in commercial sites, too. But a UNIX machine, unlike the PC that may sit next to it, does not function fully without a lot of care and feeding, or more precisely, administration. Before you place that order, let's take a look at what's required to install and manage a UNIX system.

A UNIX administrator's job covers a wide range of tasks. The administrator performs machine installations, integrates new hardware devices, configures network access, compiles and installs software packages, and answers user questions, to name but a few duties. He or she works to keep the machine or machines available to the users, a job that involves a significant amount of monitoring and preventive action. As it is for the system administrator of any computer, the goal is to provide a stable computing environment well suited to the needs of the organization.

Users of Macintoshes, accustomed as they are to simply inserting a floppy and dragging a new program to the disk icon to install it, may wonder what the big deal about system administration is. But even a single UNIX machine requires a different level of administration from that of a personal computer. A newly installed UNIX machine has great potential, but limited immediate functionality. It cannot print to an attached printer, talk to another machine connected to its network, allow a login on a terminal other than its console, use disks not present at installation, or permit a user to log in under his or her own name. UNIX can provide a great deal of functionality, but almost none of it is there by default.

The majority of PCs are just what their name implies, personal. The owner installs software to augment the functionality of the PC operating system. One user with a single set of demands determines the configuration of the PC, and the machine may be ill-suited to another person's requirements. In contrast, UNIX provides many capabilities as part of the basic operating system. A standard installation will meet the needs of a wide range of users, from those interested only in electronic mail, to researchers creating complex programs. The multi-user capability of the UNIX machine also differs significantly from the PC, introducing the whole area of user account management.

A UNIX machine is rarely an island. The majority of UNIX machines are connected to a local network, and many have access to the Internet, an international network of educational, governmental, and commercial sites. Electronic mail, news, and file transfer across this network require well behaved, fully configured communications software. Installing and maintaining connectivity has become a major part of the UNIX administrator's job.

UNIX has been in existence for more than 20 years. The many versions of UNIX now available arose from the original work done by Ken Thompson and Dennis Ritchie at Bell Laboratories. There is no single standard UNIX; rather there are two major threads in UNIX development. These threads, System V and the Berkeley Software Distribution (BSD), diverged at a UNIX version called the UNIX Time-Sharing System, Seventh Edition. System V was produced by AT&T, and BSD was produced by the University of California at Berkeley. The many vendor implementations draw from these two sources to create their unique versions. BSD-based versions include SunOS through version 4.1, 4.3 BSD, and Digital Equipment Corporation's ULTRIX. HP-UX from Hewlett-Packard, IRIX from Silicon Graphics, and Sun's Solaris are all System V-based.

BSD and System V differ significantly in their administration. Add to that the enhancements each vendor includes to set their systems apart from the others, and you end up with substantial differences between the UNIX variants. Consequently, this chapter does not attempt to make the reader an accomplished administrator of any particular version. Instead, it concentrates on the range of activities involved, with some specifics on how each of these tasks is accomplished. The following discussion emphasizes BSD-style administration, but also includes some information on System V procedures. The terms *BSD* and *System V* used in this chapter refer to the general classes of operating systems based on these two versions. Even within one of these classes, vendor innovation can produce significant variations from the original.

Most sites with more than a few UNIX machines have found it effective to hire one or more full-time administrators. This greatly improves the efficiency of the individual workers, since they do not have to handle complex administrative tasks. It also creates a group of people with a larger view of the computing environment, who can then recommend appropriate hardware and software improvements.

The UNIX administrator is responsible for installing machines and software, maintaining day-to-day operations, handling emergency situations, and responding to user needs. Each of these duties is discussed at length below. To make that discussion clear, we need to first describe some pertinent aspects of the architecture of the UNIX operating system.

5.1   The Architecture of UNIX

5.1.1   The UNIX Kernel

The kernel is the controlling process that provides the basic system functions of the UNIX operating system. It schedules processes to run, manages memory, maintains the file system structure, and performs I/O for other processes.

The kernel is loaded at machine startup time from the system disk, where it is called /vmunix, /unix, or another name selected by the vendor. It contains the operating system code, as well as hardware interface routines called device drivers. The UNIX administrator configures the kernel to include the base system, the device drivers for attached hardware, and any software options needed for running in his or her particular environment. On most systems, a machine can access only those hardware devices that are built into its kernel and that were connected at the time the kernel began running.

5.1.2   UNIX Boot Procedure

The UNIX startup procedure, also known as the *boot procedure*, is a multistage process. First, the bootstrap program is read from disk, loaded into memory, and executed. This program then reads the kernel into memory and prepares the CPU to execute it. As the kernel begins to run, it tests to determine how much memory is available on the machine. This allows the kernel to size data structures needed during execution. The kernel probes each hardware device that has been configured into it, and initializes the ones it finds. The partition

containing /, called the *root*, is mounted next. The kernel then begins
to execute programs stored in directories in the root partition.
/etc/init is one of the first started, and it controls the rest of the
boot process. Under normal circumstances, /etc/init executes startup shell scripts that continue the boot process until the devices are
enabled and users can log in.

The startup scripts have names that contain the characters *rc*: rc,
rc.boot, rc.local, brc, netrc, etc., and they vary quite a bit
between UNIX versions. These scripts perform housekeeping chores
and start special purpose processes called daemons to handle tasks
like printer control and mail delivery. Housekeeping chores include
setting the machine's name, configuring the network software, and
checking that the file systems have a valid hierarchical structure (see
below).

On BSD systems, there are normally two rc scripts: a basic script
/etc/rc that starts standard UNIX processes, and a locally modified
script /etc/rc.local that starts the machine-specific processes.
Most administrators don't edit /etc/rc, but may repeatedly change
/etc/rc.local to add daemon invocations. Figure 5.1 shows an
abbreviated /etc/rc file, which in turn executes /etc/rc.local
(Figure 5.2). A complete tour through sample startup files can be

```
# @(#)rc        4.5      (ULTRIX)        10/15/90

HOME=/;
PATH=/bin:/usr/ucb:/usr/bin
export HOME PATH

/etc/startcpu   >/dev/console

date >/dev/console
if [ $1x = autobootx ]# normal boot process
then
  echo Automatic reboot in progress... >/dev/console
  case $? in
     0)
        ;;
     4)
        /etc/reboot -n
        ;;
     8)
        echo "Automatic reboot failed. Unable to insure" >/dev/console
        echo "file system integrity. Run the fsck"      >/dev/console
        echo "command manually." > /dev/console
        exit
        ;;
```

Figure 5.1   ULTRIX /etc/rc file

```
    *)
        echo "Unknown error in reboot" > /dev/console
        exit 1
        ;;
  esac
fi

/etc/mount -av -t ufs   >/dev/console # mount local file systems
/etc/swapon -a          >/dev/console # initiate swapping
# initialize license manager
/usr/etc/lmf reset                        >/dev/console 2>&1
# run the local startup script, which sets machine name, starts many
#daemons, and mounts any remote file systems
sh /etc/rc.local
echo 'preserving editor files'       >/dev/console
(cd /tmp; /usr/lib/ex3.7preserve -a)
echo clearing /tmp                   >/dev/console
(cd /tmp; rm -f *; chmod 1777 /tmp)
echo -n 'standard daemons:'          >/dev/console
/etc/update;                echo -n ' update'      >/dev/console
/etc/cron;                  echo -n ' cron'        >/dev/console
/etc/accton /usr/adm/acct;  echo -n ' accounting'  >/dev/console
[ -f /etc/inetd ] && {
        /etc/inetd;         echo -n ' network'     >/dev/console
}
[ -f /etc/snmpd ] && {
        /etc/snmpd;         echo -n ' snmpd'       >/dev/console
}
cd /usr/spool
rm -f uucp/LCK.*
[ -f /usr/lib/lpd ] && {
        rm -f /dev/printer
        /usr/lib/lpd &      echo -n ' printer'     >/dev/console
}
                            echo '.'               >/dev/console
[ -f /etc/elcsd ] && {
        /etc/elcsd &   echo 'start errlog daemon - elcsd' >/dev/console
}
date                                               >/dev/console
exit 0
```

Figure 5.1 (continued)   ULTRIX /etc/rc file

found in *UNIX System Administration Handbook* by Nemeth, Snyder, and Seebass.

BSD machines operate in one of two modes, single-user or multiuser. In multiuser mode, all devices are available and users can log in at the console, over the network, or at connected terminals. Single-user mode, also called *maintenance mode*, is used for system installations or emergency repairs. When a machine is booted to this level, /etc/init executes a single shell on the system console instead of the startup scripts. Often only the root partition is accessible in this

```
# @(#)rc.local  4.2      (ULTRIX)         1/25/91
/bin/hostname oberon
# configure the network device
/etc/ifconfig ne0 `/bin/hostname` broadcast 152.2.128.255 netmask
255.255.255.0

/etc/ifconfig lo0 localhost
echo -n 'check disk quotas: '  >/dev/console
/etc/quotacheck -a
/etc/quotaon -a
sync
/etc/savecore /var/adm/crash
echo -n 'local daemons:'                   >/dev/console
[ -f /etc/syslog ] && {
        /etc/syslog & echo -n ' syslog'    >/dev/console
}

[ -f /usr/lib/sendmail ] && {
        (cd /usr/spool/mqueue; rm -f lf*)
        /usr/lib/sendmail -bd -q1h -om& echo -n ' sendmail'
            >/dev/console
}
# time synchronization daemon
if [ -f /usr/local/etc/xntpd ]; then
        /usr/local/etc/xntpd  -c /usr/local/etc/ntp.conf &
        echo -n ' xntpd'                   >/dev/console
fi
```

Figure 5.2   ULTRIX /etc/rc.local

state. When the single-user shell is exited (by typing exit or ^D on the console), the multiuser startup scripts begin to execute.

In contrast, System V versions of UNIX can operate at a number of different modes called run-levels. A vendor may define up to eight run-levels, labeled 0 to 6 and *s* or *S,* but in practice most implementations use fewer. A different set of actions is performed at each run-level. During the boot process, /etc/init reads its control file /etc/inittab and executes the commands for the run-level requested. Each line is of the form

id:runlevel:action:command

id is a four letter identifier, and the action field describes when and how often to execute the command. If the run-level field is empty, the command is executed for all levels. In the example in Figure 5.3, the machine normally boots to run-level 3 (line 3), at which time the console and various terminals are available (lines 11–13). The startup scripts rc, brc1, and brc2 are run when the system is booted to any

```
1   # NOTE: run-level 6 is reserved for system shutdown.
2   # default run-level is set by initdefault entry.
3   init:3:initdefault:
4   brc1::bootwait:/etc/bcheckrc </dev/console >/dev/console 2>&1
    # fsck,etc.
5   brc2::bootwait:/etc/brc >/dev/console 2>&1          # boottime commands
6   stty::sysinit:stty 9600 clocal icanon echo opost onlcr ienqak ixon
    icrnl ignpar </dev/systty
7   rc  ::wait:/etc/rc </dev/console >/dev/console 2>&1 # system initlzn
8   powf::powerwait:/etc/powerfail >/dev/console 2>&1    # pwr fail routines
9   lp  ::off:nohup sleep 999999999 </dev/lp & stty 9600 </dev/lp
10 halt:6:wait:/usr/lib/X11/iiapps/haltsys.sh
11 cons:0123456:respawn:/etc/getty -h console console  # system console
12 ttya:34:respawn:/etc/getty ttya0 9600 vt100
13 ttyb:34:respawn:/etc/getty ttyb0 9600 vt100
14 xdm :34:wait:/usr/local/etc/xdmrc
```

Figure 5.3   /etc/inittab. Line numbers added for the purpose of explanation.

run-level (lines 4, 5, 7). The line numbers in Figure 5.3 and other fig-
ures in this chapter have been added for the purpose of explanation.

If the startup scripts finish successfully on a BSD-based machine,
/etc/init creates copies of itself to run on all valid terminals listed
in the /etc/ttys file. These copies execute /etc/getty, which
issues the login: challenge on the terminal. On System V-based
machines, /etc/inittab specifies the getty invocations. /etc/ttys
and /etc/inittab are discussed further in the section on configuring terminals.

As mentioned above, the multiuser boot process includes a file system check. UNIX files are arranged on disk drives into structures
called file systems. A *file system* is a collection of files organized into
directories. The directories are linked in a hierarchical tree structure
whose top level is referred to as the *root* of the file system. The file system check done at boot time by the program fsck ensures that the
links that form the hierarchical structure are maintained.

5.1.3   UNIX File Organization

In addition to the kernel process, UNIX consists of the many programs
and utilities used by the system administrators and users. Primary
among these are the command interpreters, called *shells*, such as csh
and sh. From within these, users have access to language compilers
(e.g., cc), data manipulation tools (grep, awk), devices (lpr, mt) and
communications (telnet). There is also a suite of utilities run only by
the system administrator to configure devices, monitor system behavior, and control access to the machine.

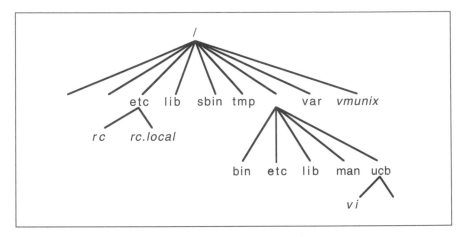

Figure 5.4   BSD file organization

The files that make up UNIX are organized into directories according to their function. The more significant directories found on BSD
and System V systems are described below. Figure 5.4 shows a typical
BSD hierarchy. Your machine may be organized in a slightly different
manner, depending on the vendor's preferences.

/ is the root directory, which contains the kernel and a number of
directories required for the operating system. Every file on a UNIX
machine can be addressed by a pathname composed of directory
names starting from the root.

/bin and /usr/bin contain common user commands, such as ls,
cat, login, rm, and chmod. Traditionally, the utilities in /bin were
basic commands that the system administrator might need to perform
maintenance or recovery tasks while in single-user mode. This distinction is less true today as many operating systems need /usr access
even to run in single-user mode.

/sbin or /5bin on BSD-based UNIX systems contain System V
versions of utilities such as ls, sh, mv, and mkdir. These commands
are in /bin or /usr/bin on System V machines.

/usr/ucb contains utilities originally added by the University of
California at Berkeley, where BSD was developed. Examples include
vi, dbx, grep, rlogin, and w. System V-based operating systems may
have these binaries in /usr/bin or /usr/ucb.

/etc and /usr/etc contain system utilities such as those that control the printer daemons, back up file systems, halt the machine, and
so on, as well as the necessary configuration files for user access and
network communication. Some of these commands are run by the sys-

```
1    crw-r-----   2 root          9,   0 Jan 12 07:38 rxy0a
2    crw-r-----   1 root          9,   1 Oct 16   1991 rxy0b
3    crw-r-----   1 root          9,   2 Oct 16   1991 rxy0c
4    crw-rw-rw-   2 root         30,   0 Aug 21 15:19 rmt0
5    crw-rw-rw-   2 root         30,   0 Aug 21 15:19 rmt0.1600
6    crw-rw-rw-   3 root         30,   8 Jan 18 16:42 rmt0.6250
```

Figure 5.5   Device files. Line numbers have been added for the purpose of explanation.

tem at boot time, and others are used by the administrator. Most users do not run any of the commands in these directories.

/lib and /usr/lib contain the compiled subroutine libraries and the programs and text files that are needed by other programs but that the users do not access directly. Both static and shared subroutine libraries may be available. Routines from static libraries, usually named with the extension .a, are included in the compiled programs. This can make executable programs enormous, such as when the X Window System libraries are used on a Reduced Instruction Set Computing (RISC) machine. Static libraries also necessitate recompiling many binaries when changing a single library routine. The alternative available on many versions of UNIX is a shared library, where the routines are read in from the library at execution time. This saves disk space, but if the shared library is damaged or missing, many executables cease to work, possibly including those required to recover from the problem. Shared libraries usually have the extensions .so or .sa.

/var is a BSD directory for dynamic data files, such as system logs and accounting files. These files were previously kept in /usr, but that required that the /usr partition be writable and backed up frequently. With the development of client workstations that did not have a local /usr but instead shared that of their server, it became useful to have a read-only /usr available to the clients. The dynamic files were moved into /var, which is separate for each client. In this way, the security risk to /usr from the clients was eliminated, as was the problem of filename conflicts for system log files. Subdirectories under /var include adm (system logs, accounting files) and spool (mail, news, printing).

/tmp and /usr/tmp are publicly writable directories used as temporary space by users and programs such as compilers and editors. Most files in these are small and short-lived. In fact, most machine startup scripts delete the contents of these directories at boot time.

/dev contains the special files for the disk drives, tape drives, mouse, etc. Users and system utilities access hardware devices through these device files.

ls -l in /dev shows that these are not normal files (Figure 5.5). The comma-separated numbers are the major and minor numbers of

```
% ls -l /etc/printcap
lrwxr-xr-x 1 root     17 Jul 24 1992 /etc/printcap -> /usr/etc/printcap
% ls -l /usr/etc/printcap
-rw-r--r-- 1 root     6009 Jan 8 11:07 /usr/etc/printcap
```

Figure 5.6 Symbolic link

the device. The major number selects which device driver is used for access, and the minor number describes characteristics of the unit. In the case of disk drives, the minor number shows which drive and partition is being referenced (lines 1–3). For tape drives, the minor number can encode the drive number, the operating speed, and whether the tape will rewind when the access command is completed (lines 4–6).

On BSD-based machines, all devices sit in /dev, while on System V machines, disks and tapes are in separate subdirectories of /dev. Device files are created using the mknod command or running the BSD /dev/MAKEDEV script. The script simplifies the installation of special files by supplying the correct major number and calculating the appropriate minor number for the device.

The UNIX file system is not strictly hierarchical. Most versions of UNIX support *symbolic links,* which are pointers from one part of the hierarchy to another. Symbolic links are files that contain only a pathname. When a process accesses the symbolic link, the access is redirected to the pathname held in the link itself. The normal terminology is that the link "points" to the pathname it contains. Figure 5.6 shows how /etc/printcap, a symbolic link to /usr/etc/printcap, appears in a ls -l listing.

5.1.4   The Superuser

The operating system files and programs in the UNIX file hierarchy control all aspects of machine operation. Regular users are not permitted to alter the operating system configuration. Instead, UNIX has a special user called the *superuser*, who can modify all the files and directories listed above. Superuser privileges are associated simply with the user id 0 (zero), although most sites use the standard login name root. Using that account, the system administrator configures the system, fixes problems, and maintains backups of system files. root is a very powerful user on your system—it can change file ownership, create devices, change file permissions, kill a process, make disk partitions, change passwords, and modify any file. At most sites, knowledge of the root password is restricted to the system administrators.

To use the root account, the administrator can log in as root or use the su command (substitute user). On BSD systems, the user executing the su command must be in a special group, with group id 0. Terminal lines under BSD can be set up to refuse root logins. These measures improve the security of the account.

Many important system files are writable only by root. For example, the file listing the valid logins and their encrypted passwords must be protected to prevent unauthorized additions. But users need to be able to change their passwords without involving an administrator. For these sorts of accesses, UNIX has *setuid* and *setgid* programs.

Normally when a program is run, it runs with the rights of the issuer. For example, cat is a general program to print a file to a terminal. If the issuer is not permitted to read the file, the command execution fails. In contrast, setuid (from *set user id*) programs run with the rights of the user who owns the program. If the cat command were owned by root and had setuid enabled, anyone who executed cat could read any file. The passwd program that changes user passwords is setuid with owner root, since only root can edit the file of valid users. In a similar way, setgid (*set group id*) programs run with the rights of the group of the program. Setuid and setgid are powerful mechanisms for extending limited privileges to users.

root is not the only special account on most UNIX machines. System binaries are normally owned by the login bin so a less experienced class of administrators can perform simple binary updates. daemon is often the owner of printer and news spool directories. Special accounts may also exist for complex software packages such as Ingres, and for system diagnostics.

5.2   System Installation

5.2.1   Initial Installation

With this background, let's look at what is required to install and maintain a UNIX machine. Often the first task you will face is the installation of a newly arrived machine. You have to uncrate the machine, put it together, and install and configure the operating system. Depending on the vendor, the disk drive for the machine may already contain an operating system. While this can save some time, the actual operating system installation is significantly shorter than the configuration phase that follows.

More likely, though, the machine will arrive with an empty disk, a set of media containing the operating system, and system manuals. The operating system may be on tape, CD-ROM, or even diskette. Ideally, the machine was ordered with a complete set of operating system manuals. These include documents for the users, such as an introduction to UNIX, a tutorial on text editing, and descriptions of the UNIX commands. There will also be a number of manuals specifically on system administration. One will cover the machine installation, another will describe basic administration tasks and tools, and there may be volumes on configuring the network, security, and troubleshooting. The installation manual will lead you through the process from empty disk to basic UNIX operation, explaining the decisions you will need to make along the way.

The vendor will have provided an installation script or graphical installation program. These programs help the administrator get a basic machine running quickly. They handle loading the software into the correct location, installing a kernel appropriate for the machine, and some basic initialization tasks like assignment of the machine name. Additional programs may be available to assist in configuring the networking software, setting up printing capabilities, and adding user accounts. Most vendors have spent a good deal of effort to make their installation scripts easy to follow.

Our discussion of the UNIX boot process assumed there were a bootstrap program and kernel on the system disk. How do you install software on a machine that can't boot? The key is to provide the bootstrap program from another source, such as from a tape or over the network. That program in turn loads and executes a reduced operating system or *miniroot*. The miniroot contains enough commands to create a root partition on the disk and copy files into that partition. Then the machine is booted off the newly created root partition, and the installation script creates the /usr partition. Into that partition are loaded the basic system files, discussed in Section 5.1.3. You may also get an opportunity to install optional software, such as additional compilers or mail readers, after the mandatory software is loaded.

The operating system thus installed provides only the basic working configuration. It must be customized to fit the environment and meet the needs of the users. Hardware such as the network interface, additional disk drives, and terminals must be made accessible; the kernel must incorporate drivers for such devices; and system software such as electronic mail must be fully configured.

5.2.2 Building a Kernel

The installation process may leave a generalized kernel in the root partition, or it may build a customized one for the particular machine and its peripherals. A generalized kernel that contains all the hardware devices supported by the vendor is referred to as a *generic* kernel. As the generic kernel boots, it initializes only those devices actually installed on the machine, and so this kernel operates on a wide range of possible configurations.

The kernel created by the installation, whether generic or customized, will eventually need to be replaced. The most common reason for rebuilding the kernel is the addition of a hardware device. On most machines, a new device cannot be used until the appropriate interface routines are built into the kernel. One reason for rebuilding immediately after installation is that kernels built by the installation scripts will not include hardware not supported by the operating system vendor. Most sites replace a generic kernel with one closer to their actual hardware configuration, to save disk space and memory.

Software changes may also necessitate rebuilding the kernel, such as when the vendor supplies new kernel routines to correct system problems. System performance tuning often involves changing kernel parameters. Certain software installations require that additional kernel options be defined, as in the case of system call tracing, disk quotas, and network packet filters.

Rebuilding the kernel requires attention to detail. The following discussion covers BSD-style kernel building in some detail, and defers discussion of the System V method to the end. Your operating system may vary slightly in file location and format, so read the kernel building section in your manuals carefully before beginning.

The files required for kernel building are located in the directories /sys or /usr/sys. Central to the process is the configuration file, usually named for the machine. ULTRIX stores the configuration files in /usr/sys/conf/*arch* (i.e., vax, mips), SunOS stores them in /usr/sys/*arch*/conf, and other BSD systems may keep them in /usr/sys/conf. Other files in the configuration directory include lists of supported devices and a file containing formulas for system parameters. In the rest of /usr/sys are kernel header files plus either source or object files from the vendor.

Figure 5.7 shows a simple ULTRIX configuration file. At the top is the name of the configuration, which is usually the machine name (line 1). Kernel parameters such as the cpu type and the amount of machine memory are next (lines 3–8), followed by options to be enabled in the kernel (lines 10–15). Line 22 describes the root and swap configuration on the machine. Swap space is an area on the disk reserved for the segments of processes or the entire processes that are removed from main memory to allow other jobs to execute. The configuration file continues with the specific hardware devices on the machine (lines 25–52). At the end of the file are the pseudodevices, which are required keywords to include software routines that act like hardware device drivers (lines 56–64).

The disks, controllers, and other devices are listed in the configuration file in the same relationships as they exist on the machine. For example, the machine Chimaera has one disk controller with four

```
1      ident            "CHIMAERA"
       machine          mips
       cpu              "DS5500"
       maxusers         128
5      processors       1
       maxuprc          50
       physmem          32
       timezone         5 dst 1

10     options          QUOTA
       options          INET
       options          NFS
       options          RPC
       options          DLI
15     options          UFS

       makeoptions      ENDIAN="-EL"

       #  the built kernel will be called 'vmunix'. Its root partition is
20     #  on the the disk partition rz0a, it will swap on rz0b, and dumps
       #  created by a machine crash will be temporarily written to rz0b.
       config           vmunix   root on rz0a   swap on rz0b    dumps on rz0b

       #  the primary bus
25     adapter          uba0        at nexus?
       adapter          msi0        at nexus?
       #  a disk controller with 4 attached drives
       adapter          ibus0       at nexus?
       controller       asc0        at ibus?      vector ascintr
30     disk             rz0         at asc0       drive 0
       disk             rz1         at asc0       drive 1
       disk             rz2         at asc0       drive 2
       disk             rz3         at asc0       drive 3
       #  a different disk controller and 2 drives
35     controller       uda0        at uba0
       controller       uq0         at uda0       csr 0172150   vector uqintr
       disk             ra0         at uq0        drive 0
       disk             ra1         at uq0        drive 1
       #  another disk controller like the previous one
40     controller       uda1        at uba0
       controller       uq1         at uda1       csr 0160334   vector uqintr
       disk             ra3         at uq1        drive 0
       disk             ra4         at uq1        drive 1
       disk             ra5         at uq1        drive 2
45     #  the Ethernet controller
       device           ne0         at ibus?      vector neintr
       #  the FDDI network controller
       device           fza0        at ibus?      vector fzaintr
       #  a tape controller with one tape drive
```

Figure 5.7 ULTRIX configuration file. Line numbers have been added for the purpose of explanation.

```
50    controller    klesiu0    at uba0
      controller    uq16       at klesiu0    csr 0174500    vector uqintr
      tape          tms0       at uq16       drive 0

      scs_sysid     1
55
      pseudo-device nfs
      pseudo-device rpc
      pseudo-device dli
      pseudo-device pty
60    pseudo-device loop
      pseudo-device ether
      pseudo-device ufs
      pseudo-device inet
      pseudo-device scsnet
```

Figure 5.7 (continued)   ULTRIX configuration file

drives (lines 29–33), another with two drives (lines 35–38), and a tape controller with a single tape drive (lines 50–52). Those combinations of drive and controller need to be represented exactly in the configuration file. Other devices in Figure 5.7 include the Ethernet (line 46) and FDDI (line 48) network controllers.

The first step in changing the kernel is to save the current configuration file and kernel. If the changes you make should be incorrect, the new kernel may not be able to run in multiuser mode. With a backup kernel available, it is possible to boot to single-user mode and to replace the bad kernel.

In most cases, you need to modify the configuration file if the system hardware has changed. A new device, a new arrangement of existing hardware, and a new location for the root partition all necessitate changes to this file. For new devices supported by your vendor, you will probably need only to copy the entry from the generic configuration file and perhaps change a device number. For third-party devices, locating the correct entry may be more difficult. If it is a small computer system interconnect (SCSI) device, you can probably use the vendor's SCSI driver. For more exotic hardware, you may be able to get the required configuration information from the device vendor, or you may have to work with the device's hardware manual. Such devices may also require a new driver, which goes into the kernel source or object file directories.

The kernel will be built in the directory /usr/sys/*arch*/*CONFIG-NAME*, in this case /usr/sys/MIPS/CHIMAERA. The configuration file is used to set up header files in the kernel build directory. If a device, e.g., pty, is listed in the configuration file, a corresponding header file variable, NPTY, is set to 1 so that the correct drivers will be incorporated in the kernel. This header creation is done by the config utility. Config *CONFIGNAME* generates the appropriate header files and a partial makefile for the kernel. The options and parameters defined in the configuration file become command line arguments to the compiler in that makefile. Executing make depend (done automatically by config on some operating systems such as SunOS) completes the makefile by filling in the file dependencies. Finally, make *kernelname* builds the kernel. This last step can be quite long if you are building a kernel from source.

If the make finishes without reporting errors, the kernel is ready to be installed. Since this will require the machine to be rebooted, notify the users well in advance about the schedule. Shortly before the chosen time, move the running kernel to /*kernelname*.old and copy the new kernel to /*kernelname*. Ps and w will not work from the time that the kernel is replaced until the machine is booted on that kernel. Use the shutdown command to halt UNIX in an orderly manner, preventing file system damage. Shutdown will broadcast warnings to users as the time approaches, and at the specified time will halt the operating system. When the CPU has halted and the machine has been turned off, you can attach the device.

As the machine reboots, the hardware probe should identify the new device. If it does not, either the kernel is not configured correctly or the hardware is not installed properly. If the device is recognized and operates correctly, leave the old kernel in the root partition for some time in case problems arise with the new one.

An alternative method for installing new kernels is to name the new one /*kernelname*.new and to boot the machine specifying that name in the boot command. You will have to refer to the vendor documents for the exact syntax, as it differs widely. If the hardware operates correctly, move /*kernelname*.new to the usual name and reboot again. Until you do, w and ps will not work.

System V kernel builds are somewhat different. The traditional System V configuration directory was /usr/src/uts/cf, but many vendors have changed its location. Two files in this directory need to be edited. The makefile includes the machine name, operating system release, and kernel version number. The machine's hardware and software configuration is described in another file normally given the same name as the machine. This file contains entries for the hardware attached to the machine, as well as root and swap locations. Kernel variables such as the number of simultaneous open files can be set in this file. When the description file is complete, the administrator executes config and make to create the new kernel.

There are a few versions of UNIX which do not require the administrator to replace the kernel to use a new device (NeXTstep is an example). On these implementations, device driver routines can be activated or disabled while the machine is running in multiuser mode. This dynamic driver loading can save time and effort when testing new device drivers. Refer to your manuals to determine if your operating system uses dynamic loading.

5.2.3   Hardware Installation

Often a system administrator must understand and perform some hardware installation. In addition to uncrating new machines and connecting the cables as described in the owner's manual, the administrator may be required to install memory, disks, terminals, and other devices.

5.2.3.1   Printers and Terminals

Printers and terminals are normally connected to serial ports on the system chassis. These devices require hardware handshaking signals to be provided from the computer. The cable connecting the device and the computer must be configured to deliver the needed signals. Details of these signals are beyond the scope of this chapter, but are covered in your device's hardware manual and in *UNIX System Administration Handbook* by Nemeth, Snyder, and Seebass.

5.2.3.2   Memory

Memory is added by inserting boards of single inline memory modules (SIMMs) into the machine chassis. On workstations, these boards go into slots directly on the main system board. Larger machines use separate memory boards that attach to the backplane. Install the board gently into the slot according to the manufacturer's directions. Memory slots are often quite fragile, and breaking a connector may require replacing the whole system board.

As a UNIX machine boots, the probe routine reads from the system memory until a read error is encountered. The machine reports what it found before the error as the available memory and operates using that amount. The results of this probe are printed to the console. This gives a simple test of the memory installation—if the new memory is installed correctly, the probe reports all that is in the chassis.

To complete the installation, edit the kernel configuration file and raise the value associated with `physmem` to the new total. This will be used to size tables in the kernel. Rebuild and reinstall the kernel. This kernel modification step is not required, but may improve performance slightly.

5.2.3.3   Disk Drives

Additional disk space is often needed to hold user files, swap space, and applications. Hardware installation for disk drives varies substantially. Some will attach to controllers built into the machine, as SCSI controllers often are. Other drives require that controller boards be installed in the machine chassis.

The most common configuration for a workstation is a built-in SCSI controller to which up to seven SCSI devices may be connected. The devices are connected in series, ending with a SCSI terminator.

When installing a disk, first ensure you have the required parts: disk, cables, and, if necessary, controller board and hardware mounting brackets to hold the drive stationary. As shown in Figure 5.7, the kernel configuration file must list the controller as well as the disk drive. Each disk drive on a controller needs to have a different drive number, normally set by switches on the drive. The numbers correspond to the drive entries in the configuration file.

5.3   System Software Customization

Once the vendor installation script has been run, the hardware connected, and a kernel built, the UNIX machine is functional, but it is unlikely that it is completely configured to fit your site. Network access may need to be added, layered software loaded, and printers and disk drives fully configured, to name a few items. This customization stage requires the most time in installing a new system, and is one an administrator may perform repeatedly for new machines or operating system upgrades. Time taken to automate this step will be repaid in the future. Many sites maintain extensive customization scripts that reproduce a site-standard file system hierarchy on the newly installed machine by editing the startup files, adding local versions of binaries, creating symbolic links, and so on.

5.3.1   Disk Space

An early task will be to utilize the disk space that was not required in the operating system installation. A UNIX machine installed from scratch will use the vendor's default partitioning of the system disk drive to set up the root, /usr, and swap areas. These may occupy only a portion of the available disk space, so you will want to configure the remainder for the needs of your organization.

A drive on a UNIX system can be divided into separate partitions on which the file systems reside. On most BSD-based versions, each physical disk partition is a single file system. On many System V versions, a single file system may span multiple physical partitions.

These operating systems operate on logical partitions rather than physical partitions. This approach is becoming more popular, as it can improve performance and simplify management. Operating systems that use logical partitions usually provide vendor-specific management tools, and so the management of logical partitions is not discussed here. The following discussion concentrates on the traditional partition structure.

ULTRIX, SunOS through version 4.1, and 4.3 BSD use the original approach. A drive on one of these systems can be divided into eight partitions, each of which can be mounted as a file system. These partitions, labeled *a* through *h,* are allocated to cover the entire disk. A partial description of the disk geometry (partition sizes, number of tracks and cylinders, etc.) can be found in /etc/disktab. Disk partitioning commands such as disklabel (4.3 BSD), chpt (ULTRIX), and format (SunOS) are used to specify the offsets of the partitions from the beginning of the disk. They can also change the partition sizes from the defaults in /etc/disktab.

If you are adding a new disk to the machine, you must include the disk in the kernel configuration as described above. If adding disk drives is a common activity at your site, you can save yourself some work by configuring your kernels with extra drive entries on the controllers. When a disk needs to be installed, you need only set the drive number, shut down the machine, and reboot with the device attached.

You must create a special file in the /dev directory for each of the disk partitions before you can access them. The entries in /dev are the filenames by which the devices will be addressed by system utilities such as mount. On BSD machines /dev/MAKEDEV xy0 will create all eight devices used to access the partitions on disk xy0.

The administrator must create file systems on the physical or logical partitions in order to make the space available. The commands mkfs and newfs allocate the necessary structures on the disk to hold a file system. Once that step is done, the file system exists on the drive but cannot yet be used. It must be attached to the existing file hierarchy to be accessible. This step is called *mounting the file system.* The command mount /dev/xy0e /usr1 makes the file system on the fifth partition (*e*) of drive xy0 accessible via the path /usr1. /usr1 is a *mount point,* an empty directory created with the mkdir command.

When the machine boots, one of the startup scripts will execute the mount command. This will mount all file systems listed in the file system table, commonly called /etc/fstab. HP-UX calls this file /etc/checklist, and AIX /etc/file systems, but they all perform the same function. This table is a list of all known file systems on the attached disks, and the mount points for those file systems. It also contains entries for file systems on other machines that can be

```
1    /dev/xy0a        /               4.2    grpid,rw,nosuid 1 1
2    /dev/xy0d        /usr            4.2    grpid,rw 1 2
3    /dev/xy0e        /usr1           4.2    grpid,rw 1 3
4    /dev/xy0f        /usr2           4.2    grpid,rw 1 4
5    /dev/xy0g        /usr3           4.2    grpid,rw 1 5
6    /dev/xy1a        /tmp            4.2    grpid,rw 1 6
7    /dev/xy1d        swap            swap   rw,grpid 0 0
8    gwithian:/mail   /gwithian/mail  nfs    soft,bg,grpid,nosuid,
                                             retry=1,retrans=6,timeo=28 0 0
```

Figure 5.8 /etc/fstab. Line numbers added for the purpose of explanation.

mounted across the network using a distributed file system such as
the Network File System (NFS).

Figure 5.8 shows a sample SunOS /etc/fstab. Lines 1–6 refer to
local file systems, which in SunOS have the type 4.2. Line 3 shows the
fstab syntax for the example given above. Line 8 describes an NFS
mount. There are additional mount options, such as *rw* for read–write,
that can be configured in this table. Consult your vendor's documentation for the exact syntax on your machine.

5.3.2   Swap Space

Each disk partition can be assigned a different purpose. The obvious
uses for your spare partitions are user home directories, additional
software packages, and temporary space. Another important use for
disk space is as paging and swapping space for processes. The operating system allocates some or all of the virtual address space of a process on disk space set aside for this. The traditional wisdom is that a
machine should have swap space totaling two to three times the
machine memory, but your swap allocation should reflect the programs in use at your site.

The swap space is normally allocated on the *b* partition on the same
disk as the root partition, though you can use any partition except *a*.
Many versions of UNIX store disk labels within the first partition, so
swapping there would destroy the partition map. Line 7 in Figure 5.8
shows the swap space for that machine to be on the *d* partition. The
file system type for swap space in this example is *swap*, but other vendors use identifiers such as *sw* and *paging*.

Machines with multiple disks can have swap partitions on several of
them, increasing the performance by distributing the load across separate spindles. To create additional swap space, set aside a partition
that is not in use for a file system. Add an entry to the file system table

```
ident      "OBERON"
machi      mips
cpu        "DS5000"
...
config     vmunix   root on rz0a   swap on rz0b and rz1b    dumps on rz0b
```

Figure 5.9 Configuration file with multiple swap partitions

that marks the partition as swap space (e.g., line 7 in Figure 5.8). On most machines, swapon -a, normally run in the startup scripts, is all that is needed to activate the new area. Some versions of UNIX, however, require that all swap spaces be configured in the kernel (as in Figure 5.9), as well as in the file system table.

5.3.3 Terminals

The only terminal your machine can access when first installed is the system console. Additional serial terminals must be hardware installed and software installed. Serial terminal installation is different between BSD and System V versions. The files /etc/ttys and /etc/gettytab control terminal behavior under BSD. Figure 5.10 shows an ULTRIX /etc/ttys. This file specifies the device name, the program that is run on that device, and the type of terminal attached. Several BSD versions use two files, /etc/ttys and either /etc/ttytype or /etc/ttytab, to hold the information others hold in just /etc/ttys. Changes to /etc/ttys are not effective immediately because /etc/init, which starts the programs on each terminal, reads this file only at boot time or after receiving a signal. kill -HUP 1 will force init to read the file again. /etc/gettytab contains the definitions for the terminal descriptions that are used as parameters to /etc/getty.

```
1    # name  getty                       type     status          comments
2    console "/etc/getty std.9600" vt100     on secure
     # console terminal
3    tty00   "/etc/getty std.9600" vt100     on secure
     # direct connect tty
4    tty01   "/etc/getty std.9600" vt100     on secure
     # direct connect tty
5    ttyp0   none                network
6    ttyp1   none                network
7    ttyp2   none                network
8    ttyp3   none                network
     ...
37   ttyqf   none                network
```

Figure 5.10 /etc/ttys. Line numbers have been added for the purpose of explanation.

Terminals are configured in /etc/inittab on System V versions of UNIX. Lines 11–13 in Figure 5.3 show that at run levels 3 and 4, logins are enabled on the console, ttya0, and ttyb0. Changes to /etc/inittab take effect on reboot or when telinit q is executed. The terminal descriptions are given in either /etc/gettytab or /etc/gettydefs, depending on the vendor's preference.

Full descriptions of terminal capabilities are in the termcap (BSD) or terminfo (System V) databases. These contain information on cursor positioning, initialization sequences, padding requirements, and other control sequences.

5.3.4   Printers

A printer configuration step must be performed before the UNIX machine will be able to access either printers connected to itself or remote printers on its network. Local printers are attached to a port on the machine. If the serial line was in use for a terminal, that installation must be removed. Edit /etc/ttys or /etc/inittab to remove the invocation of getty on that line.

Printing on BSD versions uses the commands lpr, lpd, lpq, and lpc. lpr is the user command to print a file. It places the file in the printer's spool directory, usually /usr/spool/*printername*. The line printer daemon lpd is started at system boot time (Figure 5.1). It is notified by lpr that something is ready to print, and creates a copy of itself to print the file. lpq and lpc check the print queue and issue control commands to lpd.

The BSD printer configuration is controlled by /etc/printcap, a portion of which is reproduced in Figure 5.11. Each printer has a list of aliases by which it can be addressed, shown on lines 1 and 11. For a local printer, the entry lp (line 2) names the port to which it is connected. The other lines describe the baud rate of the printer (line 9), input and output filters (lines 3,4), and the name of the spool directory (lines 6,15). Remote printer entries specify the name of the machine to which to pass the file for printing (line 13).

Filters are used to handle device dependencies. Most impact printers use the standard filter, /usr/lib/lpf, but more versatile devices such as Postscript printers require special filters.

Printing on System V-based UNIX uses the user command lp, the daemon lpsched, and the configuration command lpadmin. lp places the file in the spool directory, also called /usr/spool/*printername*, from which lpsched prints it. The printer is configured by running lpadmin, which creates description files in /usr/spool/lp. Many System V versions also provide the lpr command.

```
 1     2341p|lp234|21p|lp2|Second floor lineprinter:\
 2                      :lp=/dev/tty03:\
 3                      :if=/usr/lib/lpf:\
 4                      :of=/usr/lib/lpf:\
 5                      :tr=\f\f:\
 6                      :sd=/usr/spool/lpd-027:\
 7                      :lf=/usr/adm/lpd-errs:\
 8                      :pw#80:\
 9                      :br#9600:\
10                      :ff=\f\n:
11     0271p|lp027|01p|lp0|Zero floor lineprinter:\
12                      :lp=:\
13                      :rm=chimaera:\
14                      :rp=0271p:\
15                      :sd=/usr/spool/lpd-027:\
16                      :lf=/usr/adm/lpd-errs:\
17                      :ff=\f\n:
```

Figure 5.11 /etc/printcap. Line numbers added for the purpose of explanation.

5.3.5 Network Software

Unless you administer a sole machine in an isolated environment, you will need to configure the network software on the new machine. Every machine must have a hostname that is unique on the network to which it is connected. To avoid obvious conflicts with machines such as sun, mac1, and so on, machines on the Internet use the domain naming system. The chosen hostname is prepended to a string showing both the administrative grouping and the site classification. For example, dopey.cs.unc.edu was a machine in the Computer Science department at the University of North Carolina.

Each machine has a unique hardware address, set by the manufacturer, for each network interface installed on the machine. For most UNIX machines, this interface is for Ethernet. If the machine is using the networking software TCP/IP, each hardware interface also has an IP or Internet number. Before a machine can talk to another machine, it must know the remote machine's IP number. A machine's IP number and usually some of its close neighbors are listed in the host table, /etc/hosts.

Other IP numbers are supplied to many machines by BIND, the Berkeley Internet Name Domain server. BIND uses a network of servers to provide the IP address of an individual machine. The IP numbers for a site's hosts are known by several servers who will respond to requests for that information. For a full discussion of IP numbers, BIND, and UNIX network administration in general, see Chapter 7.

To use network commands such as `rlogin` and `rsh`, the system needs pseudoterminals called *ptys*. These behave like terminals, but are associated with a process rather than a serial terminal. Ptys must be configured in the kernel (line 59, Figure 5.7), and an entry made for each one in `/etc/ttys` (lines 6–37, Figure 5.10).

If you have more than one machine, you can use a distributed file system to share files and save disk space. The Network File System (NFS) is available on most UNIX operating systems. It allows you to mount a remote machine's file systems into your local file hierarchy, where normal UNIX commands can be used to access the files. To enable this sharing, NFS processes are started on the machine exporting the file systems. These file server processes provide the files to the client machine. To control access, the partitions that the server has available are listed in `/etc/exports`, along with the names of the machines that are permitted to mount these file systems.

On the client machine (the one that will read the remote files), the remote partitions can be mounted using the `mount` command. By updating the file system table (usually `/etc/fstab`), these can be automatically remounted when the client machine reboots.

While remote access and network communications can greatly enhance your system, too much access is definitely bad for its health. There are both benign and more malicious individuals traversing the Internet to see what they can find, and in some cases, modify. Access to your machine is controlled by a number of files, a partial list of which is `.rhosts`, `/etc/hosts.equiv`, `/etc/hosts.lpd`, and `/etc/exports`. `/etc/hosts.equiv` and `.rhosts` determine who can log in to your machine without being challenged for a password. It is worth checking the default `/etc/hosts.equiv` file when your system is first installed; remove any + you find in there as it allows universal access. `/etc/hosts.lpd` on BSD versions specifies which machines can deliver files to printers connected to your machine. As noted above, `/etc/exports` allows the administrator to limit the hosts that may mount the partition. For a full discussion of these issues and precautions, refer to *Practical UNIX Security* by Garfinkel and Spafford.

5.3.6   Mail

At many sites, electronic mail is a critical part of the computing environment. Users run mail utilities such as `mail`, `mh`, `elm`, and `pine` to send mail and to read messages that have been delivered into their in-box, usually named `/usr/spool/mail/login` or `/usr/mail/login`. They can save previously read articles back into the spool file, or into a local mailbox in their own directory.

UNIX machines normally come with Berkeley `sendmail`, which is a transport system for delivering local and intermachine mail. The vendor-supplied `sendmail` configuration is probably sufficient for isolated sites with a single multiuser machine, but sites with multiple machines often customize their `sendmail` installation. For example, some sites may wish to set up a centralized location for storing mail. These changes are made in the `sendmail` configuration file, `/etc/sendmail.cf`. This file specifies many parameters to `sendmail`, including the official site name to use, under what load conditions to stop receiving mail, and how the message headers should appear. It also contains cryptic *rewriting rules* that convert mail addresses from one form to another. Modifying `/etc/sendmail.cf` is not for the novice administrator. A full description of `sendmail` can be found in *TCP/IP Network Administration* by Craig Hunt.

5.3.7   News

Electronic news on an isolated multiuser machine allows users in a community to exchange information, similar to a bulletin board. Connect to the Internet, and a flood of information can be available in hundreds of technical and nontechnical newsgroups, from `rec.arts.startrek.info` to `comp.unix.aix`. Software to receive, store, and send news, such as C News or InterNetwork News (INN), is available from sites on the Internet. In addition to performing the software installation, the administrator must allocate a substantial amount of disk space. (Over 300 megabytes is common for sites receiving large numbers of newsgroups.) Another site currently receiving news must agree to provide the articles to you and accept postings from your site for propagation, and you must configure a transport agent for this (either `uucp` or `nntp`, usually). Old news must constantly be deleted, or *expired,* to make room for new.

Users can read the arriving articles with a number of news readers including `rn`, `trn`, `xrn`, `nn`, `tin`, and `gnus`, also available on the Internet. Each user decides which newsgroups to subscribe to. The file `.newsrc`, normally in the user's home directory, keeps the list of subscribed groups and which articles have been read in each, so the user does not reread articles.

5.3.8   UUCP

Some sites receive mail and news over a batch communication system known as `uucp` (UNIX-to-UNIX copy). The primary program, `uucico`, initiates and manages connections between machines. `uucp` also includes user commands to send files between hosts and execute remote commands, and administrative commands for checking the

```
1     # @(#)crontab  #

3     * * * * *         /usr/lib/atrun
4     5 4 * * *         sh /usr/adm/newsyslog

6     5 1 * * *         /usr/adm/daily.local
7     5 5 * * 1         /usr/adm/weekly.local
8     5 6 1 * *         /usr/adm/monthly.local

10    5 1 * * 1-5       /usr/local/etc/dumpdaily
                        >  /usr/adm/dump/dailylog 2>&1
11    5 * * * *         /usr/adm/hourly.local
12    5 5 * * *         /usr/etc/catman -w >/dev/null 2>&1
```

Figure 5.12   /usr/lib/crontab. Line numbers added for the purpose of explanation.

queue and connection status. Setting up uucp involves a special login, modem setup, and control files stored in /usr/lib/uucp. Many sites on high-speed networks no longer run uucp. Further discussion of this can be found in Chapter 7 and in O'Reilly and Todino.

5.3.9 Cron

cron, a daemon that executes jobs at a specified time, is used to automate certain administrative tasks. Anything that has to be done at a regular interval, but without any user intervention other than launching, is a candidate for being placed under the control of cron. Examples are disk usage reports, find commands that delete core files more than a week old, a status check of installed machines, and nightly expires of old news articles. The daemon's actions are specified in one or more crontab files whose entries include the execution date and time, the command to execute, and, in some versions of UNIX, which user should execute the command.

Figure 5.12 shows a crontab file. The first five fields specify the time at which the command should be run. In order, these are the minute, hour, day of the month, month of the year, and day of the week (1 = Monday, etc.). The wild card * in the time field matches any time. This allows commands to be repeated at regular intervals, such as hourly or daily, without explicitly listing all valid combinations. The sixth field is the sh command to be executed. Line 3 shows that /usr/lib/atrun executes every minute. /usr/local/etc/dumpdaily in Line 10 is run at 1:05 am Monday through Friday.

On most BSD versions, there is a single crontab file kept in /usr/lib or /etc. Editing the file is sufficient to schedule the job. On System V machines and some BSD ones, such as SunOS, any user can have a personal `crontab` file. Changes are made to a `crontab` file with the `crontab` command, which modifies the file and notifies the `cron` daemon to read the file again. The `crontab` files are kept in `/usr/spool/cron/crontabs` on these machines.

5.3.10 Layered Software

In addition to configuring these operating system functions, site-specific software needs to be installed. Software that is installed separately from the operating system is often referred to as layered software. Examples include compilers, CASE tools, word processing packages, and graphical user interfaces. A wide range of products is available from the workstation vendor, commercial software developers, and source depositories on the Internet.

`archie` is a service that lists the Internet locations of a particular software package. Anyone can `telnet` to an `archie` server (currently `archie.mcgill.ca`, `archie.sura.net`, `archie.funet.fi`, and `archie.au`) with the login `archie` and type `prog filename` to get a list of locations. Use the transfer program `ftp` and the login `anonymous` to copy software back to your machine. The first item to retrieve is the client software for `archie` itself, so you won't have to use `telnet`. Choose the packages you install with care; not only can you spend hours compiling and evaluating software, but some, such as the document formatter TeX, require a tremendous amount of configuration and subsequent user support.

The installation of layered software packages is quite specific to the package, but some general guidelines apply. Before ordering the software, make sure it will run on your machine and your version of the operating system, and that it is available on media your machine can read. Installation can be as simple as running a vendor-supplied script or as complex as compiling an entire product tree for your machine. Take particular care with the pathnames used in the build process, because some products incorporate those names into the executable and make it difficult for you to move the binary or libraries at a later date. If you must provide specific filenames, try to use generic names (i.e., `/usr/local/lib/PACKAGE` instead of `/oberon/usr3/local/lib/PACKAGE`). Using symbolic links, these generic names can point to the true location. This makes it much easier to move software, as the symbolic link can be changed to point to the new location at the same time the binary is relocated.

Even as your machine is being first installed, it's useful to plan for the future. Years ago, when operating systems changed every 2–3 years rather than every 6–9 months, upgrade planning was less important. Any new or modified binaries were simply placed in

/usr/bin, to be copied individually from old to new after the next upgrade. The frequency of upgrades and the sheer quantity of new programs makes this method painful today. An alternative strategy is to isolate layered products and locally modified versions of standard system utilities into a separate hierarchy whenever possible. This makes reinstalling these products after an operating system upgrade much easier, since the entire hierarchy can be restored from backups rather than by rerunning all the installations. This directory is often called /usr/new or /usr/local, but the choice of name is yours. The new location must be publicized to the users, who need to include it in their paths.

5.3.11   On-Line Manual Pages

The on-line manual pages (commonly called *man pages*) are descriptions of commands, library routines, and system calls. They give a brief definition, list the valid arguments, and provide other usage information. The man pages are stored in /usr/man as both unformatted and formatted text. The cat subdirectories (e.g., cat1, catn) contain the formatted versions, and the man subdirectories contain the unformatted versions. The different man directories correspond to sections of the UNIX manuals. There are usually directories for local and new pages, called manl (not to be confused with man1) and mann. Manual pages for programs installed in the separate hierarchy (as described in the last paragraph) should be isolated in a separate directory such as /usr/man/mann or /usr/local/man to facilitate upgrades.

The man program is configured to search the directories in /usr/man. Some versions also search directories specified in the user's MANPATH environment variable. These versions are preferable, because they allow the administrator the freedom to put layered product manual pages outside /usr/man. If your version doesn't understand MANPATH, you can replace it with one of those available on the Internet.

The man command has a useful flag to search for a keyword in the subject lines of the manual pages. This is man -k or its alias, apropos. These commands read the file /usr/lib/whatis, rather than searching the /usr/man hierarchy. The whatis file is created by catman -w, which can be run nightly or weekly, as shown in line 12 of Figure 5.12.

```
root:1oiuet13tkiTc:0:3:Superuser:/:/bin/csh
bin:kdf4EGvvKQKtI:3:3:Operator:/:/bin/csh
sysdiag:*:0:1:System Diagnostic:/stand/sysdiag:/stand/sysdiag/sysdiag
daemon:*:1:1:Mr Background:/:
branwen:newfUOvc4L5g6:2500:8:Ms. Branwen:/home/branwen:/bin/csh
```

Figure 5.13 `/etc/passwd`

5.4 Maintaining the UNIX System

By now, your UNIX machine is in good shape. Software has been loaded, networking configured, and other startup tasks completed. At this point the administrator's job turns to maintaining the system operation for the users and responding to required changes. This includes user account management, system security, file backups, status monitoring, upgrades, and problem correction. These are the day-to-day tasks that make up most of an administrator's job.

5.4.1 Account Management

Each of the machine's users needs an account with which to access the machine. When first installed, this account consists of a login of eight or fewer characters, a password, a directory in which to save files, and any startup files the administrator thinks the users will need. Many sites also have a usage policy statement that is distributed to users when they get their accounts. This reduces misunderstandings about what constitutes appropriate use of the account.

Each account has an entry in `/etc/passwd` that lists the login, user and group identification numbers, owner's name, home directory, and default shell. Figure 5.13 shows a partial `/etc/passwd` file. The second field is for the encrypted password. Because access to the password encryption makes an account potentially more vulnerable, many UNIX versions locate the encrypted passwords in a separate, unreadable file called the *shadow password file*. The user and group ids, rather than the full login and group names, are used in process control and the UNIX file system to denote the owner of a process or file.

A new account is usually given a private home directory, owned by that login. This is the work space for the user. You may find it useful to set up standard `.profile`, `.cshrc`, and `.login` files for the users to ensure their initial environment has access to all important directories and facilities. If your site uses graphical display workstations, you should include a default windowing environment for the new account. If you have installed any layered software outside the standard UNIX locations, you should add these directories to the paths in the new user's startup files.

Most versions of UNIX have an `adduser` script that will perform all the required steps to add a new account. Many large sites have modified this script to conform to their environment.

"Guest" accounts without passwords are invitations to intruders. If a guest or demo account is required, choose a password that the users will remember but that can't be easily guessed by an uninvited guest.

In a site with many users and many machines, a few additional issues become important. If numeric user ids do not match between two machines, you will not be able to share files between them using NFS. As mentioned before, all that is saved in the file system to identify the owner is the numeric user id. If a partition is mounted on a machine whose user ids don't match those on the server, a user may find he has access to files owned by another, and no access to his own files. For this reason, sites that maintain many NFS connections use the same user ids on all machines.

Adding an account to a large number of machines can be time-consuming. Several software packages have been developed to centralize account management. The best known of these is Sun's Network Information Service (NIS), formerly called the Yellow Pages. A master machine distributes its version of `/etc/passwd`, `/etc/group`, and several other files, to a few slave machines. The master and slaves then listen for requests from other machines for this information, and provide it as needed. A login addition to `/etc/passwd`, for example, needs to be executed only on the master machine for it to be distributed to all machines in the environment.

As users leave your organization, their accounts will need to be deleted. Remove accounts as soon as they are not needed, as idle accounts are often used by intruders to access a system. If an account owner is gone, there's no one to complain that files are appearing in the directory, or that the last login time is too recent.

When a user leaves, he or she may still have important files in the home directory. Ideally, the user will have transferred any crucial material to other users before leaving, but that is not always possible. In order to minimize the potential loss, announce to the remaining users that the account will be deleted, so they can copy any important files from the home directory. Then archive the account's files to some location, such as a tape or optical disk. This will preserve any files relating to your organization that no one realizes are needed until the account is gone. After the backup is done, remove the home directory and the entry from `/etc/passwd` to free the disk space and disable the account.

```
wheel:*:0:user1,user2
games:*:6:user1,games,user3,user4
pxp1:*:1002:user6,user1,user5,user4,user7,user8
```

Figure 5.14 /etc/group

UNIX allows a group of users to share files with each other, while excluding other users. A UNIX group can be constructed using the logins of all the people who wish to share a particular file. The file owner then executes the chgrp command to place the file in the group. The group mode bits also need to be set with chmod to enable permissions for that group.

UNIX groups are added by editing /etc/group, which is shown in Figure 5.14. The group entry consists of the name, a password field, a unique numeric group id, and a list of logins in that group. On older System V-based UNIX versions, a user was a member of only one group at a time, and changed between groups by executing newgrp. A number of recent System V-based operating systems have adopted BSD group handling, in which the user is a member of all of his or her groups at the same time. After a change is made to /etc/group, however, the BSD user must log out and back in again before the new group is available to him.

5.4.2 Security

Another major task in system administration is maintaining operating system security. This divides into three areas: password management, access control, and monitoring. Passwords are often the weakest part of a site's security plan. The standard UNIX password program will allow users to use almost any easily guessed password if they are simply persistent enough. Some versions of UNIX have corrected this, and you should test your vendor's implementation to see if the changes are sufficient to prevent guessable passwords from being entered. The best password programs deny dictionary words, dates, names, and other easily guessed values. Sites with weak password programs should consider installing one of the replacement programs available on the Internet, such as npasswd or passwd+.

It is also important to encourage proper password security among your users. Some users cavalierly distribute their password to their friends. Others post it on their workstation or program it into their function keys. All of these undermine the best security.

The password on the root account is critical, because once a user can become root, he or she can read, modify, or destroy any part of the system. Make sure it cannot be guessed, is known by as few people as necessary, and is changed immediately after a root user leaves the work group.

Regardless of how good your password checking program is, it is a good idea to run the best available password cracking program on the password encryptions in use. These programs gather all the encryptions in use at a site, and then encrypt a huge list of words and other strings to compare against the encryptions. These cracking programs will fill in for gaps in the `passwd` program, and allow you to warn users before their accounts are compromised. A good source for these programs is the Internet.

Access control is another major element in system security. `/etc/hosts.equiv` and `.rhosts` files were mentioned earlier as files that control whether a user must type a password when connecting over the network. Some sites disallow `.rhosts` files entirely. A good rule is to list only machines run by knowledgeable administrators in `/etc/hosts.equiv`, if you choose to have any there at all. Limit the machines listed in `/etc/exports` to machines administered by your group, because of the userid-based permissions (discussed under account management).

Set file and directory permissions so users cannot change machine configuration information. Files executed by root, such as `crontab`, need to have restrictive permissions. If users can write into one system binary directory, they probably can compromise the entire system. Some vendors provide a list of suggested permissions for system directories and files you can follow. Any other system directories you create, such as `/usr/local/bin`, should be similarly protected.

An excellent tool in improving and monitoring system security is COPS by Dan Farmer, available on the Internet. It checks file and directory permissions, scans `/etc/passwd` for invalid entries, and looks for setuid root programs, to name but a few.

5.4.3   File Backups

Another task of the system administrator is to configure and maintain a backup schedule for the machine. Unless the site is large enough to employ an operator, the system administrator may be the one running the backups as well. During a system backup, copies of files in a disk partition are written to another location for restoration in the case of disk damage, or more likely, user error. Every site should have a regular backup schedule that covers all the important files on the system.

The files on a machine change with different frequencies, so they need to be backed up at different intervals. User files often require daily backups, while system binaries, which rarely change after initial installation, need only weekly or less frequent backups. This is one of the reasons for keeping user files on a separate disk partition from system binaries.

To keep the quantity of backups manageable, not all backups are complete dumps of all files in a file system. Instead, incremental backups are used to save only what has changed since the last backup was done. Each incremental backup is much smaller than the entire file system, so many can be saved between full dumps. Often the daily backups of user files are incrementals only, with a full dump done at a regular interval of a week or so.

Backups can be done to a variety of media, including tape, optical disk, or another disk drive. Most sites use tape because of the low cost of the media. Eight millimeter tapes can hold more than five gigabytes when used on drives with compression capabilities. Tapes can wear out or break, so optical disk may be used for more critical backups.

UNIX provides the commands dump and restore to perform the backups and restorations. dump writes a full or incremental backup of a disk partition to the backup device. Dump levels are numbered from 0 to 9, with 0 denoting the full dump. A level 1 dump copies all files modified since the last level 0 or 1 dump, a level 2 dump backs up files changed since the last level 0, 1, or 2 dump, and so on. For greatest reliability, dumps should be done when file systems are inactive.

restore allows the administrator to read the backup and extract one or more files from it. In the case of a disk failure, several entire partitions will need to be restored. If there are incremental backups more recent than the latest full backup, restoration becomes a multi-step process. First the full backup is restored to the empty partition, and then incrementals created since that full backup are restored, ending with the most recent.

UNIX vendors sometimes provide additional backup facilities. AIX, for example, has a mksysb command that will build a bootable copy of the system in a single command. For backing up less than an entire partition, tar or cpio can be used. Other backup systems designed for large, networked sites are available from commercial sources.

5.4.4 Monitoring the Operation

As an administrator, one of your goals is to provide a reliable computing environment. To do this, you must observe the system, both to correct existing faults and prevent future problems. Some part of each day is devoted to checking the operation of hardware devices and examining resource levels such as disk space and processor availability. Many times a problem can be corrected before it becomes a serious inconvenience to the users.

5.4.4.1 Checking Hardware Operations

At the beginning of your shift, check that all the machines are running. If a machine crashed during the night it may need assistance rebooting. Most machines will reboot after a crash, but those with a hardware failure or file system damage will not.

File system damage can occur when there is a cable or controller problem, but most often it is simply a matter of timing. UNIX systems do not perform an immediate disk write when a file is closed. The file is held in system buffers temporarily, and written to disk asynchronously. These buffers are written out either when the buffer is needed for another file, or regularly by the update daemon (usually every 30 seconds). In the intervals between updates, the data in the buffers may be newer than that on disk. If the machine crashes for any reason during the interval, it is possible the file system structure may be damaged.

The file system integrity checker fsck is run during the boot process by the startup script. Fsck will make some repairs, but will stop if it finds certain serious errors. The machine stops rebooting and drops into single-user mode so an administrator can rerun the command and explicitly authorize the required action. This gives you an opportunity to see what files fsck is planning on removing, so a restoration can be ordered, but in practice the actions fsck asks about are almost always required to get the file system back into usable shape.

Peripheral devices can develop problems, so their operation should be checked regularly. One simple way to test the printers is to set up a script that runs under the control of cron and prints a test page to each printer in the early morning. These pages can be collected every morning and corrective action taken quickly if a printer is not operating.

In the case of a malfunctioning printer, the problem may be in the connection to the host or in the line printer daemon, lpd (BSD) or lpsched (System V). The daemon is more likely the problem, and killing it and restarting may clear the error condition. The serial line can be tested by attaching a terminal and reenabling getty on the line. If a login is successful, the line is operating correctly. Problems on established terminals are more likely to be hardware in origin unless a change has been recently made to /etc/ttys (BSD) or /etc/inittab (System V).

Network disruptions can be crippling in today's distributed systems, so network monitoring is important. By using rsh, ping, and other network commands, an administrator can check the network status and determine what machine or network segment cannot be reached.

5.4.4.2 Resource Monitoring

The most common resource problem is disk space. If the partition with /usr/spool fills to capacity, mail and news will be lost. When the home directory partitions are full, users will be unable to save or modify any files. In each case, running out of disk space can cause a serious disruption. Administrators commonly keep scripts running that alert them to problems with disk space.

The solutions to the space problem are varied, depending on the files involved, and the priorities of the organization. When the appetite for user disk space or network news grows to the limits, some sites have the luxury of purchasing more disks. More likely, however, strategies to reduce the existing files are employed.

In the system directories, old versions of binaries can be deleted and the remaining ones stripped of their symbol tables, at a loss of debugging information. Source directories often have extraneous object files that a make clean in the build directory will delete. Less used documentation or source files can be compressed to reduce space. System logs, such as /usr/adm/wtmp, /usr/adm/messages, and /usr/adm/usracct can be copied to tape and truncated. If your machine retains crash dumps, these can be compacted or discarded after examination. Files named core, which result from program segmentation faults or other errors, can also be removed. Many system daemons have verbose logging mechanisms used for debugging that can get out of hand quickly. For example, /usr/spool/syslog files may contain an entry for every mail message sent or newsgroup read, so these should be rotated to tape quickly. Unless you need the logs, turn off their production to avoid wasting disk space.

In the user directories, the problem is more difficult. Many sites enforce the migration of files that have not been accessed in a long time. These are copied to another media, such as tape or optical disk. User education and even peer pressure can persuade users to remove files, particularly old core files and files copied from the Internet. Users' home directories can be reallocated among the user partitions to spread the free space to more users, or to let a few disk hogs fight over entire partitions. In a distributed environment, it is possible to keep copies of large, less frequently accessed software packages on only a few servers, and have other machines mount those partitions using NFS to access the software. This frees what had been system space for home directory space, but still leaves the software accessible.

A more draconian but often necessary option is the imposition of disk quotas. These set an upper bound on the amount of disk space a user can acquire. Users receive warnings when they exceed the quota until ultimately they cannot save any additional files. Quotas must be configured into the kernel before use.

Another resource to check is the processor itself. When a machine has a high load average, as seen by the command uptime, the running processes should be reviewed using ps. The programs and load vary considerably from site to site, but after a short time you should be able to gauge the normal load for your machines. Any processes that have accumulated a large amount of CPU time are worth looking into, since a program under development can simply be in a loop. You can terminate, pause, and restart processes using the kill command, and adjust priorities of running processes with renice.

The ps listing is also a good place to check in case other parts of the system are not operating correctly. The manual page for ps explains how to interpret the state field for each process. Processes that are permanently in a wait state (except for swapper and pagedaemon) are problems. These processes are waiting for an event, and may be tying up resources waiting for something that will never happen. Processes in this state cannot be killed, and the only cure is to reboot the machine.

BSD machines have several system monitoring commands you can use, but their output can be difficult to understand. Pstat can provide a wide range of information, of which the most useful are swap space utilization (-s) and how full various tables are (-T). vmstat describes the virtual memory state, while iostat provides disk I/O information. netstat is used to monitor some network statistics. Additional monitoring commands may be present on your system.

If a machine is constantly performing below expected levels, the cause may be a hardware limitation or a badly tuned kernel. Hardware bottlenecks could be the CPU, disk drives, memory or network. The CPU could simply be too slow for the load that is placed on it. Sometimes distributing the load across multiple machines will improve the situation, but often a hardware upgrade, such as adding a floating point coprocessor or replacing the CPU, is required.

Some disk configurations can cause performance problems. Disks come in very different sizes and access rates, and the disks on the problem machine may be older, slower drives. The placement of files on the disk affects performance, because disk arm movement adds to the response time. By keeping files that will be accessed at the same time on the same disk partition, arm movement can be minimized. If your machine swaps or pages frequently, allocating auxiliary swap space on a second or third disk will distribute the load to multiple disks. Excessive swapping can be due to an undersized main memory, so adding memory will reduce disk accesses in that case.

The network may be creating the perceived performance problems on the UNIX machine. Diskless workstations obtain the operating system over the network and must swap over it as well. This swapping loads the network and slows response time. (Because of this, most sites require local disks on their workstations, even if they are only used for swapping.) Excessive broadcast traffic will slow machines down as they process the packets. Ethernet collisions require retries, so a congested network means the processor may have to attempt transmission several times before it is successful.

Tuning kernel parameters can sometimes ameliorate performance problems. This involves changing values in the kernel configuration file or header files, and rebuilding the kernel. For a complete discussion of performance tuning, see your vendor documentation or *System Performance Tuning* by Loukides.

5.4.4.3 System Accounting

UNIX provides system accounting utilities that can gather information on disk usage, CPU utilization, pages printed, connection times, and other resource usage. The related log files grow as the system runs, and these must be summarized and either archived or discarded to avoid running out of disk space.

BSD and System V versions of UNIX track the same information, but they do it in entirely different ways. BSD machines normally have accounting on by default, running `/etc/accton` out of the `rc` startup scripts. Other BSD commands are `quot` (disk usage), `sa` (summarize CPU accounting), and `last` (connection time). System V versions require the administrator to initiate accounting by running the scripts in `/usr/lib/acct` from `cron`.

BSD versions commonly use the `syslog` daemon to deliver error, information, and status messages for a number of daemons. The destinations for these messages are determined by entries in `/etc/syslog.conf`.

5.4.4.4 Error Reports

`syslog` may log the error reports and boot messages, or that work may be done in a vendor-specific manner. The error file produced tells what devices were recognized at the last boot, what `panic` message accompanied the crash, and various operational warnings, such as full file system messages. The messages can be the first warning of failing hardware or other imminent problems, so they are worth reviewing at least weekly.

5.4.5 Software Upgrades

Nothing is static in the computer industry, and before long your well installed, carefully monitored systems have out of date operating systems. Operating system vendors release new versions fairly frequently. The new system may offer new features, correct bugs, support new hardware, or some combination of these. Operating system updates are organized around major releases in which significant new functionality is added. In contrast, some updates are considered to be minor or *patch* releases. These usually contain bug fixes and security patches, but may also introduce new hardware support. Refer to your vendor's documentation for their naming standards.

Major operating system releases are distributed to be applied to an empty disk, as you might do with a new machine. Some vendors also provide upgrade distributions to install the major releases. With an upgrade distribution, it is possible to upgrade from, say, 2.1 to 2.2 without losing all of your existing configuration. Minor operating system upgrades are normally distributed as upgrade distributions only, but may occasionally appear as complete installations as well.

The timeliness with which you apply the upgrade, and in fact whether you apply it at all, are up to your individual site. If your machine has devices that aren't supported by the workstation vendor, you may have to wait until the device manufacturer has a compatible driver. If your users demand the latest versions for their work, upgrades need to be performed as soon as all the required elements are available. If, on the other hand, your organization values stability over new features, you should consider installing only well-tested upgrades, ones that have been released for several months. During that time, the vendor support staff will have been trained on it, and any serious problems may have been discussed on network news-groups.

It is not necessary to apply every minor operating system upgrade. If the benefit to your site is less than the time and expense to upgrade, it is possible to omit an upgrade. Indeed, if your organization does not have a support contract, it may be cost prohibitive to apply every one. The major drawback in remaining with an older version is that the vendor's phone support may be unavailable, or at least unhelpful, if you don't have the latest version. Your site will also not be able to utilize any new hardware introduced with that release. There is also the possibility that you may have to apply the upgrade later, if the vendor releases a new version that is based on the release you omitted.

Major version upgrades require substantial organization and time. In preparation for the upgrade, take full backups of the machine. All of / and /usr will definitely be overwritten, and other partitions on those disks may be affected. If a customization script has been maintained from the time the machine was first installed, you can predict what files will need to be reinstalled to customize the newly upgraded systems. By saving those files to a single directory and putting them on a separate tape, they will be available for quick retrieval after the upgrade. The final preparation step is to read the upgrade documentation and make sure all the media are present.

The choice of time for the upgrade depends on the requirements of the user community. Most sites do major systems work only at off-shift times such as weekends or evenings. Risky work shouldn't be undertaken on Friday afternoon if you have weekend workers, since they may not be able to reach you to solve problems that arise. You need to be cognizant of the various project deadlines to avoid changing the environment just before a major release or demonstration. Once chosen, the upgrade date should be proposed to the user community to flush out any unforeseen conflicts.

The actual upgrade is done according to the vendor instructions. Then either the local customization script is run or similar steps done by hand to mount all the file systems, set up networking, etc., as was done in the initial installation. If possible, this upgrade should be done first on a machine that is not critical to the users, so the upgrade can be fully tested before installing on production machines. After the upgrade, users should be notified of any changes they need to adapt to, and local documentation must also be brought up to date. Finally, the local customization script should be fine-tuned to reflect any differences found with the new operating system version.

Upgrading layered products is simpler than upgrading the operating system. You should install or compile the new version in a separate location from the old one. When this is fully tested, it can be put in the correct place in the system directories. Save the old version under a different name so users can continue to work in the case that problems develop with the new version. You should notify the users of the upgrade so they can take advantage of new features.

Occasionally the efforts of the vendor to make layered product installation simple compete with administrative desires to maintain an older version as a fallback position. In order to put all parts of a software package in the correct locations, the vendor installation script often assumes it can write over whatever was in those locations before. In addition, the vendor's binary may include exact pathnames. Getting around the "hard-wired" locations in a vendor's script sometimes takes ingenuity, and occasionally it is necessary to abandon the ideals of always maintaining a proven version.

5.4.6 Software Errors

All operating systems and all but the simplest software packages have some errors in them. These bugs vary in severity from trivial to critical. As problems are discovered, you will be called upon to correct those that can be fixed.

As radical as it may sound, some bugs will not be worth correcting. Given the limited system administrator resources that most sites employ, those resources must be used wisely. In some cases, a simple workaround can be found for the problem. In others, the bug has to remain unfixed because of other demands on the administrator's time.

For more severe problems, you must either fix the problem yourself or marshal other resources to do so. If your site has the source for the program in question, a repair can be attempted. In the equally likely case that no source is available, the software vendor may be able to help.

The amount of help will often depend on an existing support contract. Most vendors offer at least one software support contract option. This may cover 24-hour phone assistance and all future updates, 9-to-5 support, or it may simply be a mailing address to report bugs, with the promise of "best effort" assistance. Phone support contracts are helpful to the new administrator, and may be worth the money for the site's first UNIX machine. This issue of support should be considered at machine purchase time, as support availability may factor into the choice of a machine vendor.

If a software problem has your site at a complete standstill, and you don't have a support contract, you may still be able to get help from the vendor. For such emergencies, the vendor's sales organization can sometimes set up the needed communications with the technical support staff. The likelihood of such a repair depends on the particular vendor, the severity of the problem, and past relationship between the site and the vendor. If an element is that critical to your site, a support contract is probably worth the money.

Other sites may have faced whatever problem you've encountered and may be able to suggest a fix or workaround for the problem. The network newsgroups and local UNIX user groups are possible places to look for a solution. Many newsgroups have a *Frequently Asked Questions* article that appears monthly, covering common problems and solutions. Newsgroups that end in .answers, such as comp.answers, contain many of the Frequently Asked Questions articles for newsgroups within their hierarchy. If, after reading all the available documentation and exhausting whatever other resources are available, you still can't solve the problem, you can submit an article describing the problem and your specific software environment to the appropriate newsgroup. You will probably get some suggestions, but if you post a trivial question that is easily found in the manuals, some of the responses won't be too charitable. Do your homework first, and post only as a last resort.

5.4.7   Managing a Large Installation

Over time, many sites grow from a single machine to dozens or even hundreds. This scaling-up process can be difficult, particularly when the support staff does not grow at the same time. There are several different philosophies for administering large sites.

When there are only a handful of machines, the traditional PC model of management suffices. Each machine is separately installed, upgraded, and maintained. The machines differ according to the needs of their users. This individuality is difficult to maintain as the number of machines grows, unless staffing is increased with the machines.

Sites with limited staff and tens of machines may adopt a generalized machine plan. Each workstation is, with respect to software, equally capable. Machines may differ in monitor, memory, or available disk space, but the functions made available in the operating system configuration are identical. These machines are simpler to upgrade, as a single template will suffice for the operating system files. User files may be on the workstation, which is more time-consuming to administer, or they may be centralized on a file server and supplied to the workstation through a distributed file system like NFS.

Workstations with their operating systems on the local disk and user files on a file server are quite common, but sites with many machines may take this a step further. At those sites, workstation clients with only root and swap on the local disk get /usr and user files from a file server. Booting and basic utilities are available on the local machine, but all other files are provided through the distributed file system. This reduces the number of /usr directories that must be updated when a binary is replaced. Unless this configuration is explicitly supported by your vendor, you may need to modify the client rc startup scripts to make this work.

The extremes of this client/server arrangement are the dataless and diskless clients. Dataless clients boot and receive all files from their server, though swap space and sometimes /tmp is on the local disk. Diskless clients must swap over the network, which can put a significant burden on the local network. Dataless configurations may be appropriate for large, severely understaffed sites. Not all versions of UNIX support dataless and diskless clients.

Each version of UNIX supported is an additional burden for the support organization. It is significantly easier to manage 30 machines of one architecture running the same operating system than it is to manage 10 workstations of three different architectures. As you can see from this chapter, the system administration of UNIX versions differs, sometimes significantly. Knowing one version well will assist in learning a second and third, but does not eliminate the learning step. The fewer variants a small staff has to support, the more effective they will be. On the basis of this, some large UNIX sites will limit the types of machines they own. Instead of buying the latest, one-of-a-kind machine, they will concentrate on getting more from their fleet, either by tuning or site-wide upgrades.

There are also software utilities that make administering large sites easier. Project Athena at MIT developed a number of tools such as Hesiod (network name server) and Kerberos (distributed authentication server). Sun's Network Information Service allows a single, master password file for multiple machines. The distributed file systems AFS and DES can be used both for account control and file system services. Backups of an entire site can be done from a central location using a variety of commercial packages. System binaries on different machines can be kept synchronized by `rdist` and other utilities. All of these reduce the management required for additional machines.

5.4.8   Emergency Procedures

At times, the problems you face will be greater than just software bugs. A critical machine may go down just before a major deadline, and diagnosis and correction will have to be done under great pressure. Disaster recovery and emergency repairs require all of an administrator's knowledge and ingenuity. No book, and certainly no chapter, can hope to cover the range of problems and solutions an administrator will face. Here, instead, are a few types of problems and standard solutions. Experience is the best teacher on this topic.

First, a few words of caution. If you are faced with a serious problem you've never handled before, get help before trying a solution that is in any way destructive. Help in emergencies may come from a coworker, vendor support organization, or other administrators in your area. You will learn a lot and will avoid getting yourself into a more serious situation.

An important component to disaster recovery is a complete set of backups. The individual files are extremely valuable to your organization. Disk drives can and do fail, and their files need to be restored. Many sites keep their backups off-site so they are not damaged in any disaster that eliminates the main computer room, such as fire, tornado, or earthquake. Computers and peripherals can be rented if there is substantial hardware damage, but it could take years to reproduce all the files.

A common emergency is a machine that won't boot. The fundamental question to answer is whether it is a hardware problem or a software one. That's not always easy to determine, so the administrator either needs some basic hardware knowledge or the help of a hardware technician.

Once you've found the problem to be hardware, the simplest approach is the part swap. Take a working machine with similar hardware and switch only the suspect part—CPU, memory, monitor, and so on. By moving only one part at a time, the defective component can be determined.

An alternative is running the vendor-supplied diagnostics, if any are available. These range from user-friendly utilities to cryptic tools only the vendor's hardware support staff can understand. If you have neither a similar machine for a part swap nor a maintenance contract, these may be the only sources of information.

When you suffer a hardware failure, there may be software steps that will regain some of the lost functions of that hardware. If a disk drive fails on a workstation, for example, it may be possible to reconfigure the machine to receive /, /usr, and swap over the network. While this is not an ideal configuration, it does keep the workstation functioning until the repaired disk can arrive. If a disk drive on the server fails, the administrator can reconfigure existing disk space, moving files to tape if necessary. Files from the damaged disk can then be reloaded from the last backup.

If a machine will not boot into multiuser mode while the hardware appears to be operating normally, some portion of the operating system has been damaged. The kernel may have been corrupted, critical binaries may have been lost, the root file system may have been damaged, or some program in the startup scripts may be hanging. There are two major strategies for restoring the machine to service. If the machine completes the probe routines and begins to run the startup scripts, it should be possible to boot it to single-user mode using the root partition on disk. The single-user shell runs on the system console with the permissions of the account root. Once the machine is in single-user mode, the administrator can remove the sections of the startup script that are causing problems, and boot to multiuser mode. Work would still remain to debug the problem with the startup script, but the users could have most functionality back while the diagnosis proceeds.

If the boot does not start, or aborts before the startup scripts begin, the machine may be incapable of a single-user boot. The administrator needs to provide it a kernel and root partition from another source. This is not unlike what is done when the machine is first installed, when a small operating system is read off tape or CD-ROM into the swap space or memory and used to build the true root partition on disk. The miniroot boot process usually presents a menu from which you can select either a machine installation or a single-user shell you can use for maintenance activities. Once you are in the shell, devices for the root partition can be created in the miniroot's /dev, and the root partition on disk can be mounted on a mount point in the miniroot. You can modify the system's root partition because the operating system is running off the miniroot only. The source of the problem, perhaps a corrupt kernel or missing /bin directory, can be corrected. In an environment with workstation clients and servers, another mechanism for booting a disabled machine is to set it up temporarily as a diskless client of one server. Once booted off the network, its disks can be mounted and modified.

5.5   User Support

Everything an administrator does supports the user community at least indirectly. System administration includes direct user support as well. Administrators must answer questions, investigate problems, train new users, and obtain software and hardware to fulfill user needs. To support the users, you must know their level of knowledge about the computing systems, and what they are trying to accomplish on the systems. Some groups will require much leading and training, while others will outstrip the administrator in finding and mastering the latest products. Knowing what kind of help they need will determine how to structure the support.

No two UNIX sites are identical. A certain amount of locally written documentation is needed for the users. This includes machine locations, security policies, local software paths, printer rooms, and disk space policies. More technical topics, such as using particular software packages or customizing a .login, can be covered depending on the users' needs. If you find yourself answering the same question many times, it's a likely candidate for your local documentation.

Users can get help on problems either by approaching the administrators directly, or by asking whoever is on call at the particular time. The advantage of direct contact is that the most competent people are there to solve the user problem quickly. The difficulty is that the administrators lack quiet time to accomplish tasks requiring concentration, and jobs can easily be overlooked in the turmoil of a busy day. Most large sites employ a *help desk* model, where junior staff members answer user questions as well as they can, but log work requests for anything beyond their abilities. The most frequent user complaint about help desk organizations is the length of time it takes to solve a problem. Neither of these is ideal; each site must develop a support plan appropriate to the available staff and the needs of their users.

Good communications between the user and administrators are crucial. System maintenance activities can be disruptive to the users, so schedules should be well publicized. Electronic news, bulletin board notices, and memoranda are all possible ways to get the message across. By keeping users advised of progress on existing problems, they can see that efforts are being made to improve the situation. This by itself can improve the relationship of users and support staff. Many sites actively solicit the opinions of their users before making major decisions involving the computing environment.

The system administrator participates in or is completely responsible for the formulation of hardware and software plans for the future. As the organization expands, computer facilities need to keep pace. The administrator must be ready to specify what additional purchases must be made to handle growth or reorganization in the group.

Because of the system monitoring portion of the job, the administrator is qualified to influence hardware purchases. Organizations have a limited hardware budget, and bottlenecks must be targeted and removed with only those resources. If the organization has enough machines for its staff, buying more memory to reduce swapping is more effective than purchasing another machine. With today's modular machines, it is simple to replace a slow disk with a fast one, add memory, and in some cases even upgrade the CPU.

The computer industry is constantly changing, with new hardware and software products appearing daily. It is important to stay aware of the major industry trends, so planning and purchases can reflect what the site really needs. New machines or upgrades to existing machines are constantly being introduced. Operating system technologies change, and you may find yourself with a choice of operating systems to run on a particular platform. Important layered products in the areas of graphical interfaces, compilers, and file systems are released. All these areas have to be considered in your planning. The trade press and network newsgroups are excellent sources for operating system and layered product information.

5.6 Conclusion

This brief discussion of system administration gives a survey of the responsibilities of a UNIX administrator. There are a number of resources that will provide you more information. As you install and maintain your UNIX machine, your primary reference should be the operating system manuals. Each vendor adds some features to the UNIX operating system, so there is no substitute for a complete set of manuals, either printed or on CD-ROM.

In concentrating on how to accomplish specific tasks, the manuals rarely address the larger issues of UNIX administration. They will show you how to execute the backup command, but not what media to use, what sequence of incremental dumps to run, etc. A good source for some of these configuration topics is *UNIX System Administration Handbook* by Nemeth, Snyder, and Seebass.

USENIX and other UNIX conferences are excellent places to find out what other system administrators are doing. Many have faced the same problems that a new administrator will, and some elegant solutions have been found. Conferences offer exposure to current ideas, contact with fellow administrators, and often classes. In some areas, there are local UNIX user groups that sponsor talks and meetings. And if you are connected to the Internet, there are people all over the world discussing UNIX.

You've now seen the scope of the work of a UNIX system administrator. Unpack your manuals, uncrate the machine, and good luck!

5.7   Bibliography

The following books are useful resources for the system administrator.

A. Frisch, *Essential System Administration,* Sebastopol, CA: O'Reilly & Associates, 1991.

S. Garfinkel and G. Spafford, *Practical UNIX Security,* Sebastopol, CA: O'Reilly & Associates, 1991.

C. Hunt, *TCP/IP Network Administration*, Sebastopol, CA: O'Reilly & Associates, 1992.

M. Loukides, *System Performance Tuning*, Sebastopol, CA: O'Reilly & Associates, 1991.

E. Nemeth, G. Snyder, and S. Seebass, *UNIX System Administration Handbook*, Englewood Cliffs: Prentice Hall, 1989.

T. O'Reilly and G. Todino, *Managing UUCP and Usenet*, Sebastopol, CA: O'Reilly & Associates, 1988.

6

Customizing the UNIX User Environment

Stefan Gottschalk and Sue Stigleman

6.1 Why Customize?

You have a brand new UNIX account, or you have an old account, but you want to speed things up. One of the nice things about UNIX is that you can customize it: trim, stretch, and color it to suit yourself. Have your computer call you *master* and hang on your every word. Have an electronic mailperson notify you when electronic mail arrives. Energize your screen with fuschia and chartreuse windows, calm it with restful blue, or show your school spirit with the colors of your *alma mater.*

Customization is not just about whimsy or ease of use. It can also be essential for getting things done. For example, while writing this chapter, one of the authors wanted to print the man pages for the C shell. The pages printed with a number of words missing. After some exploration, it turns out that she needed to set an environment variable to specify the location of some page formatting macros. (Environment variables are one of the major tools for customization and are discussed at length later in this chapter.)

UNIX has a host of tools which can be mixed and matched to create an environment tailored to your own work habits and personality. A very cursory explanation of each of these tools would be sufficient to tell you how to customize your environment, but this chapter goes into somewhat more detail. We hope this will help UNIX users understand the system's behavior, help the programmers work *with* the system rather than in spite of it, and help the system administrator with trouble-shooting and administrative tasks.

6.2   Tools for Customizing

The main tools for customizing UNIX are:

- Shells
- Variables
- Aliases
- Programs, commands, and shell scripts
- Initialization files

Shells   Your interaction with a UNIX workstation is controlled by a program called the *shell*. The shell reads what you type in and executes the commands you request. There are several shells available, including the C, Bourne, Korn, and extended C shells. Although you will be assigned a default shell when your account is created, you can choose the shell you wish to use from those available on your system. (You could even write a shell of your own!) You can further customize a shell by setting environment and shell variables, using aliases, and creating initialization files.

Environment and shell variables   When you are logged onto a UNIX system, the shell maintains two sets of variables, one used solely by the shell and the other passed to the programs you run. By setting these variables, you control how your shell, your programs, and your workstation environment will behave.

Aliases   If you are using the C shell, you can give a nickname, or alias, to a command to make it easier and faster to use. Shorten lengthy command names or lengthen UNIX's short and cryptic names. Aliases are also used in electronic mail, saving you from having to remember long and awkward email addresses for your correspondents.

Programs, commands and shell scripts   A number of UNIX programs and commands can create a personalized UNIX world for you and your work. If you are expecting an important email message, run a program that notifies you immediately when mail arrives. If you want to keep track of the time, display a clock on your screen automatically each time you login. You can use the programming-like capability of the shells to create your own customized commands using shell scripts.

Initialization files   Aliases, programs, and shell and environment variable settings can all be stored in initialization files. Shells and many other programs read these files when they start, to determine their initial setup configuration.

6.2.1 Shells

The shell is your interface with the UNIX operating system. It handles a number of tasks for you: executing programs, managing variables that control your environment, and even functioning as a programming language.

6.2.1.1 The Shell as a Program Executor

The shell displays a prompt at which you issue commands. (The default prompt for the C shell is % and for the Bourne shell $. As we'll see later, you can change the prompt to suit your own needs.) When you want to do something like list the files in a directory, run an editor, or compile a program, you type the appropriate command. The shell in turn will execute the programs that carry out the task.

To examine the operation of the shell, consider the common UNIX command ls, which lists the files in a directory. When you type ls, the resulting list of files is not produced directly by the shell. Instead, the shell takes the ls, searches your path for an executable program called ls and if it finds one, asks the UNIX kernel, the heart of the UNIX operating system, to run it. Using the system call fork, the kernel creates a process which becomes the ls program. Each time you type ls, a new process is created to run ls and display the list of files you've asked for.

Meanwhile, the shell waits for the ls process to finish. When it is done, the shell prints out its prompt, telling you that the ls program has completed and the shell is ready for the next command.

6.2.1.2 The Shell as a Shell Variable and
Environment Variable Manager

Besides executing programs, the shell can also be used to set and alter the variables that control your work environment and the behavior of the shell. The shell maintains an environment, which it passes to each process it asks the kernel to create. The environment consists of a series of character strings, such as HOME=/usr/users/gottscha. These character strings, the environment variables, allow you to control aspects of the process's behavior, such as how it should expect your terminal to behave, where to find your home directory, and what printer to use. Shell variables are similar, but are used only by the shell. Environment and shell variables will be discussed in Sections 6.2.2, 6.2.3, and 6.2.4.

6.2.1.3   The Shell as a Programming Language

The common shells also have their own programming language with a variety of control structures. A few of the programming capabilities of the shell are often used in the `.cshrc`, `.login`, `.logout`, and `.profile` files, which are described later in the chapter. You can also create your own commands, simple or intricate, by writing shell scripts in the shell's own command language.

6.2.1.4   Choosing a Shell

The two most common shells are the Bourne shell (named after its author, Steve Bourne), and the C shell (written by Bill Joy and named for the C programming language.) The Bourne shell is the traditional one, present in almost all versions of UNIX. We recommend the C shell if available because it is easier to use and more tolerant of mistakes.

You'll be assigned a default shell when your account is created. The name of the shell is stored as the last field of your entry in the password file (usually `/etc/passwd`.) You can choose another shell from the ones listed in the file `/etc/shells` on your system. If you were assigned the Bourne shell and want to change your default to the C shell, type

```
$ chsh
Changing login shell for stigle
Shell []: /bin/csh
```

You will then be prompted for your password as a security measure.

For further information on your shell, see the appropriate online man pages.

6.2.2   Environment Variables

Environment variables store information about you and your work environment, such as the path of your home directory and the name of your preferred text editor. Environment variables are passed by the shell to any program the shell calls for you.

Although some environment variables are set for you automatically when you log in, several comands let you set and modify your environment variables. To list all of your environment variables, use the `printenv` command by itself:

```
% printenv
HOME=/usr/users/gottscha
SHELL=/bin/csh
TERM=xterm
```

```
USER=gottscha
PATH=/usr/ucb:/usr/bin:/bin:/etc:.
EDITOR=/usr/ucb/vi
TERMCAP=vs|xterm|vs100|xterm terminal emulator (X window
system):cr=^M:do=^J:nl=^J:bl=^G:le=^H:ho=\E[H:co#80
:li#65:cl=\E[H\E[2J:bs:am:cm=\E[%i%d;%dH:nd=\E[C:up=\E[A
:ce=\E[K:cd=\E[J:so=\E[7m:se=\E[m:us=\E[4m:ue=\E[m
:md=\E[1m:mr=\E[7m:me=\E[m:ku=\EOA:kd=\EOB:kr=\EOC
:kl=\EOD:kb=^H:k1=\EOP:k2=\EOQ:k3=\EOR:k4=\EOS:ta=^I
:pt:sf=\n:sr=\EM:al=\E[L:dl=\E[M:ic=\E[@:dc=\E[P:MT
:ks=\E[?1h:ke=\E[?1l:is=\E[r\E[m\E[2J\E[H\E[?7h\E[?1;3;4;6l
:rs=\E[r\E<\E[m\E[2J\E[H\E[?7h\E[?1;3;4;6l:xn
:AL=\E[%dL:DL=\E[%dM:IC=\E[%d@:DC=\E[%dP
:hs:ts=\E[?E\E[?%i%dT:fs=\E[?F:es:ds=\E[?E
```

(Don't be intimidated by the strange appearance of the TERMCAP variable. As we'll see in Section 6.5, it is usually set for you.)

To see the value of a single environment variable, use printenv with the name of the variable:

```
% printenv EDITOR
/usr/ucb/vi
```

(The EDITOR variable specifies the text editor you want to use to edit or create files within another program such as mail or readnews. EDITOR will be described further, later in this section.)

To set or change the value of an environment variable in the C shell, use setenv with the name of the variable and the desired value:

```
% setenv EDITOR /usr/ucb/emacs
% printenv EDITOR
/usr/ucb/emacs
```

If you are using the Bourne shell, creating an environment variable is a two-step process. First, create the variable by typing the variable name and its value, connected with an equal sign (with no spaces around the equal sign):

```
$ EDITOR=/usr/ucb/emacs
```

Then "connect" it to the environment by using the export command:

```
$ export EDITOR
```

To remove an environment variable in the C shell, use `unsetenv` with the name of the variable:

```
% unsetenv EDITOR
```

To remove an environment variable in the Bourne shell, set it to nothing:

```
$ EDITOR=
```

You can define any environment variable you like. If you want to define an environment variable called `MYVARIABLE`, you can do that:

```
% setenv MYVARIABLE "This is my variable"
```

As environment variables are created, they are stored in memory. A particular environment variable does not exist until it is set. If you have not set a value for `EDITOR`, the `EDITOR` variable isn't empty—it doesn't exist at all and will not appear in response to `printenv`.

To find information about which environment variables a particular program uses, check the program's man page. For example, the man page for the news reading program `rn` describes the 46 environment variables used by `rn`.

Some common environment variables are described in alphabetical order below. It would be impossible to include them all. New variables appear almost constantly as users and software producers create them. In addition, not all environment variables are supported on all versions of UNIX. The variables listed below are common to most versions of UNIX.

6.2.2.1   EDITOR/VISUAL *path*

The variables `EDITOR` and `VISUAL` are used in similar ways by various programs, so they are described together here. Historically, `EDITOR` refers to line editors (e.g., `ed`) and `VISUAL` to display-oriented, or full-screen editors (e.g., `vi`, `emacs`).

Some UNIX programs will invoke a text editor so you can create and edit files. Examples are `mail` (for writing and editing electronic mail messages) and `readnews` (for writing and editing news postings). These programs look at `EDITOR` or `VISUAL` to find which editor you prefer to use. Some programs look for the `VISUAL` variable first and then for `EDITOR` if `VISUAL` isn't found. Others look only for the `EDITOR` variable. If you don't specify an editor, programs will default to the editor specified in the man page for the program (usually `vi`).

Some common values for the EDITOR and VISUAL variables are ed, edit, ex, vi, and emacs. Use the whereis command to identify the correct full path for the editors you choose.

6.2.2.2 DISPLAY *host:display.screen*

The environment variable DISPLAY is used by programs in the X Window System, discussed further in Section 6.7. For example, the command

```
% setenv DISPLAY rosman:0.0
```

or in the Bourne shell,

```
$ DISPLAY=rosman:0.0
$ export DISPLAY
```

specifies that you are looking at the monitor (a.k.a. DISPLAY) on the computer rosman, that that monitor is the first or only monitor (:0) attached to rosman, that the screen is the first screen (.0) within the display, and that X programs should display their output on that screen.

6.2.2.3 EXINIT *command*

If you use vi, edit, or ex, you can store in EXINIT commands you want executed automatically when the editor starts. If you want line numbers on the screen while editing, you can put set nu in your EXINIT variable, using for the C shell

```
% setenv EXINIT "set nu"
```

and for the Bourne shell,

```
$ EXINIT="set nu"
$ export EXINIT
```

You can set or disable several options in one command. So if you want line numbers turned on (nu), autoindent turned off (noai), and tab stops set every 4 instead of 8 spaces (tabstop=4), you would set EXINIT thus in the C shell:

```
% setenv EXINIT "set nu noai tabstop=4"
```

6.2.2.4 HOME *path*

HOME contains the absolute pathname of your home directory. As you login, the login program asks for your username and password. The login process consults the system password file to verify that you have an account and that your password is correct. From the same file, login gets your home directory pathname, sets the HOME variable, and sets your current directory to your home directory.

The HOME variable is used by programs looking for initialization files, which are typically stored in your home directory. For example, the programs of mh, a message handler, look for the file $HOME/.mh_profile. The variable HOME is also used by programs that need to create files in a person's home directory. alex, one of the programs in the mh suite, creates alias files, which it attempts to place in $HOME/Mail/aliases.

6.2.2.5 MAIL *path*

The environment variable MAIL refers to the file where incoming mail is stored. As we will see in the section on customizing mail, this variable is used to determine when to notify you that mail has arrived.

6.2.2.6 PAGER *path*

A pager is a program that lets you look at files one screen at a time. The most common one is /usr/ucb/more.

6.2.2.7 PATH *path*

PATH is used for finding executable programs. Without the PATH variable, you would have to know the full path name for each program you want to run and type it each time you run the program. PATH contains a list of pathnames separated by colons. It is usually set to PATH=:/usr/ucb:/bin:usr/bin by login. You should expand it to include all of the directories containing software you use, a task normally done using the C shell variable path described in the next section.

6.2.2.8 PRINTER *string*

PRINTER is used by various printing-related programs like lpr (which prints files), lpq (which examines the print spool queue), and lprm (which removes jobs from the print queue). If the PRINTER variable is not present, these programs use the default printer for your system. PRINTER should contain the name of the printer you use most often. If you usually print on your office printer opie set that printer as your default by typing:

```
% setenv PRINTER opie
```

Then you can issue the `lpr` command and know that the printouts are going to `opie`. If you use more than one printer, you can always override the variable `PRINTER` for a particular print job with a parameter to the `lpr` command.

6.2.2.9   SHELL *path*

`SHELL` contains the path and name of the program which is your preferred shell. It is initially set by `login` to the value contained in the password file (usually `/etc/passwd`). `SHELL` is used by programs which allow *shell escapes*. For example, the command `:sh` in `vi` will take you temporarily out of `vi` to the shell so you can check a file name, read a mail message, or check the time without having to exit from `vi` and then start it again. `mail` and many other programs have the same facility, although the specific command to get to the shell will vary.

6.2.2.10   TERM *string*/TERMCAP *string*

`TERM` contains the name of the terminal the shell thinks you are using. `TERMCAP` stands for *terminal capabilities,* and as you might guess, contains a description of the capabilities of your terminal. `TERM` and `TERMCAP` are discussed further in Section 6.5.

6.2.2.11   USER *string*

This variable is set by the program `login` to contain your username. A few programs check this environment variable to find the username of the person who executed them. A common use is finding the files that contain incoming mail, usually `/usr/spool/mail/$USER`, where `$USER` is the username of the user. For example, the authors' mail would be stored in `/usr/spool/mail/gottscha` and `/usr/spool/mail/stigle`. (Notice that both authors have last names that are too long to be standard UNIX usernames, so their usernames are only part of their last names.)

For more information on how environment variables work, see the man pages for your shell and *Advanced Programming in the UNIX Environment* by Stevens. For further information on which environment variables the programs you run use, see the man pages for the specific programs.

6.2.3   C Shell Variables

C shell variables control the behavior of the C shell. They come in three types: string, numeric, and binary. String variables contain strings, such as a prompt or the name of your terminal type. Numeric variables contain numbers such as the number of command lines you want saved for possible recall. (These variables are really stored as strings, not as true numbers, but they are interpreted as numbers and you can do mathematical operations on them.) Binary variables are like light switches—they can be turned on and off.

Several C shell commands allow you to examine and modify the values of shell variables. The operations on C shell variables are similar to those on environment variables, but some of the specific commands are different. To list the values of all of your current C shell variables, use the `set` command:

```
% set
argv()
cdpath/usr/users/gottscha
cwd   /usr/users/gottscha/book
history 50
home /user/users/gottscha
ignoreeof
mail (600 /usr/spool/mail/gottscha)
path (/usr/ucb /usr/bin /bin /etc .)
prompt    louvre.cs.unc.edu>
shell    /bin/csh
status   0
term xterm
user gottscha
```

To see the value of a single variable, use the `echo` command and the variable name prefixed with a dollar sign:

```
% echo $term
xterm
```

To set or change the value of a string or numeric variable, use the `set` command with the name of the variable followed by an equal sign and the desired value:

```
% set prompt = Hello
% set history = 50
```

If the value of the variable contains any blank spaces, it must be surrounded by quotation marks:

```
%set prompt = "Yes, Master"
Yes, Master
```

You can set the value of a variable to a list of words by enclosing them in parentheses, as in

```
set path = ($HOME $HOME/bin /usr/ucb /bin)
```

To turn on a toggle variable, use the `set` command with the name of the variable:

```
% set ignoreeof
```

To remove a toggle variable, use the `unset` command with the name of the variable:

```
% unset ignoreeof
```

To define a new variable, use the `set` command with arguments:

```
% set firstname = stefan
```

Then you can `echo` its new value:

```
% echo $firstname
stefan
```

You can also use programs when creating and setting variables. The command

```
% set host = `hostname`
```

runs the program `hostname`, which returns the computer name, and then stores the name into a variable called `host`.

You may have noticed that the environment variables in Section 6.2.2 were in all uppercase letters, while the C shell variables we've seen are in all lowercase. This is not a requirement, but a useful convention which helps us remember which are environment variables and which are C shell variables. (To add to the confusion, Bourne shell variables are usually in uppercase.)

Later in this chapter, you will learn how to store C shell variable settings in an initialization file to save you from the effort of typing them in each time you log in.

Several common C shell variables are described below. As with environment variables, it is impossible to include them all, because users and software producers can create new ones.

6.2.3.1   argv

You may notice this variable when you use set to see all of your shell variables. argv refers to the arguments passed to the shell. It isn't used for customization.

6.2.3.2   cdpath = *path*

Use cdpath to store the directories that you want the shell to search when you issue a cd (change directory) command. If cdpath is not set when a cd command is issued, then the shell checks only subdirectories of the current directory. For example, watch this user trying to change into a directory called /usr/users/stigle/test/test2, two levels down from her present working directory:

```
% pwd
/usr/users/stigle
% cd test2
test2: No such file or directory
% set cdpath=/usr/users/stigle/test
% cd test2
%pwd
/usr/users/stigle/test/test2
```

Normally the cdpath is set to a directory or directories you will be visiting frequently. As with the PATH environment variable discussed in Section 6.2.2.7, multiple path names can be stored in the cdpath variable. Unlike PATH, you can put the current directory (.) first here.

6.2.3.3   cwd = *path*

cwd stands for *current working directory*. This shell variable is set automatically to a new current working directory whenever the cd command is used. However, $cwd, just like any other variable, can be set to whatever you like and will retain that value until you issue another cd command:

```
% cd /usr/bin
% echo $cwd
/usr/bin
% pwd
/usr/bin
% set cwd = "hi there"
% echo $cwd
hi there
% pwd
/usr/bin
% cd /etc
% echo $cwd
/etc
```

6.2.3.4 echo

The shell variable `echo` controls whether command input is echoed to the screen. For example, watch the display of the `date` command as `echo` is set and unset:

```
% set echo
% date
date
Sun Jan 17 15:53:15 EST 1993
% unset echo
unset echo
% date
 Sun Jan 17 15:53:24 EST 1993
```

6.2.3.5 filec

The variable `filec`, on some versions of UNIX, is needed to turn on file completion, in which pressing ESC fills out a partially typed command or filename.

6.2.3.6 histchars = string, history = n

The shell variables `history` and `histchars` and the command history are great timesavers. If `history` is set, the C shell saves commands as you type them. The number of commands saved is set by the shell `variable` history. The command `history` will list these saved commands in numerical order. To illustrate,

```
% set history = 4
% echo hi there
hi there
% echo lo there
lo there
% history
1   set history = 4
2   echo hi there
3   echo lo there
4   history
```

Saved commands can be reexecuted by using the `history` character, the exclamation point (`!`). (In UNIX, the exclamation point is often referred to as *bang*.) `!3` will be expanded to command number 3. Fragments of past commands can also be used. In the example above, `!d` will reexecute the `date` command. `!?4` would reexecute a command containing the string 4; so from the list above, it would repeat command number 1 (`set history = 4`). The `history` character can be used for commands relative to the current command by placing a negative number after the `history` character. `!-2` (bang minus 2), would execute the command two commands ago. To reexecute your last command, type `!!` (sometimes referred to as *double-bang*).

There is a second special `history` character: the carat (^). Commands of the form `^oldpattern^newpattern` will execute the previous command, except the substring `oldpattern` will be replaced by `newpattern`. For example,

```
% ls -l bio*
No match
% ^bio^bib
[list of files with names beginning with bib]
```

The bang and the carat are the default history characters. By typing

```
% set histchars = ',;'
```

you can tell the shell that you want the comma to do what the bang did above, and that the semicolon should perform the carat's duties.

6.2.3.7   home = *path*

Shell variables with certain names have special meanings to the C shell. The shell variables `home`, `path`, `user`, and `term` have a special property in common: they are tied to their respective environment variables (HOME, PATH, USER, TERM). If you change the value of one of the pair, the value of the other changes to match it. For example,

```
% setenv HOME house
% echo $HOME
house
% echo $home
  house
  % set home = garage
  % echo $home
garage
% echo $HOME
garage
```

This same process happens for the `path`/PATH, `user`/USER, and `term`/TERM pairs also.

6.2.3.8   ignoreeof

Setting `ignoreeof` prevents the C shell from accidently being killed by a ^D. You would then use the `exit` or `logout` commands to leave the shell.

6.2.3.9   mail = *path*

The shell variable `mail` specifies the file in which your incoming mail can be found. The C shell looks at the modification time of the file, and if it has changed since the last check, it will print the message *You have new mail* just before presenting a prompt.

The C shell checks for mail every 5 or 10 minutes, depending on your specific operating system, but you can change this by making the first word in the variable a number representing how often in seconds you want the shell to check the mail files. For example,

```
% set mail = (600 /usr/spool/mail/gottscha)
```

causes the shell to check the file `/usr/spool/mail/gottscha` every 10 minutes.

The program `biff` (discussed in Section 6.6.2) is another way of being notified when mail arrives.

6.2.3.10   noclobber

The shell variable `noclobber` is a safety feature. When `noclobber` is set, you'll get an error message if you try to overwrite an existing file when using I/O redirection. When it is not set, redirection will overwrite the file. For example,

```
% unset noclobber
% date > f
% cat f
Sun Oct 20 02:04:12 EST 1991
% set noclobber
% date > f
f: File exists.
```

This demonstrates that while `noclobber` was set, the redirection > into the file `f` failed, and the file was left unchanged.

6.2.3.11   noglob

If this variable is defined, the shell will refrain from "globbing." If you are not familiar with this term, then an explanation is in order.

Several characters (? * [{ ~) have special meanings when you use them in commands. The wildcard character ? will match any single character. For example, suppose you have six files in your current directory: a1, a2, a3, b1, b2, and c1. If you do an ls command, you will see

```
% ls
a1
a2
a3
b1
b2
c1
```

If you wish to see all of the files which start with the letter a followed by any single character, you can type

```
% ls a?
a1
a2
a3
```

If noglob is not set, the ls a? is expanded into ls a1 a2 a3 before being executed by the shell. The ls program never sees the question mark; it receives three parameters, a1, a2, and a3. Similarly, the parameter ?2 would get expanded into a2 b2.

The asterisk will match any sequence of characters. So * by itself will match everything in the directory and ab* would match any file whose name begins with ab.

The ? and * are the most common globbing characters. [] and {} are used for grouping characters to be matched. [aA]* would match all files beginning with either a or A. The tilde (~) is a shorthand way of referring to a user's home directory. For example, if you wanted to change to the home directory of user benites, you could type:

```
% cd ~benites
% pwd
/usr/users/benites
```

This feature, pattern matching on filenames, is called *globbing*. It is generally very useful, but occasionally it is a hindrance, particularly if you try to type a command that has the characters ? or * in it! For an example of this, see Section 6.5 where globbing must be turned off in order to set the TERMCAP variable with a value that has question marks in it.

6.2.3.12   notify

If `notify` is set, the shell will interrupt what you are doing to notify you when background jobs finish, rather than waiting until the next time it prints a prompt.

6.2.3.13   path = (*path path* ...)

Choose your own paths for searching for executable files by setting the `path` variable to a set of directories separated by spaces. Be sure to put the period (.) for checking the current directory last in the list. Having it first makes you vulnerable to malicious programs and security break-ins. If you have superuser privileges, don't put . in the `path` at all. `path` is automatically linked to the environment variable PATH.

6.2.3.14   prompt = *string*

Whatever is in this variable gets printed as the shell's prompt to you. Thus,

```
% set prompt = "your command, O gracious master: "
 your command, O gracious master:
```

Note that the second line is not merely the value of `$prompt` getting printed out (as if we used an `echo` command). Rather, it *is* the new prompt.

You can set your prompt to the output of a UNIX command by putting the command in single back quotes. For example, typing:

```
% set prompt = "`hostname`> "
hominy.cs.unca.edu>
```

will set your prompt to the name of the host you are connected to, a useful prompt for people who work on more than one system.

The shell keeps track of how many commands you have executed. It does this so that you can call up your commands by number, if you like (as discussed in Section 6.2.3.6). If you want the number of the next command to be printed in the prompt, you can include an ! in your prompt string:

```
% set prompt = "enter your \!th command: "
enter your 45th command:
```

Note that we place a backslash \ before the !, which has a special meaning to the shell: to make sure that the ! is not interpreted until the prompt is printed.

6.2.3.15   savehist = *n*

savehist sets the number of items in the history list that you want to have saved in the file $HOME/.history when you logout, thereby saving them from one login session to another.

6.2.3.16   shell = *path*

The variable shell contains the path and name of the shell file. See the environment variable SHELL.

6.2.3.17   status

status contains the exit status of the last command. You will see it in your list of shell variables, but like argv, it is not used for customizing.

6.2.3.18   term = *string*

This is automatically linked to the environment variable TERM.

6.2.3.19   time = *n*

If time is set, then any command that takes more than the specified number of cpu seconds will print a line giving time and utilization information when it terminates. For example,

```
% set time=0
% date
Sun Jan 17 17:28:05 EST 1993
0.0u 0.0s 0:00 66% 100+54k 0+1io 0pf+0w
% set time=1
% date
Sun Jan 17 17:28:56 EST 1993
```

The time isn't printed out for the second date command because it took less than 1 cpu second.

6.2.3.20   user = *string*

This is automatically linked to the environment variable USER.

6.2.3.21   verbose

The shell variable verbose causes the words of each command to be printed after a history substitution.

For more information on C shell variables, see the online man page.

6.2.4 Bourne Shell Variables

As with the C shell and its variables, Bourne shell variables control
the behavior of the Bourne shell. Several Bourne shell commands
allow you to examine and modify the values of shell variables. These
operations are similar to those we've already seen for environment
and C shell variables. To list the values of all of your current Bourne
shell variables, use the set command:

```
$ set
DISPLAY=:0.0
EXINIT=set redraw wm=8
HOME=/usr/users/stigle
IFS=
MAIL=/usr/spool/mail/stigle
PATH=/usr/users/stigle/bin:/usr/ucb:/bin:/usr/bin:/usr/etc:
/usr/local/X11R2/bin:/usr/bin/X11:/usr/local/bin:
/usr/local/hacks/bin:/usr/new:
.PS1=$
PS2=>
SHELL=/bin/csh
TERM=vt100
TERMCAP=vs|xterm|vs100|xterm terminal emulator (X window
system):cr=^M:do=^J:nl=^J:bl=^G:le=^H:ho=\E[H:co#80
:li#65:cl=\E[H\E[2J:bs:am:cm=\E[%i%d;%dH:nd=\E[C:up=\E[A
:ce=\E[K:cd=\E[J:so=\E[7m:se=\E[m:us=\E[4m:ue=\E[m
:md=\E[1m:mr=\E[7m:me=\E[m:ku=\EOA:kd=\EOB:kr=\EOC
:kl=\EOD:kb=^H:k1=\EOP:k2=\EOQ:k3=\EOR:k4=\EOS:ta=^I
:pt:sf=\n:sr=\EM:al=\E[L:dl=\E[M:ic=\E[@:dc=\E[P:MT
:ks=\E[?1h:ke=\E[?1l:is=\E[r\E[m\E[2J\E[H\E[?7h\E[?1;3;4;61
:rs=\E[r\E<\E[m\E[2J\E[H\E[?7h\E[?1;3;4;61:xn
:AL=\E[%dL:DL=\E[%dM:IC=\E[%d@:DC=\E[%dP
:hs:ts=\E[?E\E[?%i%dT:fs=\E[?F:es:ds=\E[?E
```

(You'll see your environment variables in this list also.)

To see the value of a single variable, use the echo command and the
variable name prefixed with a dollar sign:

```
? echo $PS1
$
```

To set or change the value of a variable, type the name of the variable followed by an equal sign and the desired value:

```
$ PS1=MyPrompt:
MyPrompt:
```

Many Bourne shell variables are the same as their C shell counterparts. Three common variables unique to the Bourne shell are IFS, PS1, and PS2.

6.2.4.1   IFS *string*

IFS stands for *internal field separator,* which tells the shell what characters to use to parse commands into the appropriate pieces. It is usually set to space, tab, and newline.

6.2.4.2   PS1 *string* and PS2 *string*

PS1 holds the primary Bourne shell prompt, and PS2 the prompt for a continuation line.

6.2.5   Aliases

UNIX comes in for a fair amount of criticism because its commands are cryptic, and for the uninitiated, hard to remember. "Surely there must be a copy command," you say as you struggle unsuccessfully to copy a file using the word *copy.* Eventually, you discover that the UNIX copy command is just cp. If it helps to understand why UNIX is so pithy, here's a bit of history from *The Little Gray Book: An Ultrix Primer* (p. 7-1):

> When the UNIX system was invented, there were no television-like terminals. Computers and users communicated through teletypewriters, which printed infuriatingly slowly. For this reason, UNIX commands were designed to print as little as possible and thereby speed up interactions.
>
> This philosophy of "speak softly, then shut up" did not change when the need for it disappeared. The result is a terse, sometimes cryptic user interface. The good news is that you can change it to suit you.

Let's look at that last sentence again: "The good news is that you can change it to suit you." If you are a C shell user, one very helpful change is to use aliases to rename commands into forms that are easier for you to remember. For example, the command

```
% alias copy cp
```

will rename the UNIX cp command to copy for you. The command

```
% alias dir ls
```

will let you use the UNIX ls command by typing dir instead. This particular alias is useful for MS-DOS users accustomed to typing dir to see a list of files. Other useful aliases for MS-DOS users are

```
% alias move mv
% alias delete rm
% alias type more
```

One of the authors created the alias

```
% alias loogut logout
```

which compensates for her frequent misspelling of the `logout` command.

UNIX neophytes often forget how to get online help. The `man` command will display online manual pages for a command, but the word `man` is not usually thought of as a synonym for help. If you would prefer to use the word `help`, set up the following alias:

```
% alias help man
```

Once you become comfortable in UNIX, you may decide you like terse commands and create aliases to shorten command names:

```
% alias h history
% alias g gnuemacs
% alias e emacs
% alias gmake gnumake
```

Aliases can be used to store standard options or arguments for commands. Another alias using the `ls` command is

```
% alias ls 'ls -l'
```

This alias resets the meaning of `ls` to the long form (`-l`) of the `ls` command, which gives a more informative list of files. The alias

```
% alias mag "magic -d X11"
```

lets you call the program `magic` with a default library (`X11`) by typing only one word.

Aliases can get quite elaborate. The alias

```
% alias report "vi reportfile; nroff -ms reportfile | lpr"
```

starts `vi` so you can edit the file `reportfile`. After you finish `vi`, the alias will run `nroff` (a text formatter) and then print the output.

Aliases can use other features of the C shell, such as shell variables and history characters. The following alias changes the prompt to display your current directory and prompt for the next command number:

```
% alias cd 'cd \!*;set prompt="`pwd`>"'
% cd /usr/users/benites
/usr/users/benites>
```

The outer layer of the alias changes the `cd` command to everything within the single quotes (i.e., cd \!*;set prompt="`pwd`>"'). The fragment `cd \!*` will call the `cd` command and pass to it the directory you asked to change to (in this case /usr/users/benites). The final fragment, set prompt="`pwd`>" uses the command pwd to reset the prompt. As you see, the final result is a prompt that shows your current directory.

Aliasing can be addicting. Once you start, you'll find more and more ways to save time and reduce typing errors by creating aliases.

6.2.6   Programs, Commands, and Shell Scripts

Even greater customization can be obtained by running various UNIX programs and commands. Several specific commands will be discussed later in the chapter, but here is an example: umask. In Section 6.3, we'll see how we can put this command into a file called .login so it is run every time you log in, safeguarding your files without you having to remember it.

UNIX is a very open environment. The default on many systems is for your files to be readable by other users. Each of your files has three types of permissions for the three types of users—you, the file's group owner, and everyone else. For each type of user, there are three types of permissions—read, write, and execute. If you wish to set your own default file permissions, you can use the umask command. Here are two sample umask values:

```
umask 022    gives user read, write, execute;
             gives group and others read and execute
umask 077    gives no access to group or others
```

The umask *subtracts* permissions from the default permissions, which are usually 666 for ordinary files and 777 for directories and executable files. Each digit represents the addition of three possible values: 4 for read, 2 for write, and 1 for execute permissions. For example, if you subtract the umask value 027 from the default 777, the result is 750, which represents all permissions for the user (first digit), read and execute permissions for the group (second digit), and no permissions for other (third digit).

Files created in the future will have their permissions set according to the umask value. (The command chmod is used to change the permissions for existing files.)

Other commands for customizing particular functions will be discussed in later sections.

A related mechanism for customizing is the shell script. These are programs, similar in some ways to MS-DOS batch files. Shell scripts can get quite elaborate. Here's a fairly simple example:

```
#!/bin/csh
cat $1 | mail $2
```

Once you create this simple two-line file and save it under the name mailfile, make it executable by typing

```
% chmod +x mailfile
```

Then you can use this new command, mailfile, by typing something like

```
% mailfile chap3 brock@cs.unca.edu
```

which will send the file chap3 to the user brock@cs.unca.edu. The $1 in the script refers to the first argument following the script name, which is the name of the file, and the $2 refers to the second argument, brock@cs.unca.edu. These arguments are passed to the shell script and used in its execution.

6.2.7   Initialization Files

In the UNIX world, many programs look in your home directory for initialization files when they start. By convention, these files' names begin with a period. To see a list of the ones you have, type

```
% ls -a
```

while in your home directory. (You'll see a list of all of your files, not just the ones that start with a period.)

To display the contents of one on the screen, use the more command. For example, to see your C shell initialization file, type:

```
% more .cshrc
```

You can create and edit initialization files using an editor such as `vi` or `emacs`. Some of the most common initialization files and their uses are

- `.login`   Login settings
- `.cshrc`   C shell initialization
- `.logout`   Executed at logout time
- `.profile`   Bourne shell initialization
- `.mailrc`   Berkeley mail
- `.forward`   Forward email to another address
- `.twmrc`   `twm` window manager
- `.Xdefaults` X Window
- `.newsrc`   News file
- `.emacs`   `emacs` initialization
- `.rhosts`   Allow permission for remote login without password

For information about initialization files used by particular programs, see the man pages for those programs.

6.3   Customizing Your Environment Using the C Shell

A new C shell starts with no aliases and only a few predefined environment variables. In order to use your personalized aliases and variable settings, you have to make the C shell execute a series of `alias`, `set`, and `setenv` commands.

It would be impractical if you had to type these commands yourself, one by one, at the beginning of each session. Fortunately, when the C shell starts, the first thing it does is read the file `.cshrc` (sometimes pronounced *dot-SEE-shark*) from your home directory and executes the commands it finds there. You can place a number of `alias`, `set`, and `setenv` commands in the `.cshrc` file, along with other commands and programs.

This process of executing commands from a file is called *sourcing* the file. Two other files are sourced by the C shell: `.login` and `.logout`. The file `.login` is sourced at startup, just after `.cshrc` is sourced, and `.logout` is sourced just before the shell exits. All three files, `.cshrc`, `.login`, and `.logout`, are normally kept in your home directory.

When you login, the system starts a C shell and tells it to behave as a login shell. This shell then knows to source .cshrc, .login, and .logout as described above. Since the C shell is just a program like any other, it can be executed from the existing C shell. Doing so will cause a new C shell process to be run but *not* as a login shell. This new C shell sources only the .cshrc, and neither .login nor .logout.

Why make the distinction between login shells and nonlogin shells? Generally, you will want most customizing commands to be executed by all your shells, whether they are login shells or not. However, there may be certain commands which you want to execute only once during your session, even if you start multiple shells during that session. Typically, such commands concern terminal settings, discussed in Section 6.5, modifying special files, or changing file permissions. These commands would be put in your .login file.

As we've said, these three files, .login, .cshrc, and .logout can contain variables, commands, and aliases, as well as comments to document any unusual features. The files can be created or modified using an editor such as vi or emacs. Changes to .login won't be read (i.e., the file won't be sourced) until the next login. Changes to .cshrc will be sourced when the next shell is opened. To force the shell to source these files immediately, type

```
% source .login
% source .cshrc
```

Let's look at some sample files and see how the various elements of customization are used. The following .cshrc illustrates typical uses of this file: setting shell variables and aliases. The first line specifies that this is a C shell script. The lines prefixed with # are comments and are ignored by the shell:

```
#!/bin/csh # sample .cshrc #

# set ignoreeof to prevent a Control-D from killing the shell
set ignoreeof

# set to 50 the number of previous commands saved for recall
set history = 50

# determine the name of the computer you are on using the
# hostname command, strip of the last part of the name
# (.cs.unca.edu),
# and then use the remainder as your prompt
set host = `hostname` set host = `basename $host
.cs.unca.edu` set prompt = "$host> "
```

```
# notify you immediately when background jobs on done
set notify

# set up some aliases for common commands and programs
alias mag "magic -d X11"
alias cl "cd .; clear"
alias ll "ls -la | more"
alias h history
alias gmake gnumake
alias rn "/usr/local/bin/rn -i=1 -h -N -q"
alias 221 "lpq -Prbh221"
```

The following `.login` file illustrates some slightly more complex uses of a `.login` file. In addition to setting environment variables and running some programs, it has some conditional statements. The default printer is set based on which computer is being used, and mail is run automatically only if there is new mail:

```
#!/bin/csh
# sample .login for book
#

# set the paths you want searched for programs
set path=($HOME $HOME/bin /usr/ucb /bin /usr/bin /usr/etc \
/usr/bin/X11 /usr/local/bin /usr/local/hacks/bin /usr/new .)

# set the default file permissions for new files
umask 022

# turn on biff so you will be notified of incoming mail
biff y

# set your default editor
setenv EDITOR /usr/local/bin/emacs

# set your default printer based on host name
if ($host == ivy) then
  setenv PRINTER opie
endif
if ($host == enka) then
  setenv PRINTER auntbee
endif

#display who is on system
echo "${prompt}users";users
```

```
#check to see if have mail, and if so, start mail.
#the check for mail is done by creating environment and shell
#variables called MAIL and mail, and then checking to see if
#mail exists.
setenv MAIL /usr/spool/mail/$USER
set mail = $MAIL
if (-e $mail) then
  echo "${prompt} mail"
  mail
endif
```

.logout files are not nearly as common as .login, but one good use for this file is cleaning up after yourself when disk space is limited. For example, the Digital Equipment Corporation's version of PHIGS creates 8-megabtye executable files. A class of 30 students creating these files will rapidly fill up all available disk space. If each PHIGS student has the following .logout, those mammoth executables will be deleted automatically each time the student logs out:

```
# sample .logout
#
#clean up PHIGS executables
find ~/graphics -type f -size +15000 -exec rm {} \;
```

This .logout consists of a find command, which looks in the student's graphics directory (~/graphics) for files (-type f) larger than 15,000 blocks, which is approximately eight megabytes (-size +15000), and then removes them (-exec rm {} \;).

6.4   Bourne Shell Initalization

The Bourne shell is initalized in a way similar to the C shell, but it reads the file .profile, rather than .cshrc and .login. The primary purpose of .profile is to set shell and environment variables. Aliases can't be used in the Bourne shell, although shell scripts can serve the same role.

6.5   Terminal Initialization

A terminal, to the inexperienced eye, is a relatively uninteresting object that lets you talk to the really interesting machine, the computer. The experienced eye sees terminals as a field of land mines in the user interface. In order for a terminal to relay information successfully from you to the computer and back, the computer has to know how to talk to and listen to the terminal. In UNIX, this understanding is accomplished using the commands tset, stty, and tty and the environment variables TERM and TERMCAP.

Many terminals are hardwired to the computer via a dedicated port called a tty (pronounced *TEE-TEE-WHY*), an abbreviation for teletype. When you log on, the program that handles the login process knows the tty port through which you are logging on, looks it up in the tty database (usually the file /etc/ttys) to find out what kind of terminal is connected to that port, and sets the environment variable TERM accordingly. It then looks up the terminal type in the terminal capabilities database (usually the file /etc/termcap) to find the terminal parameters (width, height, and so forth) and sets the TERMCAP. This login process then transforms itself into your shell, which inherits the environment variables TERM and TERMCAP, among others.

However, things get a little more complicated if you are connecting over a modem. In this case, there is no longer a one-to-one correspondence between the tty and the terminal type. You may dial in through your PC at home at times and connect from a Wyse 50 in your office at other times.

Because the operating system cannot be certain what kind of terminal is on the other end of the line, it usually associates the tty that a dialup line is connected to with generic terminal type names like plugboard, dialup, or unknown. The termcap database should have entries for these terminal types, which define very simple default behavior. Consider the termcap entry for dialup:

```
sd|du|dialup:co#80:os:am:
```

This specifies an 80-column terminal (co#80), with overstrike capability (os) and automatic margins (am—lines going off the right side scroll down one line and continue from the left)—in short, a *dumb* terminal. Otherwise, vi would not even know how to clear the screen or move the cursor correctly, and consequently would refuse to run in full-screen mode. More sophisticated terminals have entries ten times longer, detailing every capability, right down to whether the terminal is able to print the tilde character (~).

Fortunately, if you know what kind of terminal you are using, you can correctly set the environment variables TERM and TERMCAP yourself. There is no need for you to look up the entry for your terminal in the termcap database and enter a hideously long setenv command. This is automated by the tset (terminal set) command.

Executing tset -s will reinitialize your terminal and cause four C shell commands to be printed to stdout (standard output) and two lines to be printed to stderr (standard error). Here's the tset command with its output displayed on the screen:

```
% tset -s
set noglob;
setenv TERM vt100 ;
setenv TERMCAP
```

```
'd0|vt100|dec-vt100|vt100-am:cr=^M:do=^J:nl=^J:bl=^G:co#80:l
i#24:cl=50\E[;
H\E[2J:le=^H:bs:am:cm=5\E[%i%d;%dH:nd=2\E[C:up=2\E[A:ce=3\E[
K:cd=50\E[J:
so=2\E[7m:se=2\E[m:us=2\E[4m:ue=2\E[m:md=2\E[1m:mr=2\E[7m:mb
=2\E[5m:   me=2\E[m:is=\E[1;24r\E[24;1H:rf=/usr/lib/tab-
set/vt100:rs=\E>  \E[?3l\E[?4l\
E[?5l\E[?7h\E[?8h:ks=\E[?1h\E=:ke=\E[?1l\E>:ku=\EOA:kd=\EOB:
kr=\EOC:kl=
\EOD:kb=^H:ho=\E[H:k1=\EOP:k2=\EOQ:k3=\EOR:k4=\EOS:ta=^I:pt:
sr=5\EM:vt#3:x  n:sc=\E7:rc=\E8:cs=\E[%i%d;%dr:';
unset noglob;
Erase is Delete
Kill is Ctrl-U
```

(This example and the others in this section use C shell commands. For information on using `tset` within the Bourne shell, see the `tset` man page.)

The commands printed to `stdout` can be executed immediately using command substitution with the shell command `eval` or can be redirected to a file and sourced. Suppose, for example, that we have logged in through a modem from a PC emulating a vt100, but we find that our `TERM` variable is set to `unknown`. We can set our `TERM` variable and then use `tset` to reinitialize the terminal:

```
% echo $TERM
unknown
% setenv TERM vt100
% eval `tset -s`
Erase is Delete
Kill is Ctrl-U
```

The two lines following the command `eval` are the `stderr` lines mentioned above. (These two lines can be suppressed by adding the `-Q` option to `tset`.) The `stdout` text is captured by the back quotes and sent to the shell, which uses the `stdout` text to set the variables `TERM` and `TERMCAP`.

Further terminal setup is done with the command `stty`. The following command lets you look at the current terminal driver mode:

```
% stty everything
new tty, speed 9600 baud , 10 rows, 80 columns
even odd -raw -nl echo -lcase -tandem tabs -cbreak
crt: (crtbs crterase crtkill ctlecho) -tostop
-tilde -flusho -litout -pass8 -nohang -autoflow
-pendin decctlq -noflush
erase kill werase rprint flush lnext susp intr quit stop eof
^?   ^U   ^W    ^R     ^O    ^V   ^Z/^Y ^C   ^\  ^S/^Q ^D
```

To reset some of the terminal setup values, use the command `stty`. For example, to set the end of file character to ^Z and the suspend character to ^S, type

```
% stty eof ^Z
% stty susp ^S
```

This is a very brief introduction to the complex topic of terminal initalization. For more information, see the appropriate man pages. Stevens' *Advanced Programming in the UNIX Environment* has a good chapter on terminal operation in UNIX.

6.6   Customizing Mail

Electronic mail is a major activity on most UNIX systems. Your mail is stored in a mail box, typically `/usr/spool/mail/$USER`, where `$USER` is your login name. You read mail with a mailer, also known as a mail user agent. There are a number of agents, including the Berkeley mail program, the Seventh Edition mailer, `mm`, `mh`, `elm`, and the `emacs rmail` program. Behind the scenes, the mailer interacts with a mail transport agent like `sendmail` or `smail`. You will probably never see a mail transport agent directly: the mailers handle all of the details of reading, sending, storing, and deleting messages.

This section will focus on customizing the Berkeley mail program, hereafter referred to as `mail`. Other mailers can also be customized, usually through methods similar to those described below.

The major tools for customizing mail are variables, aliases and commands. Because it is tedious (and pointless) to type in all of your desired customized settings each time you use mail, store them in a mail initialization file called `.mailrc`. Mail is also controlled by a system-wide mail customization file called `/usr/lib/Mail.rc`. Your own `.mailrc` will override the settings in `Mail.rc`. A sample `.mailrc` looks like

```
% more .mailrc
set ask
set crt = 20
ignore Received Status Message-Id
alias me stigle
alias joe darty
alias chinesedinner daniels smith me snoyette lange darty
```

The individual elements that you can use to assemble your `.mailrc` are discussed below.

Another file related to customizing mail is .forward. It is particularly useful if you receive mail on several UNIX systems but want to read it all on one. On the others, set up a file called .forward containing your address on the system where you want to read your mail. A .forward file could also be used to forward your mail to another person, although this would not be done very frequently.

6.6.1 Mail Variables

Mail is controlled by a number of variables, which can be set using the mail command set:

```
set ask
```

To unset a variable or to override a variable that is set in Mail.rc, use the command unset:

```
unset dot
```

Most mail variables are binary: they are either set or unset. Others are string or numeric. Some common mail variables are discussed below. If you store set or unset commands in a .mailrc file, they will be in effect each time you use mail. Any set or unset command you type while in mail will only last until you exit from the mail program.

ask   If ask is set, you will be prompted for a subject line when you send a message.

askcc   If askcc is set, you will automatically see the cc: prompt when you finish creating a message. Fill in the names and addresses of people you want to receive carbon copies of the message.

crt = *n*   To keep a long mail message from scrolling rapidly off the screen as you are reading it, set the crt variable to the number of lines the pager program should display before pausing:

```
& set crt = 22
```

dot   When dot is set, you can end a message by typing a period on a line by itself. The other way to end a message is to type a ^D, which is controlled by the ignoreeof variable below. Do not unset dot and set ignoreeof, or you will be left with no way to get out of creating a mail message!

EDITOR = *path*   We've seen this variable before. As you might guess, it specifies the path and name of the editor you want to use to edit mail messages when you use ~e or the edit command. Set EDITOR by specifying the name and path of your desired editor. For example,

```
& set EDITOR = /usr/local/bin/emacs
```

escape = *character*   This variable allows you to specify the so-called escape character, the character for calling one of the escape commands like e (for edit), p (for print), and f (for forward). Because the default escape character is the tilde (~), escape commands are often referred to as tilde commands. Set this variable to a single character, for example,

```
& set escape = ^
```

header   The header variable causes the headers of messages in your mailbox to be displayed when you first enter mail.

ignore   Normally, two ^Cs will interrupt the sending of a mail message. If ignore is set, the ^Cs are simply printed as @ signs and there is no interrupt.

ignoreeof   If ignoreeof is set, mail will not accept ^D as the end of a message. (Make sure you don't have ignoreeof set and dot unset!) The ignoreeof in mail is not the same as the shell's ignoreeof variable.

msgprompt   When msgprompt is set, mail will prompt you for the text of your message and display instructions for terminating the message.

nosave   Normally, an aborted message (one in which you have typed two ^Cs) will be stored in $HOME/dead.letter. If nosave is set, aborted messages will not be saved.

PAGER = *path*   The PAGER variable sets the command (more, less) you want to use as a pager for displaying long messages.

record = *path*   If you want to automatically save copies of all messages you send, use the record variable with the name of the file where you want to store the messages:

```
& set record=/usr/users/stigle/outgoing.mail
```

save   The opposite of nosave, the variable save will cause an aborted message to be saved in the file $HOME/dead.letter.

SHELL = *path*   The variable SHELL specifies the shell you want to use when you do a shell escape in mail.

screen = *n*   The variable screen allows you to set the number of message headers you want to see at a time.

VISUAL = *path*   The variable VISUAL contains the name of the editor you want to use when you use ~v or the visual command in mail to edit a message.

6.6.2 Commands

Three commands are commonly found in `.mailrc` files: `alias`, `biff`, and `ignore`.

alias   Aliases were discussed earlier as a method for renaming UNIX commands. The most common use of aliasing, though, is probably in `mail`. If you can't remember your friend Bob's login id, you can set up an alias:

```
& alias bob kratchet
```

This is particularly useful for long and awkward mail addresses, such as `123456.1234@compuserve.com`, and for groups of addresses. Suppose you regularly send mail to three fellow members of a committee whose addresses are

```
rezik@ca.uni1.edu
mystery.user@well.sf.ca.us
wfk65@north.carolina.edu
```

These addresses are awful to remember, let alone type accurately time after time. So save them in an alias:

```
& alias committee rezik@ca.uni1.edu \
mystery.user@well.sf.ca.us \
wfk65@north.carolina.edu.
```

Separate the individual mail ids with commas, spaces, or backslashes. The backslash continues the command on the next line. Some other useful aliases are

```
& alias me your_email_address
```

for quickly sending copies to yourself and something like

```
& alias myvax your_vax_address
```

for sending mail to yourself at another computer. To see your aliases from the shell, do a `more` on your `.mailrc`:

```
% more .mailrc
[contents of .mailrc]
```

To see your aliases from within the mail program, type alias at a mail prompt:

```
& alias
[list of aliases]
```

As with the mail environment variables, aliases defined within the mail program are only temporary. Permanent aliases should be put into your .mailrc file.

biff   If you want to be notified when mail arrives for you, use the biff command:

```
% biff y
```

To turn biff off, type

```
% biff n
```

To see the current setting of biff, type

```
% biff
is n
```

The biff command operates at the shell level, not inside mail. To have it on automatically, put it in your .login.

If you are wondering where the name biff came from, UNIX legend tells that it was named for a dog Biff, who barked when the mail was delivered.

ignore   Mail messages pick up a number of header lines as they work their way through various computers. If you want to suppress the display of these lines, use the ignore command. The command

```
& ignore Received
```

will suppress the display of header lines beginning with Received.

If you want to ignore multiple lines, put them in one ignore command separated by spaces:

```
& ignore Received Message-Id Return-Path cc X-Vms-To
Status In-Reply-To
```

The ignore command is not the same as the ignore mail variable discussed above. The ignore command begins with the word ignore and controls the display of mail header lines. The ignore variable is set using the set command and controls the mail response to ^C. For other mail variables and their meanings, check the man pages for mail.

6.7   X Window Customization

The X Window System, usually referred to simply as X, is a portable network-based windowing software standard developed as part of Project Athena at the Massachusetts Institute of Technology. X programs are displayed in windows, which can be opened and closed, moved, enlarged and shrunk, and iconified. The type of window you'll probably use most frequently is an xterm window. xterm is a terminal emulator, a program that acts like a terminal. In an xterm window, you can read mail, compile programs, enter commands—all of the typical character-based UNIX operations. You can even have a window for each operation and click back and forth between them using the mouse.

Windows are managed by a program called a window manager. There are several window managers available, including Motif, Open Look, uwm (universal window manager), and twm (tab window manager). Your interaction with X occurs primarily through a window manager rather than directly with the underlying X system itself.

X is described in more detail by John Mauney in Chapter 3. Here I will concentrate on the basic mechanisms for customizing your X environment. X is extremely flexible, particularly in the power you have over your X environments and programs. There are four main areas of configuration: starting X, setting your display, choosing and configuring a window manager, and managing resources.

6.7.1   Starting X

How you start X will depend on how it is configured on your local system. Some workstations have an X server running automatically, usually started from xdm or by init. In either case, since the X Server is already running, you need not be concerned with starting one.

On other workstations, you may have to start the X server yourself. Usually, this involves running xinit, which starts an X server and a client program. Contact your system administrator for the appropriate commands for your system. Typically, these commands can be run manually from the command line or can be put into your .login or .profile for automatic execution.

As with most X programs, xinit can be quite complex. Its basic operation, though, is to look in your home directory for a file called

.xinitrc. This small sample .xinitrc contains commands to start an xterm, the xclock program, and the Motif window manager:

```
% more .xinitrc
#! /bin/csh -f
xclock &
xterm &
mwm
```

6.7.2   Setting Your Display

X is designed to be network-transparent. In other words, an X application that appears on your workstation could in fact be running on a different workstation altogether. Consequently, X programs need to know where to expect your input and where to display the results for you. The main mechanism for communicating this information to X programs is by setting the DISPLAY environment variable discussed in Section 6.2.2. The general format for the DISPLAY variable is

```
host:display.screen
```

For example, the command

```
%setenv DISPLAY rosman:0.0
```

specifies that you want applications to use the monitor (or display) on the computer rosman, that that monitor is the first or only monitor (:0) attached to rosman, and that the screen is the first screen (.0) within the display. The generic value unix:0 sets the server to be the same machine the application is running on.

6.7.3   Window Managers

Your interaction with X is handled by a window manager. The standard window manager for Digital, IBM, and HP is Motif (mwm), which has a similar look and feel to MicroSoft Windows. The standard for Sun has been Open Look (olwm), but soon will probably be some marriage of Open Look and Motif. The Tab window manager, twm, is distributed with version 11 Release 5 (X11R5) of the X Window System.

Motif can be customized in several ways. The easiest way is to use the customizing menus built into the window manager interface. Using these menus, you can modify the border colors for your windows and set the size, color, and placement of icons. Motif also uses the .Xdefaults file discussed below. If desired, you can do further customizing with a file called $HOME/.mwmrc.

6.7.4 Managing resources

Applications in X are controlled by a set of variables called resources. Common resources are background and foreground colors and the size and placement of windows.

Resources are stored in a resource database as a series of key/value pairs, similar to the system of environment variables discussed in Section 6.2.2. A typical key/value line has the form

```
appname*resource: value
classname*resource: value
```

The first part of the key is the application name or class name. Each application is a member of a class. For example, xclock is a member of the class XClock, xterm is a member of XTerm, and xmh (an X mail program) is a member of the class Mail. In general, class names begin with a capital letter, or if the first letter is an X, with two capital letters.

Applications will query the resource database for the values of keys beginning with their application and class names. The program xclock will check the resource database for lines that begin with xclock or XClock.

The remaining parts of the key specify the resource requested, and may have a variable number of segments. Asterisks (*) can be used as wildcard characters which match a range of keys, in a manner similar to file globbing with asterisks. The following examples tell the xclock program to make its foreground color red and its background color black:

```
xclock*foreground: red
xclock*background: black
```

The line

```
*foreground  red
```

would set the foreground color on *all* applications to red (unless otherwise specified.)

6.7.5 Geometry Specifications

The dimensions and location of a window are called its *geometry* in X. An example of a geometry specification for an xterm might be

```
term*geometry:   80x25+50+100
```

This specifies a window 80 columns wide by 25 rows tall. (Note that xterms interpret the height and width parameters in units of characters, but many applications interpret them in terms of pixels.) The window is to be placed 50 pixels from the left edge of the screen and 100 pixels from the top edge. The plus signs mean that the location parameters, 50 and 100, are offsets from the upper left corner. The first of the two is the offset along the *x*-axis, the second is the offset along the *y*-axis. Frequently, screens have the upper-left corner as their origins, the positive *x*-axis is rightward, and the positive *y*-axis is downward. In this context, the use of plus signs makes sense since the location can be interpreted as positive offsets from a screen corner.

Similarly, the geometry specification allows you to use minus signs to denote negative offsets from a corner. 80x25-50-100 would put the same size window 50 pixels from the right edge and 100 pixels above the bottom edge. 80x25+50-100 and 80x25-50+100 are valid, too, of course. So the general format for a geometry statement is

```
<width>x<height>{+-}x{+-}y
```

6.7.6   Color Specifications

You have a great deal of control over the colors displayed on a color monitor in X. You can set the colors of the windows, buttons, borders, and cursors. Colors in X can be specified in two ways. The first is simply a name, such as *black* or *SkyBlue*. The second method uses the form #RRGGBB or #RRRRGGGGBBBB, specifying a shade in terms of its red (RR or RRRR), green (GG or GGGG), and blue (BB or BBBB) components. RR is a two, three, or four-digit hexadecimal number, as are GG and BB. Thus #ff0000 has maximum red and no green or blue, and is full red; #00ff00 is full green; #ffffff is brightest white; and #555555 is medium gray.

The following two entries are equivalent:

```
xterm*foreground: wheat
xterm*foreground: #f5deb3
```

Ultimately, X works with colors as red-green-blue mixtures. When you specify a color by name, the Server simply looks the name up in /usr/lib/rgb.txt or /usr/lib/X11/rgb.txt and gets the color mixture from that. This database is human-readable, and we suggest you browse through it to get an idea of what color names are installed on your system. Reading it is a bit like visiting a paint store (antique white, misty rose, thistle), a dessert cart (papaya whip, honeydew, mint cream, chocolate), or a large box of Crayola crayons (violet red, blue violet). The program xcolors, available by anonymous ftp from several sites, will display the color names and corresponding colors for you.

6.7.7 Fonts

You can also specify fonts for particular applications. The available fonts can usually be found in the various directories of /usr/lib/ X11/fonts. The command xlsfonts will list the names of the available fonts. Fonts in X are not fully standardized, so you may need to do some experimenting.

6.7.8 Building the Resource Database

Values in the resource database can come from a variety of sources. If the developer of the application has created a file of resource values, it will usually be stored in /usr/lib/X11/app-defaults. An X application will look for a file named for itself and load the values in it. For example, the xclock program will look for the file /urs/lib/X11/ app-defaults/Xclock.

You can create your own resource file for a specific application also. These files are usually stored in your home directory, or you can set the environment variable XAPPLRESDIR to point to another directory which contains the desired resource file. Well-behaved X programs will check for these files and load the resource values they contain. Any resources at this stage that are identical to ones in the app-defaults file will override the ones from the app-defaults file.

The general resource file is $HOME/.Xdefaults. Of all of the files used to build the resources database, .Xdefaults is the one most users create and modify to customize their X environment. Each line in an .Xdefaults file, as in the other resource files, should be a blank line, a comment, or a key/value pair. Comments are helpful—they help you remember what a resource is for, or why you chose a particular value for it. Comments have an exclamation point (!) as the first character of the line. All text on such a line is ignored by the resource manager. The bulk of an .Xdefaults file will be key/value pairs. Below is a sample .Xdefaults annotated with comments:

```
! sample .Xdefaults
!
! set some general values
*font: terminal18
*highlight: black
*borderColor: black
*foreground: black
*background: white
*doubleClickDelay: 250
*language_preference1: 6
! set values for session manager
```

```
! turn on screen saver sm.screen_saver_enable: enable
sm.screen_saver_period: 10
! set foreground and background colors and pattern for root
window
sm.display_foreground:  #ccccb8b8ffff
sm.display_background:  #9c9cffffffff
sm.display_pattern: 43
! set colors and pattern for mouse pointer
sm.pointer_foreground: white
sm.pointer_background: black
sm.pointer_shape:    -26
! set colors for emacs
emacs.pointerColor: green
emacs.cursorColor: red
! set values for xclock program
XClock*font:            9x15
XClock*foreground:      black
XClock*background:      white
XClock*highlight:       black
XClock*hands:           thistle
XClock*mode:            cat
XClock*update:          1
XClock*alarm:           off
XClock*bell:            on
XClock*chime:           on
XClock*period:          5
```

How .Xdefaults is used by X programs will vary depending on system configuration. The old style (prior to X11 Release 2) was that each X program read .Xdefaults looking for resources for it and its class (after it looks for and reads resources from the app-defaults directory and your home directory or a directory specified by XAPPLRES-DIR.) This method causes problems in networked systems where the applications can be running on a different computer from the server, and even running themselves on different machines from time to time.

The newer style is to use the xrdb program to load resources into a global resources database on the X server. Each X program has access to the same resources database, regardless of which machine the X program is running on. In some cases (as with Digital's session manager), .Xdefaults is loaded automatically. In other cases, you will need to do this yourself (a good candidate for your .login file) using the command

```
% xrdb .Xdefaults
```

To determine the current values in your resource database, type

```
% xrdb -query
```

You have yet another chance to set resources by specifying a resources file using the environment variable XENVIRONMENT. The values in the file pointed to by XENVIRONMENT will override the settings stored in the resource database. If the color of the xclock hands is set to thistle in .Xdefaults and to blue in the XENVIRONMENT file, the clock's hands will be blue when you run xclock.

Finally, you have one last chance to specify resources by putting them on the command line when you start a specific program. For example,

```
% xclock -hd green
```

will start up xclock with green hands, regardless of hand colors set elsewhere.

And finally, although this is discouraged, the developer of the application can hard-code resource values into the program.

6.8   Conclusion

One of the reasons UNIX inspires such devotion is its flexibility. You can customize almost every aspect of your work in the UNIX environment, beginning with which shell you use. The shell can be further configured with shell variables and (if you're using the C shell) aliases. Another type of variable, the environment variable, can store preferences you want passed to the programs you call. Use the many existing UNIX commands or create your own. The variables, aliases, and commands can be saved in initialization files to be run automatically when a program begins.

UNIX users typically use electronic mail. The various UNIX mail programs can be customized. We looked specifically at customizing the Berkeley mail program by storing commands and aliases in the .mailrc initialization file.

The X Window System is particularly rich in customization opportunities. Choose your colors, arrange your windows with geometric precision, or design your icons. The major mechanism for customizing X is resources, which can be set in a variety of files. A key piece of customizing an X environment is the window manager. The window manager controls your interaction with the X System. It, too, can be customized to make that interaction as powerful and as comfortable as you like.

This chapter offers an introduction to the key mechanisms of UNIX customization. Try out some of the examples offered here, experiment a little, and soon you'll have created a UNIX tailored especially for you, an environment which doesn't hinder you, but enhances your ability to work effectively.

6.9   Bibliography

P. W. Abrahams, B. A. Larson, *UNIX for the Impatient*, Reading: Addison-Wesley, 1992.

GNU Emacs Manual, Cambridge, MA: Free Software Foundation.

O. Jones, *Introduction to the X Window System*, Englewood Cliffs: Prentice Hall, 1989.

The Little Gray Book: An ULTRIX Primer, Maynard: Digital Equipment Corporation, 1990. Chapter 7: Customizing Your Environment.

"Mail Reference Manual," *Supplementary Documents Volume 1, General User*, Maynard: Digital Equipment Corporation.

E. Nemeth, G. Snyder, and S. Seebass, *UNIX System Administration Handbook*, Englewood Cliffs: Prentice Hall, 1989.

J. D. Newmarch, *The X Window System and Motif: A fast Track Approach*, Sydney: Addison-Wesley, 1992.

W. R. Stevens, *Advanced Programming in the UNIX Environment*, Reading: Addison-Wesley, 1992.

J. Wilson, *Berkeley UNIX: A simple and comprehensive guide*, New York: John Wiley & Sons, 1991.

6.10   Appendix I: Shell and Environment Commands

	Environment	C Shell	Bourne Shell
Displaying all	setenv	set	set
Displaying one	echo $NAME	echo $name	echo $NAME
Setting/ Changing	setenv NAME value	set name = value	NAME=value export $NAME
Unsetting	unsetenv NAME	unset name	NAME=

6.11   Appendix II: Common Environment Variables

EDITOR *path*	Preferred editor
EXINIT *cmd*	Initial commands for vi and ed
HOME *path*	Absolute pathname of user's home directory
MAIL *path*	Directory and file where user's incoming mail is stored
PATH *path*	Pathnames to be searched for executable programs
PRINTER *string*	Default printer
SHELL *path*	Preferred shell

TERM *string*	Terminal type
TERMCAP *string*	Terminal capabilities
USER *string*	User's login name
VISUAL *path*	Preferred editor

6.12   Appendix III: Common Shell Variables

cdpath = *path*	Directories to be searched during cd command
cwd = *dir*	Current working directory
echo	Controls whether command input is echoed to the screen
histchars = *string*	Characters to be used by the history commands
history = *n*	Number of previous commands saved for reuse
home = *path*	User's home directory
ignoreeof	Prevents ^D from killing shell
mail = *path*	File where incoming mail can be found
noclobber	Prevents redirection from overwriting an existing file
noglob	Prevents shell from doing file name substitution
notify	Causes shell to notify you when background jobs finish
path = *path*	Path to search for executable files
prompt = *string*	Form of shell prompt
savehist = *n*	Sets the number of commands saved in $HOME/.history
shell = *path*	Name of shell file
term = *string*	Terminal type
time = *n*	Sets limit for duration of commands to be reported
user = *string*	User's login name
verbose	Causes the words of each command to be printed after a history substitution

6.13   Appendix IV: Initialization Files and Programs that Use Them

.login	Login settings
.cshrc	C shell initialization
.logout	Executed at logout time
.profile	Bourne shell initialization
.mailrc	Berkeley mail
.forward	Forward email to another address

.twmrc	twm window manager
.Xdefaults	X Window
.newsrc	News file
.emacs	emacs initialization
.rhosts	Allow permission for remote login without password

6.14   Appendix V: Berkeley Mail Variables

ask	Prompts for a subject line for a message
askcc	Automatically prompts for carbon copy recipients
crt = n	Sets number of lines displayed at a time
dot	Sets period as character to end a message
EDITOR = *path*	Path and name of editor used for ~e or edit command
escape = *char*	Specifies the escape character
header	Displays message headers on entering mail
ignore	Ignores ^C interrupts
ignoreeof	Do not accept ^D as the end of a message
msgprompt	Prompts for text of message
nosave	Don't save interrupted message in dead.letter
PAGER = *path*	Command to be used as a pager
record = *path*	Automatically saves all sent messages to named file
SHELL = *path*	The shell to be used for shell escapes
save	Aborted messages will be saved in dead.letter
screen = *n*	The number of messages to display for headers command
VISUAL = *path*	The name of the editor to use for ~v or visual commands

Network Administration

Sue Stigleman and Robert Benites

7.1 Introduction

Network administration has become one of the major tasks of a system administrator. Due to the advent of inexpensive, powerful RISC-based hardware, seldom does a system administrator have the luxury of administering just one computer. More than likely, the system administrator now manages a number of distributed machines in several rooms or buildings, connected via a local area network (LAN), and running one or more networking protocols.

To make things more complicated, that LAN is probably connected to a wide area network (WAN). The system administrator must manage not only the many different distributed data services and resources available in the LAN but also must contend with issues raised from the user community when services on the WAN are interrupted or malfunctioning.

This chapter is organized roughly by the steps taken to set up a new network or to install a new host on a network:

1. Installing network hardware (Section 7.2)

2. Assigning names and addresses (Section 7.3)

3. Setting the default router (Section 7.4)

4. Getting ready for network applications (Section 7.5)

5. Configuring the name server (NIS, BIND) (Section 7.6)

6.   Configuring network file service (NFS) (Section 7.7)

7.   Setting up network printing (Section 7.8)

8.   Routing mail with `sendmail` (Section 7.9)

9.   Installing UUCP (Section 7.10)

10.   Using diskless mode (Section 7.11)

11.   Some security and reliability considerations (Section 7.12)

12.   Simple network debugging tools (Section 7.13)

Sections 7.2 through 7.4 cover subjects essential to networking. The middle sections (7.5 through 7.11) cover several important networking tools whose use is optional, though common. Finally, the chapter ends with a discussion of network security and some useful network debugging tools. Because a single chapter cannot cover all details involved in networking, for each section within the chapter we refer the reader to relevant works listed in the bibliography.

7.2   Installing Network Hardware

At its most basic level, a computer network is a collection of computers connected together. There are many types of networking hardware, but in the context of UNIX system administration, physical networking usually means Ethernet.

Although Ethernet will run on several types of physical media, the two primary choices are thinwire and twisted pair. Thinwire Ethernet (also called 10Base2) uses coax cable which runs from host to host in a long string. The individual hosts are attached to the cable via a T-connector. In twisted pair Ethernet (also known as 10BaseT), each host is wired into a central hub using telephone-like wire and telephone-like jacks. 10BaseT hubs can be chained together with more twisted pair wire. Thinwire and twisted pair can be mixed on the same local area network with special interconnection devices. Not only can the wiring types be mixed: today's heterogeneous networks allow mainframes, PCs, Macintoshes, and UNIX workstations to mingle on the same Ethernet.

Figure 7.1 shows a general schematic for our department network. It contains two older thinwire segments, represented by solid lines. There are also two twisted pair hubs. One is located in our machine room on floor 0. It connects the two thinwire segments, a file server (`ivy`), and a bridge that attaches to the rest of the campus network. The other twisted pair hub is located on the second floor. Several hosts are attached to this hub, which in turn is attached into one of the thinwire segments.

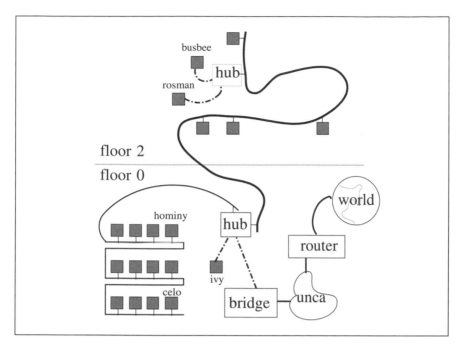

Figure 7.1 General network schematic

The evolution of this network is typical of Ethernet development over the last few years. When the original workstations were networked, thinwire was the dominant medium and therefore an obvious choice for us. However, thinwire presents one problem solved by a twisted pair configuration: should the thinwire cable be disconnected at any point along its length, the entire network segment stops operating. Our network has been brought down by users' feet, chairs, and impatient painters. As a result, the network is gradually being converted to twisted pair. A broken twisted pair cable affects only the host on that cable. The other hosts attached to the same hub continue to operate. Another consideration is that today (early 1994), workstations are usually manufactured with built-in twisted pair Ethernet jacks, thereby reducing the cost of implementing twisted pair networking.

If you are incorporating older machines into the network, you may need to install external transceivers. These small hardware components translate the analog signals on the cable to digital signals the host can understand. Most newer machines have built-in transceivers and connect directly to either thinwire or twisted pair network cables.

Each workstation in an Ethernet network must have an Ethernet interface. For most UNIX machines, Ethernet interfaces are built into the motherboard at the factory. They can also be bought and installed as separate interface boards. An Ethernet interface has a name such as `ln0`, `il0`, or `lo0`, which is the operating system's name for the interface. Each Ethernet interface also has a unique built-in 48 bit number known as its Ethernet address, or alternatively, its hardware address.

If thinwire segments become too long (more than 500 feet or so) or too big (more than about 25 hosts), repeater devices should be added to amplify the signal. If a network spans more than one building, consider running optical fiber between the buildings and using repeaters that converse over optical fiber. Optical fiber provides electrical isolation: a lightning strike can't induce a damaging current in an optical fiber, as it may with thinwire or twisted pair cable.

Another type of network hardware is a bridge, which will isolate network traffic to appropriate parts of a network based on Ethernet addresses. For example, looking again at Figure 7.1, there is a bridge between the department network and the larger campus network. Purely local traffic, such as a request from workstations for a file located on the department file server, will not leave the local network. On the other hand, traffic destined for the rest of the campus or the outside world will be passed through the bridge. While bridges isolate and filter some network traffic, they are transparent in some other respects. Programs like NIS (Section 7.6.1) and diskless operation (Section 7.11) are able to operate through bridges. With these programs, two network segments connected with a bridge look like one larger network, or a single logical network. In general, anything that can be done on a single Ethernet segment can be done across a bridge.

Yet another possible network component is the router. This device routes network traffic based on IP addresses (discussed in the next section). Routers divide a network into two separate subnets and are impenetrable to Network Information Service and other programs that use LAN broadcasting (discussed in Section 7.3.4).

After installing your computers and cables, do the normal system administration tasks of configuring and booting the operating system of each host as specified in your vendor documentation. UNIX versions now usually come with networking enabled by default, but you might need to make some changes to your local configuration. Refer to Chapter 5 on system administration for more information.

7.2.1   Learning More

See *UNIX System Administration Handbook* by Nemeth et al. for more detailed information on hardware installation. Stallings' *Data and Computer Communications* goes into extensive detail on the characteristics and functionality of networking hardware.

7.3   Assigning Names and Addresses

In the last section, we mentioned the built-in Ethernet addresses that come with each Ethernet interface card. However, not all networks are Ethernets. What is needed is a type of network addressing that will work for a variety of types of networks: Ethernet, token ring, FDDI, ATM, and so on. That type of addressing is Internet Protocol (IP) addressing. Each network is assigned a network IP number, and within that network each host has a name and a host IP number. Setting these addresses correctly is essential for proper network operation.

A host IP address is composed logically of two parts: a network part and a host part. The network part is assigned by the Internet Network Information Center (InterNIC). The host part is left to the local site to assign. For example, `hominy`, one of the workstations at the University of North Carolina at Asheville (UNCA), has the IP number 152.18.52.54. The UNCA network address is the first two numbers: 152.18. The final numbers which identify this specific host, 52.54, were assigned by the local network administrator.

7.3.1   Obtaining an IP Network Address

If your network is a private one with no external connections to other networks, then the IP host addresses could be generated by the network administrator. However, if there is any chance that your network will be connected to other networks or to the Internet, you must have a unique IP network address.

Obtaining a network address is usually easy: contact your local network administrator and ask for it. If your site does not have a network address, you'll need to contact InterNIC, a nonprofit organization that manages the distribution of Internet network numbers. To register your network with InterNIC, contact:

Internet NIC Registration
Network Solutions, Inc.
505 Huntmar Park Drive
Herndon, VA 22070
(800) 444-4345 or (703) 742-4777
Email: hostmaster@internic.net

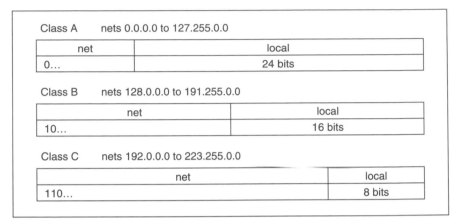

Figure 7.2   Address classes

InterNIC divides networks into three classes—A, B, and C—based on the number of hosts attached to a network. Classes are a system for dividing up the four bytes associated with an IP address, as shown in Figure 7.2. IP addresses are commonly represented as four decimal numbers separated by dots. Each of the four numbers can range from 0 to 255 (the range of values possible for a single byte.)

Class A networks are the largest, allowing more than 16,000,000 hosts. Of the four bytes allocated for the IP address, only the first byte is designated to represent the network number. The last three bytes represent host numbers. This can be represented as N.H.H.H, with the first byte between 0 to 127. In this scenario, the IP address is configured to provide a small number of networks that can support millions of hosts. Class A network numbers are almost never assigned anymore.

Class B networks are for medium sized networks, allowing up to 65,534 hosts. Class B networks use two bytes to represent the network number and two bytes to represent the host number (N.N.H.H), with the first byte between 128 and 191. This provides a good number of networks that can support a large number of hosts.

Class C networks are the smallest, providing addressing space for only 254 hosts. In this case, three bytes are used for the network number and only one for the host number (N.N.N.H), with the first byte between 192 and 223. This supports a large number of small networks.

The class or classes of your network will depend on how many hosts your organization foresees requiring access to a network. Large organizations may require a class B network where small organizations might require only a few class C numbers.

7.3.2   Assigning Individual Host IP Addresses

There is no right or wrong way to assign IP addresses for the individual hosts on your network. Find a convention that best suits your environment. In our department, specialized machines like the file servers are given numbers beginning with 1. UNIX workstation numbers begin with 50 and PC numbers with 100.

Most vendors supply a script or program to add a host to the network. Look for a program with a name like `netsetup`. These tools edit the various files where networking information is stored and may enable the networking daemons. We strongly recommend using a script if one is available.

On BSD-variants of UNIX, the network is enabled by the startup command script on your host, usually `/etc/rc.local`. Within the startup script, Ethernet interfaces are defined and configured with the `ifconfig` command. `ifconfig` associates a host's IP address to its Ethernet interface, turns an Ethernet interface on and off, and sets options for the interface. This is also how you will specify the broadcast mask and netmask, discussed below. The `ifconfig` command must be executed before any networking daemons are started. Here is an `ifconfig` statement for `hominy.cs.unca.edu`:

```
/etc/ifconfig ln0 152.18.52.54\
broadcast 152.18.255.255 netmask 255.255.0.0
```

This statement sets `hominy`'s IP number, its broadcast address, and netmask. You can enter a host's name rather than its explicit IP number if you have an entry for the host in the `/etc/hosts` file (discussed in Section 7.3.6). In other words, the `ifconfig` statement for `hominy` could be

```
/etc/ifconfig ln0 hominy\
broadcast 152.18.255.255 netmask 255.255.0.0
```

if `hominy` is given the IP number 152.18.52.54 in `/etc/hosts`.

In addition to the `ifconfig` statement for the `hominy` Ethernet interface, `hominy` must have an `ifconfig` statement for the local loopback, which allows a host to send packets to itself without going through the network.

7.3.3   Subnet Routing and Setting the Netmask

If your organization is large and uses a variety of networking protocols, the networks will probably be connected using routers. In this situation, IP addresses can be refined further by using part of the host number as a subnet number.

For example, say you have 16 subnets and have been assigned the Class B number 152.18.0.0. Normally, you would use the final two bytes for the host numbers. However, you can assign some or all of the bits from the third byte to be a subnet number. You specify these bits with a netmask. The netmask is a 32 bit number, just like an IP address. If a bit in the netmask is set to 1, that bit is interpreted as part of the network number. If the bit is set to 0, it is interpreted as part of the host number. The netmask allows you to "shave" a specified number of bits off the front part of the host number and use them to extend the network number. A host's IP address now consists of three parts: the network number, subnet number, and the host number. Here's an example of how a netmask of 255.255.240.0 is used to determine what subnet and host the IP address 152.18.213.17 refers to:

```
IP address 152.18.213.17      10011000 00010010 11010101 00010001
subnet mask 255.255.240.0      11111111 11111111 11110000 00000000
                               ------------------------------------
network number 152.18.208.0    10011000 00010010 1101
host number 5.17                                       0101 00010001
```

Therefore 152.18.213.17 represents host 5.17 on subnet 152.18.208.0. In this example, 4 bits of the local address are for a subnet. This divides the Class B network into 16 (or 2^4) subnets with up to 2^{12} hosts in each subnet.

Typically, you will be given a netmask by your local network administrator. The netmask, like the host IP address, is set using ifconfig.

7.3.4   Setting the IP Broadcast Mask

From a user's perspective, a network usually provides access from one individual host to another. However, there are situations where a host might want to talk to every other host on the network. When one host talks to many hosts at once, it broadcasts the information by specifying a broadcast address.

An example of the use of broadcasting is rwhod (pronounced *r-who-d*). rwhod is an optional network daemon that periodically sends out a broadcast packet containing information about users currently logged in to the host rwhod is running on. Other rwhod daemons on other hosts listen for this information and use it to maintain a database which can be queried using the rwho command.

A broadcast address is usually the network address followed by all of the host number bits set to 1. However, the IP broadcast mask allows you to tailor how broadcast addresses are generated for your network. For example, some vendors ship their workstations with the default broadcast address set to all 0s rather than all 1s. If you want to change this to follow the normal convention, you can use the broadcast mask to do so. The broadcast mask is defined using `ifconfig`. Once you have defined a broadcast mask, it is important to use the same one on every host on the network.

If you are using subnets, you might want your mask to restrict broadcasts to one subnet. For example, given a class B network number like 152.18, the usual broadcast mask would be 152.18.255.255. With this mask, any host on the network 152.18.0.0 would receive the broadcast packets. However, if subnet routing was being used and you wanted to keep broadcasts within a subnet, you would specify the network number, and the subnet number, followed by all the host number bits set to 1. Given the network 152.18.0.0 and 208 as a subnet number, the broadcast mask for the subnet would be 152.18.223.255.

7.3.5   Assigning Individual Host Names

Because humans are more comfortable using names like `hominy` than numbers like 152.18.52.54, hosts are given names in addition to their IP numbers. People aren't the only ones more comfortable with names—some applications also require host names.

Host names can be whatever you desire. We use the names of towns in western North Carolina. The University of Wisconsin uses the names of cheeses. (Pity the person whose workstation is named liederkranz!) Most people use names as a form of expression, but prudence should be shown. Once a name is chosen, it usually sticks for a long, long time! (Technically, each interface within a host has a hostname. We are assuming each of your hosts has only one Ethernet interface. If your machine has more than one, things may get messy.)

A host is set using the `hostname` command, as in:

```
/bin/hostname hominy
```

The command is usually inserted into the startup script for automatic execution at boot time, although on some machines, the hostname may be contained in a special file, such as `/etc/hostname.tr0` for the hostname associated with the interface `tr0`.

7.3.6   Creating the Hosts Table

You've now set the IP number and name for one host. What if you want `hominy` to communicate with another machine in the network, such as `ivy`?

The simplest way to tell hosts about each other is the `/etc/hosts` file, which associates IP addresses with host names. This allows users to remember remote hosts by their names instead of their IP addresses.

`/etc/hosts` is an ASCII text file that contains IP addresses, host names, and optional alias names. `/etc/hosts` usually contains entries for important hosts on the network and for the loopback device, `localhost`.

Here's the `/etc/hosts` for `hominy` in a small network of five machines:

```
# /etc/hosts
127.0.0.1 localhost
152.18.52.82 busbee.cs.unca.edu busbee
152.18.52.57 celo.cs.unca.edu   celo
152.18.52.54 hominy.cs.unca.edu hominy
152.18.52.5 ivy.cs.unca.edu ivy
152.18.52.58 rosman.cs.unca.edu rosman
```

As you add hosts, you must add their names to the `/etc/hosts` on the other hosts in your network. Otherwise, the new hosts will know the old-timers but not vice versa.

When a network gets larger, other solutions to the naming problem are required. Use of `/etc/hosts` has been extended by the Domain Name Service (DNS), discussed in Section 7.6.2. However, even networks using DNS will still have a few entries for important hosts in `/etc/hosts`.

7.3.7 Testing

After you've completed host naming and IP addressing, you should be able to use `ping` on your local network using IP numbers and names. `ping` is a quick and easy command that tells you if a particular host is "alive" and can be reached by the network. (`ping` will be discussed further in Section 7.13.1.)

For example, if you have added `hominy` to a network containing `busbee`, `celo`, `ivy`, and `rosman`, you should be able to `ping` from `hominy` to `ivy`:

```
% ping ivy
ivy is alive
```

You should also be able to `ping` using IP numbers. You won't yet be able to `ping` to remote machines using their names or IP numbers because you don't have a router defined (Section 7.4) or a routing daemon working.

If you are unsure that a host's interface is set correctly, you can use the `ifconfig` command with its Ethernet interface name, as in the following example for `hominy`:

```
% ifconfig ln0
ln0: 152.18.52.54 netmask ffff0000
flags=0x463<DYNPROTO,RUNNING, NOTRAILERS,BROADCAST,UP>
broadcast: 152.18.255.255
```

This is useful for detecting bad IP addresses, subnet masks, and broadcast addresses.

7.3.8 Learning More

Hunt's *TCP/IP Network Administration* has an extensive discussion of IP numbering and its implementation. Nemeth et al. also discuss this material in their chapter on networking in *UNIX System Administration Handbook*.

7.4   Setting the Default Router

Routers connect multiple IP networks, filtering and forwarding packets based on IP network addresses. Routers may be either special dedicated machines or a host with multiple network interfaces. How is routing of packets from a host to remote networks accomplished?

First, ask your local network guru for the IP number of the router or routers you should use. If you have only one router, which is probably the case, the easiest way to handle routing is to designate that router within the appropriate startup file, such as `/etc/defaultrouter` for SunOS, `/etc/rc.local` for Ultrix, or `/etc/routes` for OSF/1. The following sample for `hominy` sets the default router to our Cisco gateway, `unca-gw.concert.net`:

```
#    Manual route to Cisco gateway
[ -f /etc/route ] && {
    /etc/route add default unca-gw.concert.net 1 >/dev/console
}
```

If you have more than one router on your network, life isn't so easy. Basically, you have two choices: you can use multiple explicit routing statements, probably designating one router for specific networks and the other as a default router, or you can run `routed`, the routing daemon.

7.4.1   Testing

You've gotten an IP network number, assigned IP numbers and names to your hosts, and you can `ping` locally. The next test is to `ping` remotely. Try to `ping` that local router your network administrator told you about. Then `ping` a site that is not connected to your local network to see if packets are being forwarded through your router.

7.4.2   Learning More

Hunt's *TPC/IP Network Administration* has a chapter on configuring routing. Appendix B in Stern's *Managing NFS and NIS* has an extensive discussion of the mechanics of routing.

7.5   Getting Ready for Network Applications

Hosts communicate with each other by using IP numbers. The set-up we've done so far enables one host to communicate with another. However, you usually don't want to just say "Hi" to another host—you want to be able to do something with that host. In other words, you want to use a service available on that host. How is this handled?

In order for applications on different hosts to talk to each other, another protocol is required. Without getting into the details of the networking protocol stack, the two protocols within the TCP/IP protocol suite for this are TCP and UDP. TCP creates a virtual connection between applications and provides reliable communication. It is used for connection-oriented applications like file transfers and remote logins. UDP uses datagrams and does not have end-to-end reliability—reliabilty is the responsibility of the application program.

Beyond using a common method of communicating, which TCP and UDP provide, applications must also have some way of identifying themselves to each other. There are two common choices here also: ports and Sun RPC numbers. TCP and UDP use ports. The Sun RPC is yet another networking layer, on top of TCP and UDP. Each Sun RPC service is identified a Sun RPC number. Most of the network applications discussed in the remaining sections of the chapter rely on one or both of these numbering schemes.

7.5.1   Ports

Suppose you want to `ftp` some files from `hominy.cs.unca.edu` to `celo`. How does the `ftp` program on `celo` know how to talk to the `ftp` on `hominy`? The answer lies in a mechanism called port numbers, which are somewhat like telephone extension numbers for incoming network requests.

The available network services and their port numbers are identified in /etc/services. Each entry in /etc/services is composed of a service name, its associated port number, the protocol used when connecting with the service (either tcp or udp), and an alias if desired.

The following is a small segment of the /etc/services for hominy:

```
# /etc/services
ftp 21/tcp
telnet 23/tcp
smtp 25/tcp mail
```

/etc/services usually requires no modification by the network administrator, although it may be edited to add service definitions for third-party applications.

7.5.2   inetd

As with most tasks in UNIX, networking is handled by network daemons. Having network daemons running at all times for every possible network application is inefficient. The solution is inetd (pronounced *eye-net-d*). inetd, the Internet superdaemon, is an overseer daemon that manages the other network daemons. inetd sits and listens for requests for network services and starts the appropriate daemon when it is needed.

Most versions of the inetd daemon use the /etc/inetd.conf file to identify which network servers to call in response to a network service request. Each entry in /etc/inetd.conf contains a service name (which must also be specified in /etc/services), the type of delivery (stream for TCP, datagram for UDP), the protocol name (tcp or udp), the wait status (whether a new server will be started for each incoming request), the pathname to the server program that inetd is to start, and optional arguments. For example, if the following line is in the inetd configuration file:

```
ftp stream tcp nowait /usr/etc/ftpd ftpd
```

and inetd receives an ftp request, it starts the ftp daemon, ftpd, which is located in /usr/etc/ftpd. When the ftp session is done, ftpd is shut down.

/etc/inetd.conf usually requires no modification by the network administrator unless there is a service you wish to remove for security reasons or unless you need to install a new service. When adding a service, you should expect to receive detailed instructions about the changes required to this file.

7.5.3 Sun RPC

Some network programs use the Sun Remote Procedure Call (RPC). Using RPC, one host calls a procedure that is executed on another host. This is the client/server model—the host with the resource is the server for the resource, and the host using the resource is the client. Most RPC servers are started at boot time and run as long as the machine is up, although some may be managed by inetd. Client requests queue up and are processed by the appropriate server one at a time.

A Sun RPC server is designated by a program number rather than a port number. RPC program numbers are specified in the file /etc/rpc, which is very similar to /etc/services, but instead of listing service names and port numbers, it lists RPC program names and RPC numbers, along with an optional alias. Here are some sample lines from hominy's /etc/rpc:

```
# /etc/rpc
portmapper      100000      portmap sunrpc
rstatd          100001      rstat rup perfmeter
rusersd         100002      rusers
nfs             100003      nfsprog
```

Network File Service (NFS) and Network Information Service (NIS) are two major network applications that use the RPC protocol. NFS and NIS are discussed in the next two sections.

7.5.4 portmap

The daemon responsible for handling RPC information is the portmap daemon, also known as the portmapper. portmap keeps track of RPC services and maps RPC program numbers to TCP/UDP port numbers. As each RPC server starts, it tells portmap which port it will listen to for service requests and which program numbers it will serve. (This is the opposite strategy from inetd, which does the listening for the servers.) Each RPC client asks portmap for the port number for the desired server.

7.5.5 Testing

Testing the set-up of these basic networking mechanisms is generally a matter of seeing whether the desired daemons are running. The major command that will display daemons (and other processes) is the ps, or process status, command. Here's a partial list from ivy showing several major network daemons discussed in this and following sections:

```
% ps gaux
USER         PID %CPU %MEM    SZ  RSS TT STAT     TIME COMMAND
root         101  0.0  1.5   268  228 ?  I        0:00 /etc/mountd -i
root         105  0.0  0.5   140   68 ?  S        3:31 /etc/nfsd 8
root          90  0.0  1.0   188  156 ?  S        0:07 /usr/etc/ypserv
root          74  0.0  0.8   140  112 ?  S        0:01 /etc/portmap
root        2165  0.0  1.9   484  300 ?  I        0:02 ftpd
root           1  0.0  1.6   284  252 ?  I        0:00 /etc/init -a
root         116  0.0  0.2    32   16 ?  I        0:02 /etc/biod 4
root        3358  0.0  1.3   312  196 ?  S        0:00 /usr/lib/lpd
root        3345  0.0  0.8   124  112 p0 S        0:00 rlogind
root         272  0.0  0.8   184  124 ?  S        0:00 /etc/inetd
```

Another command, `rpcinfo`, makes a remote procedure call to an RPC portmapper to obtain information about services known to that portmapper. It is a handy way to determine if certain daemons have been started. A sample command and output follow:

```
% rpcinfo -p ivy
   program vers proto    port
    100024    1   tcp    1025   status
    100021    1   tcp    1026   nlockmgr
    100021    1   udp    1099   nlockmgr
    100021    3   tcp    1027   nlockmgr
    100020    1   udp    1106   llockmgr
    100005    1   udp    2333   mountd
    100005    1   tcp    1453   mountd
```

7.5.6 Learning More

UNIX System Administration Handbook by Nemeth et al. and Hunt's *TCP/IP Network Administration* discuss ports and RPC numbers. Information can also be found in books about RPC-based network applications, such as Stern's Managing NFS and NIS.

7.6   Configuring the Name Server (NIS, BIND)

As we've discussed earlier, a host has a name, an IP address, and an Ethernet address for each of its network interfaces. Mapping between names and IP addresses was originally handled by the `/etc/hosts` file on each host. However, as networks grow, the effort of adding names and numbers for every reachable host to the `/etc/hosts` of every other host becomes prohibitive. The same problem occurs with other types of information, such as user passwords. Without some way of distributing this information, users would have to change their passwords on every host in the network, one at a time.

The usual solution to this problem is a combination of the Network Information Service (NIS) and the Domain Name Service (DNS). NIS distributes a number of administrative files, such as /etc/hosts, /etc/passwd, and /etc/groups, within a single network. DNS handles mapping of host names and addresses but does this smaller task across networks, including the millions of hosts on the Internet.

While NIS and DNS serve somewhat different functions, there are a number of similarities between them. Both use a client/server model to provide information. A server is the authoritative source for whatever information is being shared, while clients make information requests to the server. NIS and DNS distribute naming information by using a single authoritative copy of the information on a host server.

NIS and DNS servers come in two types. One contains the master copy of the information, creating a single point of administration that helps prevent the hosts from working with different versions of data. NIS calls these the *master* servers, DNS calls them *primary* servers. To reduce the load on a master or primary server, other hosts can be designated as *slave* (NIS terminology) or *secondary* (DNS terminology) servers. These servers have copies of the information and can answer requests from clients. If a change is made to a database, the change is made only on the master, and the master propagates the new data to the slave servers.

NIS and DNS also share the idea of a domain. An NIS domain is the group of hosts that share the same set of information, such as a particular shared password file. A DNS domain is a group of hosts for which the server maintains name/IP address information.

Another similarity between NIS and DNS is they both use unusual record formats for the information they distribute: maps for NIS and resource records for DNS.

Let's examine these two programs in more detail.

7.6.1   Network Information Service (NIS)

NIS is a distributed database-lookup service that allows sharing of information between hosts on a network. (NIS was formerly called the Yellow Pages, abbreviated YP. You will notice that most of the NIS files and commands still contain the letters *yp*.)

The shared information can be of any type, but usually includes the groups, hosts, and password files. Some programs, such as passwd, will check for local files before going to the distributed NIS information.

7.6.1.1   NIS Domains

A NIS domain consists of one master server, its slave servers, and the clients that use the same set of NIS information. It is possible to have more than one domain on a network, but typically one will suffice and make network administration easier.

Before you can install NIS, you must select a name for your domain and decide upon the number and type of servers. Domain names can be anything but should reflect some aspect of the hosts you manage, such as the name of a department. The `domainname` command must be invoked on each host at boot time before any NIS daemons are started. This is usually handled by placing the appropriate command in the system startup file. The domain for a host is set by executing a command similar to

```
/bin/domainname physics
```

You probably won't need to insert this command manually: on most versions of UNIX, a `ypsetup` or `nissetup` script will be available to handle this and other details of installing NIS.

7.6.1.2   NIS Maps

The heart of NIS is a set of distributed databases called NIS maps. NIS creates these maps out of standard UNIX files such as `/etc/hosts`. The map files are stored in a binary format on the master and slave servers using the UNIX `make` facility. For example, given the `/etc/hosts` file, NIS would create the following files:

```
hosts.byaddr.dir
hosts.byaddr.pag
hosts.byname.dir
hosts.byname.pag
```

Files with names ending with `.dir` are key files pointing to information stored in data files whose names end with `.pag`. In our example, NIS has keyed the data on two fields: name and address. This enables NIS to access the information quickly either by name or by address.

The map files are usually stored within the directory `/var/yp/domainname`, where `domainname` is the name of the domain.

By default, NIS uses the files stored in `/etc` to create the maps, although it can be instructed to look for files elsewhere. The information used for NIS maps should be the same for all hosts in the network. It's a really bad idea to try to create an NIS map out of a file like `/etc/fstab`, which differs from host to host.

7.6.1.3 NIS Servers and Clients

As we said, NIS has two types of servers: master and slave. The master has the single copy of the maps that can be changed. There can be only one master server for a domain.

Slave servers honor requests for information using a copy of the master's databases but cannot make any changes to the databases. There can be any number of slave servers in a domain. Slave servers provide redundancy in the event of the loss of the master from the network.

Clients have no copies of the map files. They must query a server for each needed piece of information. If a client cannot reach any server, it can be rendered virtually useless. Since very little of the network and system information resides on the client, it may not even be possible to login to it.

Installing a Master Server

Once you have activated a domain name, there are two main steps in installing a master server:

1. Run `ypinit` with the `-m` option to define the server as a master server:

   ```
   ypinit -m
   ```

   `ypinit` handles the details of setting up the directory for the map files and creating the maps.

2. Start the NIS server daemon, `ypserv`. `ypserv` handles all requests from clients for information from the map files. It should be started at boot time by putting appropriate lines in the system startup file.

Before you can start the NIS server daemon, the `portmap` daemon must be running. If `portmap` is unavailable, NIS will not be able to function correctly.

An optional NIS daemon, `rpc.yppasswdd`, resides on the master server and processes password change requests from clients. It allows users to change their own passwords in the master password map using `yppasswd`. Some verisons of the normal password changing program `passwd` will check to see if NIS is managing the password file, and if so, call `yppasswd`.

Installing a Slave Server

Once the master server is running, you are ready to start the slave servers. You install a slave server in almost the same way you installed the master server:

1. Run `ypinit` to define the server as a slave server:

   ```
   ypinit -s master_servername
   ```

2. Start the `ypserv` daemon.

As the slave server is started, it will transfer the NIS maps from the master server. Like master servers, slave servers must have a domain set and `portmap` running.

Installing a Client

Any host which needs to look up information in the NIS maps is a client. Clients run the client daemon `ypbind`. It is confusing that servers are almost always also clients, so servers will be running both `ypserv` and `ypbind`. `ypbind` binds a client to a particular server. For security reasons, you should configure `ypbind` to specify a set of acceptable servers. This prevents someone from setting up a host to mimic a server and provide false information, such as forged password entries.

Before a client can access NIS services, it must have a domain name defined and a `portmap` daemon invoked. Once this is done, you may start `ypbind`. The `ypbind` daemon should be executed at boot time.

The primary benefit of having a distributed password mechanism is that a user may login to any of the hosts in the domain using the same password. There must be, therefore, some way to tell the `ypbind` daemon to search for the login and password on the server. This is done by inserting as the last line in the local `/etc/passwd` file a *magic token,* a plus sign. The form of the complete line is:

```
+::0:0:::
```

This magic token instructs the password lookup to go to the NIS server for login names that do not occur on the client.

7.6.1.4   Testing

Three useful tools for testing NIS installation are `ypwhich`, `ypcat` and `ypmatch`. `ypwhich` reports which server a client is bound to:

```
% ypwhich
ivy.cs.unca.edu
```

`ypcat` prints the entire contents of a requested map. It can also print the names of available maps. An example is the following:

```
% ypcat hosts
152.18.52.82   busbee
152.18.52.57   celo
152.18.52.54   hominy
152.18.52.5    ivy
152.18.52.58   rosman
```

ypmatch allows querying a specified map for the data associated with a key. It is like a grep command for searching NIS maps. For example, to search for hominy in the hosts map:

```
% ypmatch hominy hosts
152.18.52.54  hominy
```

7.6.1.5 Learning More

The major resource for NIS is Stern's *Managing NFS and NIS*. Garfinkel and Spafford's book *Practical UNIX Security* has a section on security issues of NIS.

7.6.2 The Berkeley Internet Name Domain Service (BIND)

While NIS is very flexible about the sort of data it will distribute across the network, it usually requires that copies of all the needed data reside on the master and slave servers. This assumes that all the information a user may desire is already known and available from a single server. This assumption works well for local information, such as passwords, and in small isolated groups of workstations where access to other networks is limited or nonexistent. However, when administrating large numbers of workstations (more than 50) or providing access to the Internet, this assumption proves false. Right now, there are over 2,000,000 systems with access through their local LANs to the Internet, and the number of systems with Internet access is growing constantly. To use NIS to serve the host names for the Internet would require a hosts map containing an entry for *every* system on the Internet. This huge map would then have to be transferred to many slave servers. Updates would have to occur almost constantly during the day. Even if one tenth of one percent of all systems joined or left the Internet in a day, this would still require updating host information for approximately 2000 systems. Clearly this is not suitable for providing host name resolution in wide area networks.

What is required is a name service that doesn't know everything but knows who to ask for the information. Ideally, this service should allow you to concentrate on administering the systems under your control while obtaining name resolution for other systems from another source on the network.

The Domain Name Service (DNS) provides this capability. BIND, the UNIX DNS server, allows client systems to obtain host names and addresses from BIND servers. Network administrators need provide only name, address, and optional mail-related information for those hosts in their network. The BIND client queries a server for the IP address for a particular host. If the local BIND server does not know

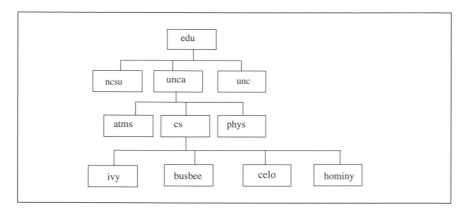

Figure 7.3   Internet domain hierarchy

the information, it queries a root server to locate a server which has the necessary information. Once the appropriate server is determined, the local server makes its request to it. If the given host name exists, its IP address is returned.

7.6.2.1   Domains and Zones

Internet domain names are organized into a tree structure. The root node defines the top level domain. Every domain is given a label. The name of a particular domain is formed by concatenating all the domain labels, separated by dots, starting at that domain and moving up to the root. This domain name forms a path from the domain up through the tree hierarchy to the root domain. Because of this, a label must be unique within a domain. (BIND also uses zones. There are slight differences between zones and domains, but we'll use the terms interchangeably here.)

A very small subset of the Internet domain hierarchy is shown in Figure 7.3. In this example, the top level domain is EDU, the educational institution domain. One zone within this domain is UNCA. The UNCA zone in turn contains a computer science zone, which contains the five hosts we've been using as examples in this chapter: `busbee`, `celo`, `hominy`, `ivy`, and `rosman`. The full name for `hominy` using DNS notation is `hominy.cs.unca.edu`.

Currently there are six "organizational" top level domains within the Internet, used primarily for United States sites:

- `COM`   Commercial organizations and networks

- `EDU`   Educational institutions

- GOV   Government agencies
- MIL   Military organizations
- NET   Network organizations including service and information centers
- ORG   Other, usually nonprofit organizations and professional societies

Along with these domains are other top level domains for individual countries, such as

- FR   France
- UK   United Kingdom
- CA   Canada
- DE   Germany

If you are planning to create a domain that will connect to the Internet, you should contact InterNIC (Section 7.3.1). Domain names need to be unique, so be prepared with some alternative names in case your first choice is already taken.

7.6.2.2   BIND Resource Records

Like NIS, BIND uses a special format for its information. BIND information is stored in resource records. While there are many types of resource records, these types are found most frequently in the BIND data files:

- A   Address   IP address for a host name
- CNAME   Canonical Name   Alias for a host
- MX   Mail Exchanger   For mail routing
- NS   Name Server   Primary and secondary servers for the domain
- PTR   Domain Name Pointer   Host name for an IP address
- SOA   Start of Authority   Beginning of information about a particular zone

Entries in resource records include a name, a type, a *time to live,* an address class (IN for Internet), an entry type, and any data needed by the particular entry type. Resource records will be discussed further in Section 7.6.3.

7.6.2.3 Root Servers

A BIND root server is an absolute authority. These special servers contain information about all the top level domains in the Internet. While they do not contain an entry for every host, they do know what servers to query in the top level domains. This is a real life example of the adage "It's not what you know but who you know." At the time of this writing, the following root servers are available on the Internet:

- `ns.nasa.gov.`
- `ns.nic.ddn.mil.`
- `a.isi.edu.`
- `gunter-adam.af.mil.`
- `aos.brl.mil.`
- `terp.umd.edu.`
- `c.nyser.net.`
- `nic.nordu.net.`

(The most current list is available from `ftp:ftp.rs.internic. net/netinfo/root-servers.`)

7.6.2.4 BIND Servers and Clients

The BIND service consists of two parts, the resolver and the server. The resolver asks questions. The server attempts to answer them.

The resolver is composed of routines that usually reside in the standard C library and are linked into any program that needs to look up IP addresses. The server usually runs as a name server daemon called `named` (pronounced *name-dee*).

Primary BIND Servers

The primary server is the absolute authority for a given local domain or zone. This is where you maintain the host information for your zone. A primary BIND server loads its information from files on a disk. In this way it's similar to a master NIS server loading information from its NIS maps. A primary server can also specify other secondary servers in its zone that have authority to respond to query requests.

Secondary Servers

A secondary server is similar in function to a NIS slave server. It can handle queries and also acts as a backup for the primary server. Any zone must have one primary master server and should have a couple of secondary servers. A primary server of one domain often acts as a secondary server for another domain.

Caching-Only Servers

It is a good assumption that if an IP address is requested for a host name once, it will be requested again. All BIND servers store information in a cache to avoid having to ask for it again. A third type of server, the caching-only server, requests information from a primary or secondary server and stores it in its cache until the data ages out.

Configuring BIND Servers

While many vendors provide some automated method for initializing BIND, knowledge of the configuration files and file formats is important. A primary BIND server uses several configuration files:

- `named.boot`   Information on server type, zone name, and location of following data files

- `named.ca`   Information on root servers

- `named.hosts`   Maps the host names to addresses for all the hosts in a zone

- `named.local`   Name and address for the local loopback interface

- `named.rev`   Maps IP addresses to host names

Aside from `named.boot`, the names of the files can be changed, as long as you correctly identify them within `named.boot`. Before a primary BIND server can be started, these files must contain the correct information for your zone. Secondary servers need only three files: `named.boot`, `named.ca`, and `named.local`.

`named.boot` is read by the `named` daemon as soon as it is invoked. `named.boot` tells the server what type of server it is, defines the zone or domain for the server, and specifies a directory path for the other configuration files. Below is the file for `ivy`, the primary BIND server in our sample network. Lines beginning with a semicolon are comments.

```
;
; BIND data file to boot a primary name server.
;
; directory where all the data files are stored
directory /var/dss/namedb
;
; type domain                        source host/file
primary    cs.unca.edu              unca.cs.master
primary    52.18.152.in-addr.arpa   unca.cs.rev
;
```

```
secondary unca.edu                152.18.1.10    unca.bak
secondary 18.152.in-addr.arpa     152.18.1.10    unca.rev.bak
;
primary   0.0.127.in-addr.arpa    named.local
;
; load the cache data last
cache     .                       named.ca
```

This file identifies the directory (/var/dss/namedb) where the other files named will reside. It also tells ivy that it is the primary server for two domains: cs.unca.edu and 52.18.152.in-addr.arpa. Data for the cs.unca.edu domain can be found in the file unca.cs.master. The second domain, 52.18.152.in-addr.arpa, is the reverse domain name, and data for it can be found in the file unca.cs.rev. (The reverse domain name information is used for looking up host names for a given address, rather than looking up addresses for a given name.)

In addition to being a primary BIND server for our little network, ivy is also a secondary server for the campus network (unca.edu). The two secondary statements indicate the domains, the primary servers for those domains, and the files ivy is to use to store the information it copies from the primary servers.

The next-to-last statement names the local server as the primary server for its loopback domain. The final statement is used to load an initial cache of root servers, which is contained in the file named.ca.

Starting a BIND Server

The BIND server daemon named must be started before queries can be resolved. Usually invoked at boot time, named scans the specified boot file and loads the listed resource records into its cache. An entry in the boot file typically looks like this:

```
echo -n 'BIND daemon:'                >/dev/console
[-f /usr/etc/named] && {
    /usr/etc/named /var/dss/namedb/named.boot;
    echo -n ' named'  >/dev/console
}
```

BIND Clients

BIND clients ask servers for IP addresses. BIND clients use a resolver file called /etc/resolv.conf. This file tells the client what domain it belongs to and which server(s) to query for name resolution. Any time a client makes a request through the resolver, this file is accessed to determine the correct server. A sample file from hominy is:

```
; sample /etc/resolv.conf
;
; BIND data file.
;
domain          cs.unca.edu
nameserver      152.18.52.5
nameserver      152.18.52.3
```

The domain line tells hominy that its domain is cs.unca.edu. Its two name servers are 152.18.52.5 and 152.18.52.3.

As with NIS, a BIND server can also be a BIND client, using either itself or another server.

7.6.3   Adding Resource Records

A detailed discussion of setting up resource records is beyond the scope of this chapter, but a few crucial highlights will be mentioned here.

A master server must have a start of authority (SOA) record. The following example is from ivy, our master BIND server:

```
@  IN  SOA  ivy.cs.unca.edu. postmaster.cs.unca.edu. (
       59           ; serial
       14400        ; refresh
       3600         ; retry
       1209600      ; expire
       86400 )      ; minimum
```

The @ in the first position refers back to the domain name declared in the named.boot file (cs.unca.edu in this case). IN is the address class, used for all Internet resource records. The SOA specifies that this is an SOA resource record. ivy.cs.unca.edu is the primary master server for this domain. postmaster.cs.unca.edu identifies the email address of the person responsible for the domain. (If you actually want to send email, you will need to replace the first period with an "at" sign @: postmaster@cs.unca.edu). The other items specify various odd options, such as the minimum lifetime of a resource record.

Another important resource record is the name server (NS), which specifies all servers for the domain. Here again are some examples from ivy:

```
IN  NS  ivy.cs.unca.edu.
IN  NS  ncnoc.concert.net.
IN  NS  tryon.cs.unca.edu.
IN  NS  balsam.unca.edu.
```

Also useful are CNAME records, which let you set up aliases for hosts. For example, the line:

```
ftp        IN   CNAME       ivy
```

specifies that incoming `ftp` requests to the address `ftp.cs.unca.edu` will be routed to `ivy`. This allows you to move a particular service like `ftp` to another machine but still leave the generic service address the same.

As hosts are added to a network, address (A) and pointer (PTR) records will have to be added for them, each in a different file on the master server. Here are the records added to `ivy` for a new host, `hominy`:

```
hominy         IN    A    152.18.52.54
54    IN    PTR   hominy.cs.unca.edu.
```

The first line is contained in a file for the domain `cs.unca.edu`. The name `hominy` will be expanded to `hominy.cs.unca.edu`. The second line is contained in a file for the reverse domain `52.18.152.in-addr.arpa`. This is used whenever `hominy` is looked up using its IP number.

7.6.4 Testing

There are several tools that can help in figuring out problems with BIND configurations.

7.6.4.1 named_dump.db

If you send `named` a SIGINT signal, it will dump its cache and database into the file `/usr/tmp/named_dump.db` for your perusal. Sending the SIGINT is easier if you use the file `/etc/named.pid`, where `named` stores its process id:

```
kill -INT  `cat /etc/named.pid`
```

7.6.4.2 nslookup

In its simplest form, the `nslookup` command will return the name, IP address, alias, and server information for a specified host. However, `nslookup` is more than a simple IP address look-up tool. In interactive mode, it allows you to query servers about any information stored in their databases, along with some information that is not, such as the people logged in on a particular host. For example, here's how to find the start of authority information for the `unca.edu` domain:

```
% nslookup
Default Server: ivy.cs.unca.edu
Address: 152.18.52.5
> set q=soa
> unca.edu
Server: ivy.cs.unca.edu
Address: 152.18.52.5
unca.eduorigin = balsam.unca.edu
    mail addr = hostmaster.unca.edu
serial=49, refresh=14400, retry=3600, expire=1209600,
min=172800
>
```

After setting the search type to soa (set q=soa), we ask for information on unca.edu. We find that balsam.unca.edu contains the start of authority record for that domain.

7.6.5 Learning More

A major resource for information on BIND is Liu and Albitz's *DNS and BIND*. The books by Hunt and Nemeth et al. also contain useful information.

7.6.6 Using NIS, BIND, and /etc/hosts Together

NIS allows distributed LAN system management, while BIND provides WAN naming services. There are also times when you may want to use /etc/hosts to resolve particular host names. It seems a natural desire to use them together, and all three methods of host look-up services can coexist. However care must be taken to understand the process of resolving names when more than one naming service is being used.

Almost all vendor implementations require some way of defining the order in which services are tried. ULTRIX uses a file named /etc/svc.conf that is used to configure services for system databases such as name resolution and security levels. Silicon Graphics systems use a modified /etc/resolv.conf file to specify service order. SunOS assumes NIS will be used with BIND. Consult your vendor manuals to see which naming services are supported and how to specify the order of their use.

7.6.7 Wide Area Distributed System Management

While NIS provides distributed system management at a local area network level, it proves cumbersome when scaled to include an entire enterprise. BIND provides a wide area network framework for distributing information, but it is traditionally used for a limited set of services such as host names. What is required is a service that provides similar information to NIS yet functions like BIND. Ideally, this service would include additional security and authentication while remaining transparent to the end user.

Such a service was designed to meet these same needs at MIT for Project Athena. This service, known as Hesiod, is one of the core components of the Project Athena environment. Hesiod provides a dynamic network database naming service that furnishes, at a minimum, much the same information as NIS but that is more suited to wide area networking. Based on BIND, Hesiod requires only the addition of one more type of BIND resource record. This single entry enables Hesiod to supply information about passwords, locations of mail stops, and more. An extension of NIS, NIS+, has similar goals.

7.7   Configuring Distributed File Systems

A distributed file system is a file service system made up of servers, clients and storage devices. These components may be contained within a single LAN or may include workstations, desktop PCs and mainframe systems on an international WAN. The ultimate goal of this file service system, whether it be small or large scale, is to provide client access to file resources consistent with the response time when clients access files on their local file system. In other words, to the end user it should seem as though a desired file is on their local file system, whether it is or not. Some distributed file system software may even hide the actual location of the data to the end user; this is called location transparency.

At one time, the Network File System (NFS) from Sun Microsystems was the only commercial offering of distributed file system software for UNIX. Since Sun's 1985 introduction of NFS, many other vendors have implemented NFS on their systems. In addition to most versions of UNIX, NFS has been implemented on MS-DOS, DEC/VMS and Novell. NFS is now the most popular and widely used distributed file system implementation. Because of its wide availability, NFS is the only distributed file system that will be described in detail in this chapter.

NFS is of particular importance in environments where a limited amount of disk storage must be shared or where a file server mechanism will reduce system administration tasks. In both instances, a single image of a file system may be shared among hosts. This reduces both the amount of disk storage needed and the amount of time required for management.

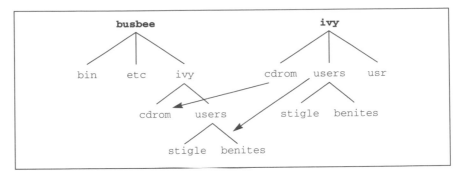

Figure 7.4   Importing file systems

Another important distributed file system is the Andrew File System (AFS) from Carnegie Mellon University. AFS is part of Andrew, a distributed computing and development environment begun in 1983. A commercial implementation, called DFS, is available from the Open Systems Foundation (OSF) as part of OSF's DCE distributed computing environment. Many UNIX vendors, along with Microsoft Corporation, have announced support for AFS. One extremely important aspect of AFS is that it is expected to be able to support over five thousand workstations!

7.7.1   Configuring NFS

NFS allows one host to access file systems on other computers. This is accomplished using a modified version of the UNIX mount command to connect a remote file system. It then almost appears as if the remote files are stored on a local disk. The location of the files, therefore, becomes somewhat transparent to the user. We say *almost* and *somewhat* because the amount of tranparency will depend on just how remote the remote file system is. If the remote file system is reasonably close, users may not be aware that the files they are accessing are physically located on another machine. Accessing very remote file systems may result in noticeable delays and time-outs.

Let's explain a couple of common NFS terms before we get started: if you can access a remote file system, then your host has *imported* the file system; if your local file systems are accessible by remote computers, your host has *exported* them.

In the following sections, we will demonstrate how to import two file systems from ivy (/users and /cdrom) to busbee. The results are shown in Figure 7.4.

7.7.2   Importing a Rremote File System

An imported (remote) file system is identified in the /etc/fstab file on the system where it will be used. The location, name, and syntax of this file vary depending on your version of UNIX; check your local man pages.

For your local file systems, /etc/fstab associates the physical partitions of a disk with a specific pathname. For remote file systems you wish to import, a path and hostname will be specified in place of a partition.

The following lines are examples of two local and two remote file systems from the /etc/fstab on busbee:

```
/dev/rz3a     /                 ufs rw 1 1
/dev/rz3g     /backup/celo      ufs rw 1 2
/users@ivy    /ivy/users        nfs rw,bg,nosuid,nodev 0 0
/cdrom@ivy    /ivy/cdrom        nfs ro,bg 0 0
```

Each file system is described on a separate line. From the example above, the root file system (/) is mounted on device /dev/rz3a, a local disk partition. Another local disk partition, /dev/rz3g, is mounted on /backup/celo. The file systems /users and /cdrom of ivy will be mounted on /ivy/users and /ivy/cdrom, respectively, on busbee. File systems may be imported with read-write (rw) capability or as read-only (ro). The file system /cdrom at ivy is mounted as read-only.

An important option on the remote file systems above is the bg option. It specifies that if the mountd daemon on the server system does not respond to the mount request, the mount is retried in the background. If this option is not specified, the system will wait until the mount completes. See the man page for the mount command for the number of times the mount will be retried.

Two other options used in our example are nosuid and nodev. The nosuid option prevents programs stored in ivy's /users file system with the setuid or setgid bits set from being executed on busbee. The nodev option will prevent access to block or character special devices through this file system. The reason for nodev is to prevent remote users from creating their own writable copy of /dev/kmem. If you can write to /dev/kmem, you can modify kernel data structures and give your processes root access.

For the mount to take place, there must be a directory, or mount point, created on the importing machine. In our example, the mount points are /ivy/users and /ivy/cdrom. Most system administrators use the convention of specifying the hostname as the first component of the mount point's pathname. For example, /ivy/users contains ivy as its first component. This convention shows users that they are using a remote file system when they use commands such as pwd. While thwarting location transparency, it does show the user that a distributed file system is in use.

7.7.3   Exporting a File System

Importing a file system is one part of NFS. Exporting is the other: you must indicate that the file system is to be exported from the system where it resides. Exported file systems are specified in the /etc/exports file. To continue our example, the following lines must be included in the /etc/exports file on ivy in order for /users and /cdrom to be mounted on busbee:

```
/users busbee
/cdrom -o busbee
```

The option -o indicates that the cdrom file system is to be exported read-only. The format of options may vary; check your man page.

It is not necessary to export the entire file system on a remote disk. Often only the part of a file system below a specific directory will be exported.

7.7.4   Other NFS Considerations

There are several daemons that must be running to support NFS, the most important of which is the mountd daemon. This daemon will be started during the boot process and is responsible for handling mount requests from clients. If you modify the /etc/exports file, this daemon must be restarted or otherwise told to reread /etc/exports. Other daemons required for NFS operation are:

- nfsd   NFS daemon
- portmap   RPC port lookup daemon
- biod   Block I/O daemon

These daemons are normally started during system boot. See Chapter 4, UNIX Internals, for the inside story.

7.7.5   Administering NFS

If your system offers an NFS management tool such as nfssetup, use it. This script or program will make administration tasks much simpler for the administrator on both the local and remote systems. It will modify the necessary system files such as /etc/fstab and /etc/exports, as well as modify boot scripts such as /etc/rc.local so that the required daemons will be started at system boot time.

If you add to or modify a file system in /etc/fstab, you may use the mount command to mount a remote file system without having to reboot the system. The command rpcinfo - p *server* will show whether the remote server has registered with portmap. If you add to or modify /etc/exports, you may also need to restart mountd, send it the HUP signal, or run exportfs. Check your man page for details.

Two other useful NFS commands are showmount and nfsstat. showmount will display all clients machines or directories that have remotely mounted a file system from an NFS server. nfsstat displays client and server NFS statistics. Unfortunately, you really must be an NFS guru to understand the output of nfsstat. showmount and nfsstat are discussed further in Sections 7.13.5 and 7.13.6.

7.7.6 Learning More

Please see the UNIX internals chapters for more information about the implementation of NFS within the UNIX kernel. Two excellent sources for information and examples regarding NFS may be found in the books by Nemeth et al. and Stern. For more information about Carnegie Mellon University's Andrew and AFS, see Nathaniel S. Borenstein's *Multimedia Applications Development with the Andrew Toolkit.*

7.8   Setting Up Network Printing

One of the challenges you will face as a network administrator will be to get printers up and running, and then keep them available for your user community. Depending on your environment, you will use differ- ent procedures to define, enable, and maintain your printers. One of the following administration tools is probably available to you: lprsetup under Digital's Ultrix or OSF/1, admintools under Solaris, lpadmin under System V, or smit under AIX. In any case, if your system offers a system management tool that assists you in installation or maintenance of printing devices, use it! It will make your life much easier, taking you step-by-step through such processes as creating subdirectories to contain the spool files and editing system files used to control the operation of a printer and define its operating characteristics.

Adding network printing capability to your system is a two-step pro- cess. First add the printer definition to the /etc/printcap file on the hosts from which you wish to print. Then add the names of these hosts to the `/etc/hosts.lpd` file on the print server, which is the host to which the printer is physically attached.

In the following excerpt from the `/etc/printcap` file on `hominy`,

```
rbh221|lp3|lw3|lw:\
    :lp=:\
    :rm=ivy.cs.unca.edu:\
    :rp=rbh221:\
    :sd=/usr/spool/lpd-rbh221:
```

the `rm` variable specifies the host machine (`ivy.cs.unca.edu`) to which the printer is attached and the `rp` variable specifies the name (`rbh221`) by which the remote machine knows the printer. (Note that both `hominy` and `ivy` call the printer `rbh221`.)

`/etc/hosts.lpd` is a simple list of host names. Here's a sample from `ivy`:

```
hominy.cs.unca.edu
busbee.cs.unca.edu
```

The print server will refuse print requests from hosts not included in `/etc/hosts.lpd`. Using our small 5-host network as an example, print requests to `ivy` from `rosman` and `celo` will be refused (they aren't in the file above), but requests from `hominy` and `busbee` will be honored.

An alternative to using `/etc/hosts.lpd` is to use the more general `/etc/hosts.equiv`, a file that specifies hosts that allow access to `rlogin`, `rsh`, and `rcp` without having to provide a password. `/etc/hosts.equiv` will be discussed further in Section 7.12.1, but for handling network printing, we recommend using the more restricted `/etc/hosts.lpd`.

7.8.1   Learning More

See *UNIX System Administration Handbook* by Nemeth et al. for a description of how to install and maintain printers under both System V and BSD systems.

7.9   Routing Mail With Sendmail

Reading and sending electronic mail is often the first introduction to UNIX for a new user. The ability to send and receive electronic messages has been one of the prime motivations for many network designs. During the 1970s and 1980s, several different methods for delivering mail were developed and put into active use. Each mail delivery mechanism worked well when used in the environment for which it was designed. However, with the arrival of the Internet and exchange of mail across heterogeneous networks and protocols, mail delivery has become a challenge.

sendmail was designed to solve the problems involved in the exchange of mail between heterogeneous networks. sendmail is a mail transport program that acts as a universal post office. sendmail can receive mail with one addressing scheme, translate the address format, and call the appropriate mailer to perform the mail delivery. It's important to note that sendmail doesn't deliver mail or interface with a user. It takes messages that have been created by mail interface programs such as mail or MH, edits the headers as required for the destination format, and calls the appropriate mailers to perform delivery or forwarding. There are several mail handlers available, but sendmail is the only one that will be discussed here.

sendmail.cf is the configuration file used by sendmail. It has three functions: defining the sendmail environment, specifying how addresses are to be modified for the receiving mailer, and mapping an address into the instructions necessary to deliver the mail. The format of sendmail.cf is very cryptic.

Some of the most important specifications in the sendmail.cf file are those that show how addresses are to be rewritten when mail is routed to its destination. This is accomplished using a series of *rulesets* numbered 0 through 29. The rulesets are processed in a very particular order depending on the type of address being modified. Ruleset 3 is always processed first. Why? Don't ask.

Individual rulesets contain instances of a rewrite macro. The rewrite macro specifies how an email address is transformed to a format more acceptable to the next "post office." For example, if a user were to specify a user address of uncavx::rkbenites1, sendmail might transform that destination address to rkbenites1@uncavx.dnet.

The main rule for modifying sendmail.cf is: find someone who has already made the changes you need. Beg, borrow, or steal a copy of those alterations and incorporate them into your copy of sendmail.cf. Volumes could be written about modifying sendmail.cf but we'll only cover a minor modification here to give you an idea of the abstruse nature of the file.

The following sendmail.cf rewrite macro,

```
#     Send BITNET mail to cunyvm.cuny.edu
#   --> next line is the start of the Rewrite macro
R$*@$-.bitnet        $1%$2.bitnet@cunyvm.cuny.edu
#   --> end of the rewrite macro specification
```

will transform the input address

```
bob@uhawaii.bitnet
```

to the new destination address

```
bob%uhawaii.bitnet@cunyvm.cuny.edu
```

The # character in position 1 of a macro line indicates a comment. The rewrite macro has an R in position 1, followed by two patterns: an input pattern and a transformation pattern. The R macro allows pattern matching using transformation meta symbols similar in appearance to shell variables, but with distinctly different effects. The meta symbol $*, for instance, causes sendmail to match zero or more tokens from the input pattern to the output pattern. $-, on the other hand, matches a single token. Particular input pattern tokens may be retrieved using another meta symbol. For example, $1 would retrieve the first token of the input parameter, $2 the second, and so on.

Because sendmail uses "canonical" addresses for most of its rewrite macros, you won't find an example this simple in your sendmail.cf.

Often the rewrite rules are used to enforce an administrative decision that an enterprise will use a particular mail server. For example, if you send mail from the host hominy but replies should go to the mail server ivy, the network administrator can configure sendmail to remove hominy from the Reply-to line, thereby ensuring that any replies to the original message won't be routed to hominy. Another common use of sendmail is to translate UUCP addresses to domain addresses.

7.9.1   Learning More

For an excellent discussion of sendmail and how to modify sendmail.cf, see Craig Hunt's *TCP/IP Network Administration*. He includes a full description of how to interpret and modify this file. For even more information, an entire book by Costales has been devoted to sendmail, appropriately titled *sendmail*. (Historically, sendmail has been the route for a number of security breaches. Costales has an extensive discussion of security in this context.)

7.10   Installing UUCP

UUCP, or *UNIX-to-UNIX Copy,* has provided rudimentary networking for over twenty years. If you have a computer and a connection to another computer in the UUCP network, UUCP networking is cheap and accessible. If an Internet connection is neither possible nor feasible, UUCP may be the only option.

Despite its name, UUCP is much more than a copy program. It is a batch processing and spooling system that enables transfer of information to remote systems, and remote execution of commands. There is also support for remote administration and maintenance.

It is important to remember that UUCP is a batch system, and usually requests are serviced only at predetermined times during the day or night. After submitting a command, do not be surprised if you receive no indication of its success until several hours later.

Most systems severely restrict which commands may be executed remotely by UUCP. It is quite normal for a restricted site to permit only mail access. Most implementations of UUCP will not return any indication of failure if a command is denied execution.

Traditionally, the connection to remote systems has been achieved using asynchronous serial lines and dial-up access through an autocall unit (ACU) or modem with autodial capability. The majority of UUCP connections are still handled this way. This underlines the major benefit of UUCP: it is a low cost method for attaining some type of general network connectivity for mail and news. For mail, `sendmail.cf` determines which messages go through the UUCP line and which remain on the local machine.

Hardware requirements for UUCP are minimal. The same hardware used to provide interactive terminal services can be used by UUCP. Systems can be connected through dedicated tty ports and a null modem cable, or through modems with autodial features.

Many vendors provide scripts to assist in installing UUCP. Good scripts can provide a safe, easy mechanism for managing general tasks for UUCP connections. System administration efforts are usually minimal once a connection has been established and debugged. Checking the log files and monitoring the status once a day should suffice for light to moderately used systems. Systems that handle a heavy load of UUCP traffic will need to be monitored more closely. Particular care should be taken to ensure that sufficient disk space is available for the amount of expected traffic.

7.10.1   Learning More

The best complete source of information is Todino and O'Reilly's *Managing UUCP and Usenet.* Garfinkel and Spafford's *Practical UNIX Security* devotes a chapter to security considerations in using and managing UUCP.

7.11   Using Diskless Mode

In large installations, workstations may use a mode of operation called *diskless*. In this mode, the individual hosts on the network boot from a file server rather than from their local disks. This saves money by reducing the need for a lot of local disk space. Its big advantage, though, is that it makes management of the network much easier. Installing operating system upgrades and many other system administration tasks can be handled primarily on the file server rather than having to be repeated for each workstation. This saves time and also ensures a more consistent environment for the network.

If you decide to use this mode, this chapter cannot offer much help. The details vary so widely among manufacturers that you will have to get the documentation for your system and read it very carefully.

7.12   Some Security and Reliability Considerations

Along with keeping a network up and running, the issue of security is one that should be of greatest importance to the network administrator. It is usually the case, however, that it isn't until there is a problem or an outright breach that security becomes a concern.

Network security is the responsibility of both the network administrator and the users of the network. One of the most important responsibilities of the network administrator is to communicate the fact that security is a responsibility for all users. Educating your user community about how the network is connected and providing some basic information about network hardware may save you the time of having to deal with service interruptions caused by something as simple as an unseated transceiver. A seemingly inconsequential task like moving a workstation may have undesirable effects, like taking down the network!

This section won't reiterate the security issues present on single isolated hosts, although they still exist for hosts in a network environment. We will turn our attention to a few specific security issues related to networking.

Specific security concerns have been mentioned in other sections of this chapter. Network administrators who use a specific network service such as NIS are encouraged to consult the recommended references for more detailed discussion of security problems and solutions for those services, as well as Garfinkel's exellent *Practical UNIX Security*.

7.12.1   Trusted Hosts

Two files, `/etc/hosts.equiv` and `~/.rhosts` (in a user's home directory) provide convenient access to users of `rlogin`, `rsh`, and `rcp` (the so-called *r*-commands), but may also be a security hazard. Systems specified in these files are considered to be *trusted*. When an `rlogin` request is received from a host that is specified in the `/etc/hosts.equiv` file or in the users `.rhosts` file and there is an entry in the `/etc/passwd` file for that user, no further verification is performed. The end result is that password checking is not performed at the remote host. The same is true for `rsh` and `rcp`.

While this seems rather innocent, it is possible for someone to remotely login to a host, circumventing local security, and have free access to what was thought to be a secure system. An unattended terminal could allow access to a remote host without a password. Also, by specifying host names in `.rhosts`, an intruder is provided with a list of systems to which a user has access. At the very least, users should protect their `.rhosts` file to prevent read access by anyone but themselves.

On the other hand, the `/etc/hosts.equiv` and `.rhosts` files limit the number of passwords that are transmitted across the network. This can increase security in an environment where potential intruders may be able to attach *sniffers* to your network.

7.12.2   Physical Security

The issue of password transmission on the network brings up another important consideration for network administrators—the proliferation of personal computers (PCs) attached to the network. Within the UNIX operating system, there is a high level of security for access and control of the network interface. With a PC, however, there is no such security control. This enables a nefarious user to operate the network interface in *promiscuous* mode. In promiscuous mode, all packets that cross the network may be examined; some could contain passwords.

7.12.3   Network Software and Services

Network software programs can be security hazards. Back doors and other weaknesses in programs such as `sendmail` have been exploited by hackers. Be sure you are using the latest version of network programs, which may contain fixes to known security holes.

Network services like `finger` are valuable ways to find and communicate with colleagues, students, and staff. However, the information could be used in a more ominous way. Some people may wish to keep personal information accessible through these services to a minimum. While there is no network equivalent to the unlisted phone number, judicious use of `chfn` command and the `.plan` and `.project` files can help your users control what information they reveal about themselves.

You can also make decisions about what network services to offer. Security experts often recommend disabling programs with little or no security, such as `tftp`. The *r*-commands (`rlogin`, `rsh`, and `rcp`), `finger`, `ftp`, and `telnet` are also candidates for disabling. However, the need for security must be balanced against the usefulness of these commands to your users.

An alternative to disabling network services is to use a firewall between an external network and your own. A firewall is a machine that will pass only approved IP packets between networks. For example, a firewall could be configured to allow mail but not remote login.

7.12.4   Monitoring

Some time spent monitoring your network will help you prevent some security problems and recognize others more quickly. Simple commands such as `ps`, `who`, `ls`, and `last` can help you become familiar with the typical users and activities on the network. It's a good idea to look periodically at crucial networking files such as `/etc/hosts.equiv` and `/etc/inetd.conf` to make sure they haven't been inadvertently or maliciously modified to allow too much access.

You can set up your own monitoring routines. There are also programs available, many of them via anonymous `ftp`, that help automate monitoring and may also control access to network services.

7.12.5   Learning More

The best place to start is with Simson Garfinkel's *Practical UNIX Security* or with Æleen Frisch's *Essential System Administration*.

If your site has access to Internet news, a good newsgroup to monitor is `comp.security.unix`, a forum where important security issues are discussed, and information and help are provided for users at all levels.

7.13   Simple Network Debugging Tools

While commercial packages exist that assist in the tracing and location of network software-related problems, many problems can be diagnosed by using commands found in almost every flavor of UNIX that supports networking. These commands are: `ping`, `arp`, `netstat`, `ifconfig`, `showmount`, and `nfsstat`.

7.13.1   Using the ping Command

Often the first question raised when experiencing network problems is whether particular hosts can be reached via the network. The `ping` command provides a quick and simple answer. Here's an example of `ping`:

```
% ping
hominy is alive
```

Named for the sound sonar makes when searching for underwater objects, the `ping` command sends an ICMP ECHO_REQUEST packet to the desired host. If the host receives the request, it returns an ICMP ECHO_RESPONSE packet. The `ping` command listens for this response and, if one is received, informs the user that the specified host is *alive*, i.e., can be reached through the network.

The `ping` command is a good first tool to use when tracking down network problems. Begin by using `ping` on hosts that you know are on your local network. Once you verify you can `ping` hosts on the local network, attempt to `ping` hosts and gateways separated by increasingly more network hardware to determine where the connection is broken.

While `ping` is extremely useful when determining problems, it should be used carefully in automated scripts due to the load it could impose on a network. Several `ping`s running out of control could generate a lot of background traffic and reduce the performance of the network.

7.13.2   Using the arp Command

The physical networks that underlie the TCP/IP network do not understand IP network addresses. They have their own addressing schemes. The Address Resolution Protocol (ARP) is used to associate a network address with an Ethernet hardware address.

The kernel of the UNIX operating system maintains a table of network addresses and their associated Ethernet addresses, commonly referred to as the ARP cache. When a program wants to send a packet to a local Ethernet host, the kernel must translate a network address to the associated Ethernet address. The ARP cache is checked first. If the address is found there, it is returned to the process requesting the Ethernet address. If the address is not found, a packet is broadcast to every host on the Ethernet. The packet contains the network address for which the associated Ethernet address is needed. If the host that owns the Ethernet address receives this packet, it will respond with its Ethernet address. These network and Ethernet addresses will be stored in the cache, and the Ethernet address will be returned to the requesting process.

Entries in the ARP cache are designated as temporary or permanent. Since the cache is a fixed size, temporary entries *age out* after a period of time and are removed from the cache. Permanent entries will not age out but are very rarely used.

The `arp` command provides a way of displaying and modifying entries in the ARP table. A sample of how to view current entries in the ARP table with the `arp` command follows:

```
% arp -a
ivy.cs.unca.edu (152.18.52.5) at 8:0:2b:1d:32:f
busbee.cs.unca.edu (152.18.52.82) at 8:0:2b:39:f4:58
rosman.cs.unca.edu (152.18.52.58) at 8:0:2b:28:b5:ef
```

The host names and IP numbers should be very familiar to you by now. The other numbers are Ethernet addresses.

7.13.3   Using the netstat Command

The `netstat` command provides access to the contents of network-related data structures stored in the UNIX kernel. The important factor to remember about the `netstat` command is that it displays information as seen from the point of view of the host where it is executed. It shows such information as active sockets, Ethernet counters, and routing statistics in either a snapshot or continuous display mode.

The `netstat` command comes in several forms. One allows viewing of network data structures such as defined interfaces, routing tables and protocol statistics. When an interval is specified, `netstat` continuously displays running statistics for packet traffic on configured interfaces.

The `netstat` command can provide a great deal of information about the state of the network. It is an excellent tool for diagnosing most networking problems. Unfortunately, picking options and interpreting their output can be difficult for network managers. In the next sections we'll look at different forms of the `netstat` command for problem diagnosis.

One thing to remember is to always use the option -n while debugging. Without it, `netstat` will try to look up addresses using the network and display then symbolically. If the network is down, `netstat` may hang up.

7.13.3.1 Displaying Active Interfaces

To display the interfaces currently running, use the option -i. This is very helpful since it allows you to see the current interfaces and their respective statistics. An example with the -i option follows:

```
% netstat -in
Name  Mtu   Network Address        Ipkts Ierrs   Opkts Oerrs   Coll
ln0   1500  152.18  152.18.52.54 6246091    21 4210588    22 70185
lo0   1536  127     127.0.0.1       1818     0    1818     0     0
```

7.13.3.2 Monitoring Routing Tables

Using the option -r with netstat displays the available routes and their status. Sample output using the -r option follows:

```
% netstat -rn
Routing tables
Destination     Gateway         Flags   Refcnt Use       Interface
127.0.0.1       127.0.0.1       UH      3      1360       lo0
152.18          152.18.52.54    U       18     3448924    ln0
default         152.18.254.254  UG      0      208105     ln0
```

The first line of this example shows the route for the local loopback. The second line specifies that packets for the local network, 152.18, go through hominy's interface ln0. The third line shows that everything else goes to the router 152.18.254.254, which is our campus router.

7.13.3.3 Obtaining Cumulative Statistics With netstat

When netstat is invoked with a number indicating a time interval, it displays continuously statistics about the number of packets received and transferred for each interface, along with collisions and errors that have occurred. The 1st line and every 24th line contain cumulative statistics since the last time the system was rebooted. Some sample output follows:

```
% netstat 1
    input    (ln0)    output                 input   (Total)    output
packets errs packets errs colls  packets  errs packets   errs colls
    0     0       0     0    0 51090293 14190 55446127   36 1101521
    0     0       0     0    0        5     0       3    0     0
    0     0       0     0    0       36     0      36    0     0
    0     0       0     0    0        5     0       5    0     0
```

Each line in this example represents statistics for one second. The data provide a means of determining whether traffic through an interface is heavy or if collisions are bogging down the network. Cumulative protocol statistics are available with the netstat option -s.

These statistics include detailed information on a protocol-by-protocol basis. For debugging purposes, this provides a good snapshot of what has transpired over time on the network. Unfortunately, you will need to be a network guru to understand the information.

7.13.4   Using the ifconfig Command

The `ifconfig` command is run as a part of the boot process to assign a network address to and configure the network interface. It may be used at other times to redefine the network address or to modify other network interface operating characteristics. Using the `ifconfig` command with only an interface id will display the current status of that interface. An example follows for the host `rosman`:

```
% ifconfig ln0
ln0: 152.18.52.58 netmask ffff0000
flags=0x563<DYNPROTO,PROMISC,RUNNING,NOTRAILERS,BROADCAST,UP>
broadcast: 152.18.255.255
```

7.13.5   Using the showmount Command

The `showmount` command may be used to display all NFS client machines that have remotely mounted file systems from an NFS server. It is a quick method to see if your NFS server is running and which clients are using exported file systems. See Section 7.7 for more information about NFS. A short example of the `showmount` command and its output follows:

```
% showmount -a ivy
celo.cs.unca.edu:/users
celo.cs.unca.edu:/cdrom
busbee.cs.unca.edu:/users
busbee.cs.unca.edu:/cdrom
rosman.cs.unca.edu:/cdrom
```

The option `-a` requests that the output be specified in the format `client:directory`. From this example, it can be seen that `celo`, `busbee`, and `rosman` all have the directory `/cdrom` mounted and that `celo` and `busbee` have `/users` mounted.

7.13.6   Using the nfsstat Command

The `nfsstat` command is a valuable tool that may be used to display current statistics for both NFS and RPC interfaces in the UNIX system kernel. `nfsstat` will display both client or server statistics. While NFS statistics are initialized to zero at each system boot, `nfsstat` may also be used to reset specific statistics in the interim. A common use for `nfsstat` is to identify server bottlenecks by displaying client timeouts.

7.13.7   Learning More

See Craig Hunt's *TCP/IP Network Admistration* or Æleen Frisch's *Essential System Adminstration* for good descriptions of management tools and strategies.

7.14   Selected References

N. S. Borenstein, *Multimedia Applications Development with the Andrew Toolkit*, First Edition, Englewood Cliffs: Prentice Hall, 1990.

D. Comer, *Internetworking With TCP/IP: Principles, Protocols, and Architecture*, First Edition, Englewood Cliffs: Prentice Hall, 1988.

B. Costales (with E. Allman and N. Rickert), *Sendmail,* First Edition, Sebastopol, CA: O'Reilly and Associates, 1993.

A. Frisch, *Essential System Administration*, First Edition, Sebastopol, CA: O'Reilly and Associates, 1992.

S. Garfinkel and G. Spafford, *Practical UNIX Security*, First Edition, Sebastopol, CA: O'Reilly and Associates, 1991.

C. Hunt, *TCP/IP Network Adminstration,* First Edition, Sebastopol, CA: O'Reilly and Associates, 1992.

C. Liu and P. Albitz, *DNS and BIND,* First Edition, Sebastopol, CA: O'Reilly and Associates, 1992.

E. Nemeth, G. Snyder, and S. Seebass, *UNIX System Adminstration Handbook,* First Edition, Englewood Cliffs: Prentice Hall, 1989.

W. Stallings, *Data and Computer Communications*, Fourth Edition, New York: MacMillan, 1994.

H. Stern, *Managing NFS and NIS*, First Edition, Sebastopol, CA: O'Reilly and Associates, 1992.

G. Todino and T. O'Reilly, *Managing UUCP and Usenet*, Tenth Edition, Sebastopol, CA: O'Reilly and Associates, 1992.

Chapter

8

Distributed Computing Environment

Kenneth Pugh

8.1 Introduction

Computer networks have become common in business and academics. Users on networks have the ability to share resources, such as data files, executable files, and printers. On most networks, especially those composed of computers from multiple vendors, this sharing is not transparent to the user. Additionally, the location of files may change due to computer failures or additional equipment. These moves may require user notification.

The Distributed Computing Environment (DCE) integrates a network into a single computing power. The user can access files across the network, regardless of the location, host computer type or operating system. Services and resources are located with a location-independent name. DCE has good performance, which is scalable to large numbers of network computers. A network security system provides protection for files and resources.

DCE strongly supports the client/server model, such as the file servers and print servers. Programmers can easily develop distributed applications where the front end (e.g., the user interface) runs on one machine and the back end (e.g., database manipulations) runs on another machine.

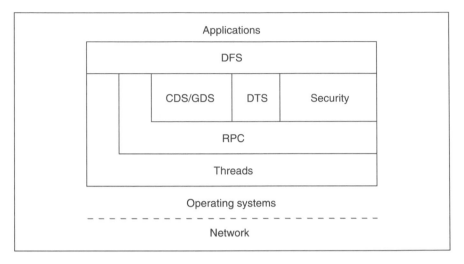

Figure 8.1   DCE overview

8.2   Overview

The basic organization of DCE is the cell. The cell is an interconnected group of machines, although not necessarily on the same physical network. DCE is optimized for intracell operations. There is an overlying set of services provided by DCE which is supported by underlying mechanisms. (See Figure 8.1.)

The upper set of services includes the directory services, the distributed file system, time synchronization, and security. The Cell Directory Service (CDS) provides for a consistent name directory within the cell. It communicates with the Global Directory Service (GDS) through the Global Directory Agent (GDA) for information about other cells. The Distributed File System (DFS) permits location-independent storage of program and data files. The Distributed Time Service (DTS) provides time synchronization between machines. The Security Service (SEC) protects resources, such as files from unwanted intrusion.

The underlying components are remote procedure calls (RPCs), threads, and diskless services. RPCs provide transparent access to operations and data across the network. Threads are multiple control flows within a single process. Diskless services permit workstations with no local hard disk to boot from the network and use its resources.

These services may be also grouped as fundamental services, which are integrated together (threads, RPCs, DTS, CDS, and SEC), and as data-sharing services (DFS and diskless support). Management tools for these services provide a central point of control for activities within the cell.

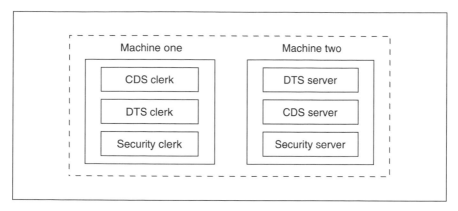

Figure 8.2   The cell—building block for DCE

The components of DCE have come from a wide variety of sources. The CDS/GDS is based on DECdns and X.500. File sharing comes from the Andrew File System of Carnegie Mellon University and Transarc. Time synchronization evolved from Digital's DTS. The Athena project at MIT contributed the Kerberos security system. RPCs were developed from NCS of Hewlett-Packard/Apollo. The thread interface follows POSIX and Digital's CONCERT Multithreaded Architecture.

The DCE components make it easy to implement client/server systems. These are implemented using RPC interfaces and threaded servers. Clients can also be threaded so that multiple servers can be accessed simultaneously.

8.3   The Cell

The cell is the basic building block of DCE. It is a group of users, systems, and resources that share common DCE services. The cell is a logical connection of resources. It does not have to be located on a particular physical network. A cell can span multiple networks, or two cells can coexist on a single network.

The size of a cell depends on the predicted usage. DCE is optimized for intracell performance. The more cells that an organization uses, the greater the amount of intercell traffic. The requirements for intercell authentication cells cuts performance. Small cells, such as for departmental groups, make management easier.

Each cell requires at least one machine acting as a server. The server provides CDS and security. To maintain time synchronization, there should be at least three machines acting as DTS servers. (See Figure 8.2.)

Each DCE client requires a few processes communicating with the server. These include the CDS clerk, the DTS clerk, and the security clerk. Applications interface to DCE through the DCE runtime library.

8.4 The Cell Directory Service and Global Directory Service

CDS provides a central naming and locating service for resources within a cell. GDS provides a similar service for inter-cell communication.

8.4.1 Names

The name of each host within a cell must be unique within that cell. In order to be part of the GDS, the name of the cell must be unique among all cells. It must use either the CCITT X.500 Global Directory Service or the DNS naming convention. The security system is not designed to support multiple cell names or aliases. X.500 and DNS names are guaranteed to be unique if you register the name.

X.500 names consist of a set of attribute values. Some standard attributes are C for Country, O for Organization and OU for Organizational Unit. The values for C and O are assigned by national organizations. In the United States, this is the American National Standards Institute in New York City. An example of an X.500 name is /C=US/O=PughKilleen. An organization can add additional attributes to make unique cell names for itself, such as /C=US/O=PughKilleen/OU=Training.

DNS names consist of an inverse hierarchy. Government Systems in Chantilly, VA assigns higher level DNS names. There are a number of domains, such as education (edu) and commercial (com). An example of a DNS name is duke.edu. As with X.500, an organization can add additional qualifiers, such as ac.duke.edu to make unique names for cells.

Because cell names and names within a cell are unique, a resource within a cell has a globally unique name. Names that include cell names begin with /... and follow the form of /.../cell/directory/. For example, suppose the X.500 cell name was /C=US/O=PughKilleen/OU=Training. To make a reference to /ultimate within this cell, you would use /.../C=US/O=PughKilleen/OU=Training/ultimate. For a DNS name, like /ac.duke.edu, a reference to /zenith would be /.../ac.duke.edu/zenith. Names referring to the local cell begin with /.:. So /.:/ultimate and /.:/zenith refer to /ultimate and zenith in their respective local cells.

Names can be searched for in both a *white pages* mode and a *yellow pages* mode. In the former, a particular name is sought. In the latter, a search is made for entries that have particular attribute values, such as a printer that supports a particular resolution.

8.4.2   Directories

Every object in a cell, such as a server, can have an an entry in CDS with a unique name. Each entry has additional attribute/value pairs. CDS names can be organized into directories. A complete CDS name consists of a directory pathname and a leaf name. The full name must be unique within the cell. The names appear like UNIX filenames, but the directories are internal to CDS.

The directory hierarchy is used to keep names unique and organized. For example, two printers on two different hosts might be named `Printer_MyHost` and `Printer_YourHost`. Using directories, these names could be `MyHost/Printer` and `YourHost/Printer`.

Directories may lead to other system servers, such as the distributed file system (`/.:/fs`) or the security system (`/.:/sec`). These directories are called *junctions* and are described below.

Like UNIX, there is a standard set of directories that should be established within CDS. `/.:/cell-profile` is used by remote cells to find the security server for this cell. `/.:/subsys` catalogs information for various servers. For example, information on security is in `/.:/subsys/dce/sec`. The directory `/.:/hosts` keeps names of groups and profiles.

8.4.3   CDS Server/Clerks

CDS is organized with a master server, read-only servers, and clerks. The master server maintains a clearinghouse—the database of names and attributes. When updates occur, these may be distributed immediately or periodically to read-only servers. The *skulk* setting determines the frequency of these updates.

Every machine has a CDS clerk. A process contacts the clerk for name entries (using the Name Service Interface, NSI*). The clerk contacts the CDS server for the information associated with the names and returns the information to the process. The clerk keeps a cache of recently referenced names, which avoids the cost of contacting the server if the requested names are in it.

---

* CDS is actually a general purpose directory service. NSI, which is used to find servers, is only a subset of the total interface. The X/Open Directory Service Application Programming Interface (XDS API) can be used for full functionality of the directory service. Thus, application-defined information can be kept in CDS.

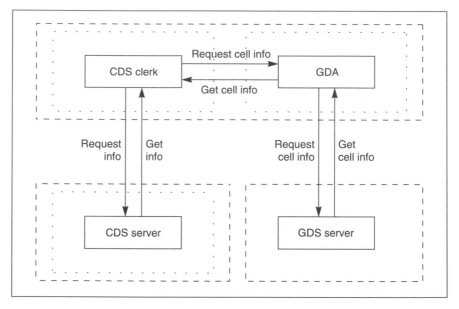

Figure 8.3   CDS/GDS

If the name refers to another cell, the clerk contacts the GDA, which routes the request to the GDS server (DNS or X.500). The information from the other cell is routed back to the clerk through the GDA. (See Figure 8.3.)

8.4.4   Clearinghouses

CDS information can be kept in more than one clearinghouse. Each CDS server has its own clearinghouse. For each directory in a CDS directory, a child pointer is created. This child pointer gives the clearinghouse in which the directory is located. The root directory in a clearinghouse contains child pointers to all its child's directories. Replicas of directories can be kept in multiple clearinghouses for efficiency purposes. Soft links, similar to UNIX soft links, can provide multiple names for the same directory entry.

An administrator of a cell can alter the contents, and perform general operations on CDS by using the CDS Control Program (cdscp). This includes adding or deleting directories, altering the locations of replicas, and creating soft links.

8.5   Distributed File System

The Distributed File System (DFS) provides transparent, efficient file sharing with security. Files have a uniform naming convention. There can be numerous read-only copies for efficiency. Maintenance, such as backing-up and restoring files, can be easily performed.

DFS can coexist with native file systems. It uses the Local File System (LFS), which is a log-based fast-restart system. It can also use the UNIX file system as an alternative to LFS. However, no replication or security protection is provided in that case.

8.5.1   Filesets and Aggregates

DFS files are kept in filesets, which are groups of related files. A fileset is the equivalent of one user's home directory and all subdirectories. Filesets themselves are kept within aggregates, which are disk partitions. DFS keeps a database of fileset names and aggregate locations. If an aggregate gets full, a fileset can be moved to another aggregate. The name used to reference the fileset does not change. Filesets may be replicated (cloned) on multiple machines, but only one can be the master copy. If a file in the master copy is altered, the read-only copies are updated.

A reference to a pathname beginning with /.:/fs joins to the DFS system. The root directory of DFS on a local cell is /.:/fs/. This can also be written as /:. Each fileset is mounted onto a directory in DFS in a manner analogous to the UNIX mount command. This links the directory name to the actual fileset location within an aggregate.

8.5.2   Access Control Lists

DFS uses an Access Control List (ACL) for each directory, rather than each file. The ACL contains user names and permissions. There are several kinds of permissions which can be granted to each user. These are the ability to read files in the directory (read), to look at the directory (test), to create new files (insert), to modify existing files (write), to remove files (delete), and to change the ACL itself (administer). A directory which is created inherits the ACL from its parents.

To limit the size of the ACL, protection groups can be created which contain a number of users. These are similar to group permissions in UNIX. Listing a group name in the ACL implicitly grants the same permissions to all users in the group. There are a few special groups. These are anyuser, which is anyone in world; authuser, which is anyone with a security ticket in cell; and administers which are the DFS equivalent of UNIX superusers.

8.5.3   Processes

There are several processes which combine to provide the DFS facilities. The Basic OverSeer (BOS) performs administration tasks and monitors other processes. The Local Filesystem process stores files in a log-based manner for quick recovery. The File Server process delivers files to requesters and keeps status information as to who is using the files. The Replication Server performs fileset manipulations, such as moving, creating, and backing up filesets. The Fileset Location Server maintains the Fileset Location DataBase, which is the key to transparent access. The Update Server keeps the DFS configuration consistent by insuring the same version of the software is running on all machines. The Scout monitors system performance and the Salvager cleans things up if there is a system crash.

The Cache Manager runs on client machines. To find a particular file, it asks the Fileset Location Broker for the host which has a copy of the file. The response may specify any of the hosts which have a copy of the file. The Cache Manager requests the File Server for that host for the file. The entire file is then transferred. It is cached on the local disk or in memory. The Cache Manager may request either a read or write copy of the file. If the file is for reading only, the File Server notifies the Cache Manager if and when its copy is no longer consistent with the master copy. If the file is for writing, the File Server will request a copy back whenever another machine issues a request for the file or when the file is closed. DFS works best for files that are generally read-only or that are updated by only one process at time. A database server is better for frequent updates to a file. (See Figure 8.4.)

There are administrative tools for mounting, cloning, and backing up filesets. Filesets are backed-up on disk before being copied to tape. The backup copy can be mounted separately, so users can access in a read-only mode, the previous version of their files.

8.5.4   Usage

The user uses native operating system commands to access files in DFS. For example with UNIX, files are listed using `ls` and directories are created using `mkdir`. The only minor difference is in how the file is referenced. The format is `/.../cell_name/fs/pathname`. For example `/.../ac.duke.edu/fs/usr/kpugh/a_file` references a file in the cell `ac.duke.edu`. The file is the one called `a_file` in the fileset mounted as `/usr/kpugh`.* Notice that this reference uniquely

---

* This could also be the file `/kpugh/a_file` in the fileset mounted as `/usr`. It all depends on the organization of the filesets.

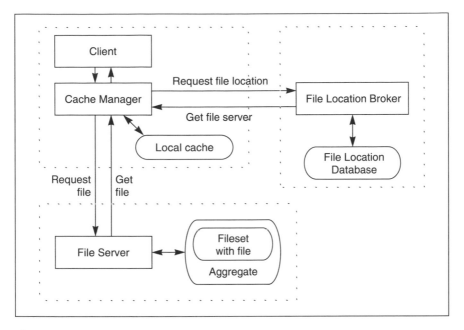

Figure 8.4   DFS

identifies the file. Any user in any cell that is connected to ac.duke.edu and has the appropriate permissions, can use this name to access that file.

A user in the ac.duke.edu cell can use a cell relative name. This would be either /.:/fs/usr/kpugh/a_file or /:/usr/kpugh/ a_file.

8.6   Security

Security on a system involves a number of different concepts. One is authentication—the identification of the users as the individuals they represent themselves to be. Another issue is authorization—does an authenticated user have permission to perform a particular operation? Data integrity insures that information passed on a network has not been altered. Data privacy guarantees that the information cannot be read by unauthorized parties.

The DCE security system uses ticket-granting concepts from the MIT Kerberos system for authentication, and protection groups and Access Control Lists (ACLs) for authorization. Optional cryptographic checksums can provide data integrity, and encryption can give data privacy.

8.6.1   Tickets for Authentication

The ticket-granting arrangement uses a central registry of principals, which are users and services. This registry contains user names with passwords and service names with keys. An authentication server (Ticket Granting Server, TGS) gives tickets to users that are used to communicate with other servers. The privilege or credential server accesses privilege groups and ACLs for resources. The registry and these servers should be on physically secure machines. The ticketing procedure is fairly complicated. The basic idea is that packets are encrypted with a secret key. The packet includes both old and new information. The recipient decrypts the packet using the key. If the old information is valid, then the new information can be trusted. The user sends a ticket to authenticate with a desired service. The ticket is encrypted with a key known to that service. The successful decryption proves the authenticity of the user.

8.6.2   Ticketing Procedure

A user logging onto a workstation enters his or her user name. This is sent to the key distribution center which looks up the name in the registry. After finding the user's password, it creates a ticket for the TGS ($ticket_{TGS}$) which is composed of a session key ($session\_key_{TGS}$), a workstation id, the name of the client, and a lifetime. The key $session\_key_{TGS}$ will be used for encoding packets sent to the TGS. This ticket is grouped into a packet with $session\_key_{TGS}$, the time, and the lifetime. This packet is encoded using the user's password.

When this packet is received, the user's password is requested. It is used to decode the packet. If the password is incorrect, the result will be garbage. If it is correct, the workstation stores $ticket_{TGS}$ and $session\_key_{TGS}$.

To get a ticket for a service, the workstation prepares an authenticator. This is composed of the user name, the workstation id, and the time, all encoded using $session\_key_{TGS}$. It sends the authenticator to the TGS along with the name of the requested service and $session\_key_{TGS}$. The TGS looks up the service name and finds a service key. It creates a session key for the service ($session\_key_{service}$). $session\_key_{service}$, along with the name of the client and time information, is encoded using the service key and becomes a ticket for the requested service ($ticket_{service}$). This ticket, along with $session\_key_{service}$ and time, is encoded in a packet using $session\_key_{TGS}$.

The workstation receives this packet and decodes it with the key $session\_key_{TGS}$ it has stored. It prepares an authenticator composed

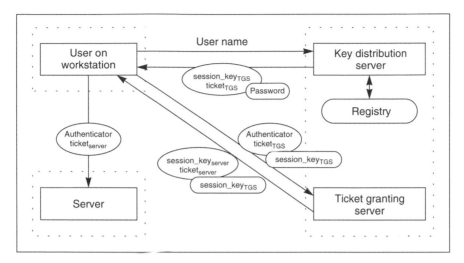

Figure 8.5   Security

of the user name, the workstation id, and the time, and encodes it using $session\_key_{service}$. It then sends this along with $ticket_{service}$ to the requested service. The service decodes $ticket_{service}$ using its own key and gets $session\_key_{service}$ and the user name. It uses $session\_key_{service}$ to decode the authenticator. It checks the user name, the times, and the workstation id. If all is correct, it can be sure the user is the right person. To insure privacy, all communication between the user and the service can be encrypted using $session\_key_{service}$. (See Figure 8.5.)

Cells communicating with other cells in a secure fashion go through an equivalent process. A cell must be registered in all cells with whom it wishes secure communications. There is no central security server, as there is a global name server.

The security system does not enforce authentication. A service does not have to require tickets, but most services do. It is up to individual applications if access via an ACL is required. However, the system does provide a secure method for maintaining and accessing the ACLs, so that an application can be sure that any permissions required are actually those of the user.

8.6.3 Names

The names of users kept in the registry (but not the passwords) are accessible via a junction to CDS, `/sec`. The users are kept in a directory called `principals`. So a user named `kpugh` on a UNIX system would be referred to as `/.:/sec/principals/kpugh`. Typically, the principal names for servers are kept the same as the name of the server itself, for maintenance purposes.

8.7   Distributed Time Service

DCE systems require time synchronization to work properly. The Distributed Time Service (DTS) insures that clocks on all machines are coordinated to within a given accuracy. Time is not an absolute quantity, but includes an inaccuracy based on distance from an absolute time source such as an atomic clock.

8.7.1   UTC and Accuracy

Time is based on Coordinated Universal Time (UTC). A time has the ASCII format:

```
CCYY-MM-DD-hh:mm:ss.fff +/-hh:mmIsss.fff
```

The first part is the UTC date and time `CCYY-MM-DD-hh:mm:ss.fff`. The next part, `+/-hh:mm`, is a time differential factor that accounts for the time zone of the machine. The third part, `Isss.fff`, is the inaccuracy. For example,

```
1993-01-31-12:00:00.0000-04:00I001.00000
```

specifies a time with one second of inaccuracy and a time zone four hours behind UTC.

DTS is called by various systems to get the time. An API is provided for programs to retrieve a timestamp, which is an opaque format of the time. The API also provides the ability to manipulate timestamps and to convert timestamps to and from readable formats. The opaque format is based on a count of 100 nanoseconds from October 15, 1582.

8.7.2   Servers

Time Provider servers periodically synchronize with each other. They may interface to an external time provider, such as WWV or an atomic clock. As timestamps contain an inaccuracy measure, the correct time is computed to be a time which falls within the inaccuracy range of all times of all servers. If a server's range falls out of the ranges of the other servers, it is assumed that the server's time is faulty. The synchronization attempts to compensate for communication delays. The synchronization process can occur periodically or when inaccuracy reaches a certain value. (See Figure 8.6.)

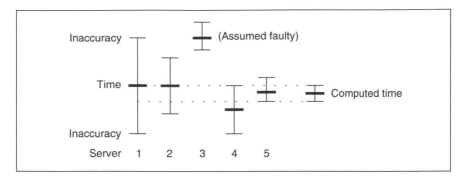

Figure 8.6 Time correction

Corrections to time on each machine are made gradually. The software clock time is adjusted at a rate of one tick per hundred ticks. If the time is too slow, a double tick is added at that time. If the time is too fast, the tick is skipped. Thus times are always monotonic and the clocks are never run backwards.

Couriers are local time servers that talk to global servers. Global time servers help to maintain synchronization among multiple networks. The time can thus be coordinated between a number of networks.

The DTS daemon process on each client contacts a Time Provider server to obtain the correct time.

8.8 Remote Procedure Call

RPCs permit distributed applications. A process can execute a procedure in another address space, either on the same machine or on a different machine in the same or different cell. An RPC server executes the procedure for an RPC client. The RPC runtime, which operates for servers and clients, provides the network communication interface and a server locator facility.

An RPC looks like a normal call to a function in the client. The underlying mechanism is somewhat more complex. A server advertises its RPC function interfaces in the CDS. The server then listens for calls. The client process calls a local interface to the remote procedure. The RPC runtime finds a server for the procedure in the CDS. It calls the server and transmits the arguments for the call. The server receives the call and converts the arguments, if necessary. It then invokes the procedure and transmits the results back to the client. The client receives the results, converting them if necessary, and then

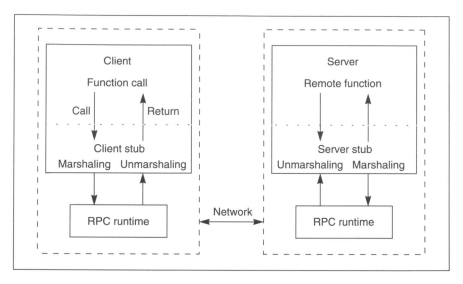

Figure 8.7   Remote procedure call

returns back to the point at which the RPC was called. (See Figure 8.7.)

RPC runtime handles any network problems, such as a timeout or server crash. It handles transparently the conversion between data representations on different machines. It also can select from multiple servers which all provide the same RPC interface.

8.8.1   RPC Interface and IDL

An RPC interface includes a set of functions that are handled by an RPC server. The interface is uniquely identified with a Universal Unique IDentifier (UUID), which is unique among all computers and interfaces in the world. The interface is described with the Interface Description Language (IDL). It includes the operations and data types, similar to an object-oriented class interface.

The UUID is generated using the UUID generator program (uuidgen). It forms a hexadecimal identifier which includes a timestamp and a host identifier. The format is opaque, but its composition insures its uniqueness.*

IDL is a high level language that resembles C. An IDL description of an interface includes a header of the UUID, its name, and a body

---

* UUIDs are also used to identify distinct computing resources such as a particular database, device, process, or processor.

which specifies the data types, constants, and function prototypes. Other IDL files can be included in a file by using the `import` statement. The data types include RPC pipes for efficient transfer of lots of data.

Unlike normal C prototypes, the access (read/write/both) is specified for each parameter. A simple IDL file might look like:

```
[
uuid(ABCDEF01-1234-5678-9ABC-123456789ABC),
version(1.0)
interface my_service
{
void remote_function([out] int * output_arg,
    [in] int * input_arg);
}
```

The execution semantics of each function can be specified. The default is that an operation must execute either once, partially, or not-at-all. The latter two would be the result of a server failure. An idempotent function can execute more than once. If a server fails, the operation will be retried on another server. A *maybe* means that the call does not have any output parameters and therefore does not require response. A broadcast function calls all servers on a network.

The IDL compiler (`idl`), using this file as input (i.e., `idl source.idl`), creates header files for the client and server, and stub code for each. Each program links with the stub code, which provides marshaling and unmarshaling of the arguments. The unmarshaling converts the argument representation from the sender's form to the receiver's form.* The programmer can specify that this conversion is to be performed by a special routine using a `Transmit_as` attribute. (See Figure 8.8.)

You can tailor an interface with an Attribute Configuration File (ACF). The ACF modifies the interpretation of RPC interface. Using the ACF, you can omit operations from a client's stub or change the type of binding. You can specify how errors should be handled—as exceptions or return values.

8.8.2 Binding

The connection of a client to a server is normally handled transparently. This relationship is called binding. It is normally performed

---

* The data are transmitted using ASN.1 BER encoding. This form includes information on the internal structure, so that the receiver can always decode the data.

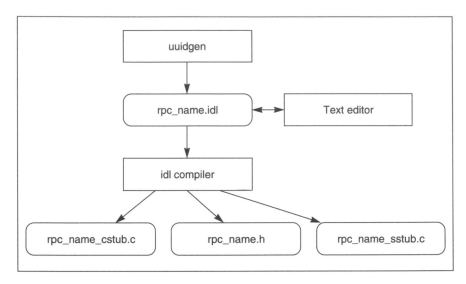

Figure 8.8 IDL compiler

automatically, but this can be overridden by specification in the IDL or by the ACF.

The binding between a client and a server is a temporary link over the network. A client binds with a server by fully specifying a network address, a protocol, and an endpoint. A protocol is a method of communications, such as the connection-oriented TCP/IP or connectionless UDP/IP. An endpoint is the identity of a logical connection for a particular protocol on a particular host. There are a few steps for how a client obtains this information, which will be described shortly. The server binds with the client by using the information supplied by the client.

The server advertises its availability by exporting the RPC interface name, version number, UUID, and the host address to the CDS. It requests endpoints for each protocol it wishes to communicate on, and registers these endpoints with the RPC daemon (rpcd). The rpcd places them in the RPC Endpoint Map.*

The client finds a server by requesting the address of a host from the CDS who has advertised that it services a particular RPC interface. A compatible interface must have the same UUID. The version number of the interface is broken into a major and a minor number.

---

* There are *well-known* endpoints that are fixed values used for particular services. Most servers will request that an endpoint be assigned to them—this is called a dynamic endpoint.

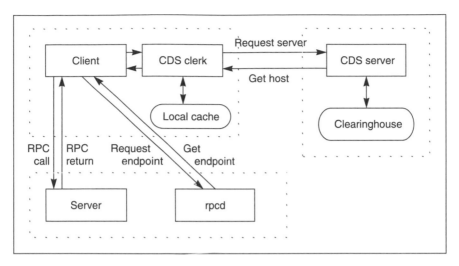

Figure 8.9   Looking up the RPC server

The server's major number must be the same as the client's, and the server's minor number must be equal to or greater than the client's minor number. (See Figure 8.9.)

The network address alone is called a partial binding. The client then contacts the RPC daemon on that host to get a protocol and an endpoint on which the server is listening. This forms a full binding. The client then calls the server on that endpoint and requests the desired operation.

With automatic binding, the RPC runtime takes care of the binding for the client. If a server fails, the runtime binds the client to another server providing the same RPC interface.

8.8.3   Managing Binding

A client can perform its own binding. It can import information from the CDS to get a partial binding, or it can translate a string representation of an address into a binding. A string binding looks like

```
object_uuid@protocol:network_address[endpoint]
```

If the server fails, it is up to the application to rebind. The client can use one of two methods of calling RPC functions. With the implicit method, the calls to RPC use the binding that is set up initially by the client. The explicit method requires that every call to RPC functions includes the binding information. This is used for specific purposes, such as checking to see if every server is working. There is also a custom binding handle for specialized purposes.

8.8.4 Error handling

Using the ACF, you can specify how any RPC errors are to be handled. Errors includes communication errors and server errors. By default, these errors cause exceptions, which if not handled, cause the program to terminate. Using the ACF, you can specify that communication errors (comm_status), server errors (fault_status), or both are to be passed back in arguments to RPC calls, rather than to be handled as exceptions.

Communication errors need be handled only if communications fail routinely. They should be handled only if the application knows that it is calling an RPC by using implicit or explicit binding. Server errors need be handled only if the client has some recovery action it can perform.

8.8.5 Management

Similar to the CDSCP, the RPC Control Program (rpccp) is a program for managing the Endpoint Map. Endpoints can be manually added and deleted from the map.

8.8.6 Servers

There are two models for RPC servers. In the service model, the servers provide a distributed service, which is independent of any resources. The client will get the same operation performed, regardless of which server is used. For example, it does not matter which DTS server is used to get the time.

With the resource model, the client has the ability to access a particular resource, such as a high-speed printer. Although all servers provide the same interface, only one server gives the access to a particular printer. Servers providing the same interface may also differ in action or quality. Some printer outputs are high quality and costly; others may be slow and inexpensive.

An object UUID can be associated with a particular resource such as a laser printer, or a particular class of resources, such as high quality, expensive printers. When a client requests the location of a server, it can specify an RPC object UUID, which must match the server object UUID. Thus, the appropriate server will be selected.

A single server can serve multiple classes of resources by grouping object UUIDs into types. Object UUIDs are grouped into types by the server. Each type has its own UUID. For each type, there is a separate set of functions (entry point vectors, EPV). The interface UUID, type UUID, and the EPV are registered with the RPC runtime. If the RPC call has an object UUID, then the type in which it is grouped is obtained. Then the appropriate EPV is called for that type.

In a similar manner, a server can perform operations for multiple versions of the same interface. Each version has its own EPV. The RPC runtime calls the correct EPV for a version.

For particular services, the server can keep a client state by using a context handle. This is information for a particular client which is passed back and forth between the server and the client.

8.8.7 Secure RPCs

RPCs can work with the DCE security service on several levels. The server needs to have its name in the security registry. Both the server and the client make calls to the RPC runtime to establish authenticated communication. Both determine the amount of protection (encryption) to apply to packets sent between them. This can vary from encryption on the first packet, to encrypted checksums on each packet, to full encryption on all packets.

Authorization is the responsibility of the server. The server can use the ACL service or Privilege Attribute Certificates (PACs). PACs are sent with each RPC call. They are checked to determine the client's permissions for a particular object.

8.8.8 Groups and Profiles

The first time a server starts up, it exports its name to the CDS. This creates an entry containing the interface UUID, version, and host address. Servers typically place themselves in groups, which are pools of entries. The servers in each group provide some similar services. For example, for printers there might be groups for types (laser, dot matrix), location (building, floor), and emulation (Postscript, Diablo).

When a CDS looks up a service, it searches its entries according to a profile. A profile is a set of prioritized references. This works similar to the PATH environment variable for executable files. The entries in a profile can be individual server entries, groups, or other profiles. A standard default profile can be included as one of the entries in the profile. Under UNIX, the profile is set up with an environment variable.

8.8.9 Server considerations

Servers can handle multiple RPCs simultaneously using threads, which are described in the next section. The number of RPCs a server

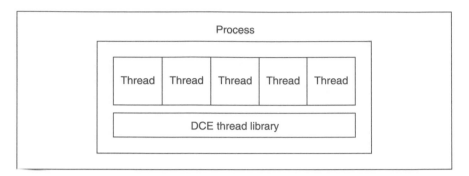

Figure 8.10   Threads in a process

can support depends on several items. Each call can require little or much processing. The host machine can be slow or fast. The calls may not be required to be performed quickly. The network traffic may cause a bottleneck in transmitting data back and forth.

8.9   Threads

Threads are individual flows of control within a single process, and are also known as lightweight processes. They are used by servers to process multiple requests simultaneously. They can be used by clients to request multiple services simultaneously without interrupts and signals. In DCE, threads are provided by a user level library.* DCE threads follow the POSIX 1003.4a standard, which was adapted from DEC's Concert Multithreaded Architecture.

Each thread has its own priority and its own scheduling attributes. Threads can be synchronized using mutual exclusion objects (mutexes) and condition variables. Each thread can keep data specific to itself (somewhat like a local global variable). Threads can terminate themselves or be canceled by other threads.

Each process starts with a single thread of control. Other threads are created by calling a library function (`pthread_create`) and passing it the name of a function. This function executes independently of the creating function. When the function terminates, the thread is terminated. (See Figure 8.10.)

---

* Threads can be supported by the kernel directly, as in OSF UNIX.

8.9.1 Priority and Scheduling

The priority of a thread is relative to other threads in the same process. The process' priority determines when it will be scheduled for execution by the operating system. Thread priorities and the scheduling scheme determine which thread will be executed within the process.*

There are several levels of scheduling. With First-In/First-Out (FIFO) scheduling, the highest priority thread runs until it blocks or terminates. With Round Robin (RR) scheduling, threads of equal priority are time-sliced. With OTHER scheduling, threads are given timeslices inversely proportional to their priorities.

Any threads that are FIFO scheduled are run first. If there are no FIFO threads ready to run, then threads with RR scheduling are run. If no RR threads are ready, then threads with OTHER scheduling are run. The OTHER scheduling insures that all threads within a group are given at least some time to run. This prevents a high priority OTHER thread from completely blocking a low priority thread. However, if there are FIFO or RR threads ready to run, the OTHER threads will not be run.

8.9.2 Synchronization

Since threads all exist in the same process, they can access the same global variables. To insure that two threads do not attempt to alter the same global variable, a mutual exclusion object (mutex) can be used. A mutex is like a lock that can be held by only one thread at a time. Other threads attempting to lock the mutex are blocked until it is unlocked by the thread holding it.

Mutexes come in three variations. The fast mutex causes a deadlock if the same thread that holds that lock attempts to lock it again. This would be unintentional, but could be caused if a thread that held the lock called another function that also attempted to get the lock. A recursive mutex can be locked by the same thread multiple times. This avoids the deadlock problem. However the mutex must be unlocked the same number of times before another thread can lock it. A nonrecursive mutex will return an error if the same thread attempts to lock it.

Condition variables are used to block execution of a thread until some shared data reach a certain state. One or more threads can wait until a condition is signaled. When another thread signals that condition, one of the threads begins executing. The other threads continue

---

* If an operating system supports threads, then the thread priorities may be based upon the threads in all processes.

to wait for the condition to occur. Alternatively, the signaling thread can broadcast the signal to all threads that are waiting for it.

8.9.3 Thread specific data

Each thread has its own copy of the automatic variables in functions. All threads share the global variables of the process. A thread may wish to have a global variable which is shared only by the functions within itself. Such variables are called thread-specific data and are identified with keys. Each key designates a single value, which could be used to hold an address of an allocated block of memory. When a thread accesses a value using the key, the value which is specific to that thread is accessed.

8.9.4 Thread termination

A thread terminates when the function which was used in the call to create it terminates (with a `return` statement). A thread may cancel itself before this by calling `pthread_exit`. Another thread may wait for a particular thread to finish by calling `pthread_join`. A single value (passed to `pthread_exit`) may be returned to the waiting thread.

One thread may terminate (cancel) another thread by calling `pthread_cancel`. The other thread may not be immediately cancelled, depending on its cancellation state. If a thread has general cancellation turned off, it will not terminate, but the request for cancellation will be queued. If general cancellation is turned on, the thread may have asynchronous cancellation turned off. Then cancellation will occur only at certain `pthread` calls. If asynchronous cancellation is turned on, then the thread will immediately terminate. Typically, asynchronous cancellation is turned off if the thread is holding a mutex, or else the mutex might never be unlocked.

8.9.5 Thread considerations

If threads are implemented using routines as in the standard DCE library, the library does the scheduling of the threads. If one thread blocks (say for an I/O call), then all threads will block. Therefore the library includes wrapper routines that turn blocking I/O calls into nonblocking calls. Threads that do I/O are thus suspended until the I/O is complete, but the process itself does not block.

All functions that thread calls should be reentrant. This basically implies that they should not contain static data items; nor should any functions that they call contain static data.

There are only four states for a thread. It can be running—in control of the CPU. It can be ready to run. It can be terminated, which is the state after it calls `thread_exit` and before another thread calls `thread_join`. Finally, it can be waiting—for a mutex to be unlocked or a condition to be signaled.

8.9.6 Signals

Traditional programming with UNIX-type signals changes with the introduction of threads. In UNIX, one sets up a handler for asynchronous signals (such as `SIGINT`) using `signal`. Instead a thread can be designated to wait for a particular signal by calling the POSIX function `sigwait()`. The thread blocks until the signal occurs, and then it can take the appropriate action. Each thread can handle its own synchronous signals (such as a divide by 0), by calling `sigaction` and providing a handler.

8.9.7 Server Applications

Using threads, servers can handle multiple requests simultaneously. A server implicitly sets up multiple threads when it calls the function `rpc_server_listen` to await client requests. When a RPC call arrives, the runtime starts up a thread, using the function for which the RPC is called. If all threads are active, calls can be queued in a request buffer.

8.10 Diskless Support

Diskless workstations can be supported in a DCE cell. These workstations need access to the file system for permanent storage. The DCE diskless support comes from Hewlett Packard's diskless support technology. A small startup program exists in the workstation. It uses the Internet BOOT Protocol (BOOTP) and Trivial File Transfer Protocol (TFTP) to transfer information. It gets configuration information from the CDS. It then connects to the DFS, which it uses as its filesystem.

8.11 Summary

Each part of DCE uses functionality provided by other parts. Clients and servers use CDS for finding out where the servers are, and use RPCs for communication. The security system depends on DTS to keep timestamps synchronized. Secure RPCs depend on the security system for authentication and authorization. DFS relies on the security system for ACLs and RPCs for communication between clients and servers. DTS uses CDS for automatically locating the Time Provider servers.

DCE administrators work on a cell-wide basis. Users are added and deleted from the central security registry. Access control lists are handled in the same way. DFS permits easy back up and restoration of files regardless of their physical location.

DCE can provide an organization-wide control of a group of computing resources. With CDS and DFS, the physical organization of the group is made transparent to the user. Programmers can easily create distributed applications as client/servers using RPCs and threads.

Index